DOVEY UNDAUNTED

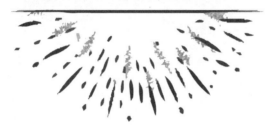

DOVEY
UNDAUNTED

*A Black Woman Breaks Barriers in
the Law, the Military, and the Ministry*

TONYA BOLDEN

NORTON YOUNG READERS
An Imprint of W. W. Norton & Company
Independent Publishers Since 1923

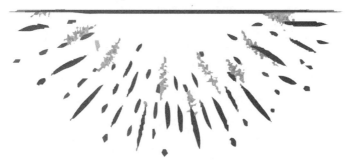

For information about permission to reproduce selections from this book, write to
Permissions, W. W. Norton & Company, Inc., 500 Fifth Avenue,
New York, NY 10110

For information about special discounts for bulk purchases, please contact
W. W. Norton Special Sales at specialsales@wwnorton.com or 800-233-4830

Manufacturing by Lake Book Manufacturing
Book design by Beth Steidle
Production manager: Julia Druskin

ISBN 978-1-324-00317-5

W. W. Norton & Company, Inc., 500 Fifth Avenue, New York, N.Y. 10110
www.wwnorton.com

W. W. Norton & Company Ltd., 15 Carlisle Street, London W1D 3BS

2 4 6 8 9 0 7 5 3 1

For Zakai Eliza Lee Brunson

CONTENTS

DOVEY UNDAUNTED

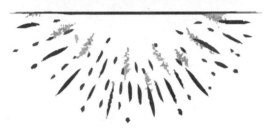

PROLOGUE

"LAWYER, WHAT IS IT they say I done?"

That was Ray on a late October day in 1964.

Black.

Twenty-five.

Eighth-grade education.

Construction worker.

Husband.

Father of five.

Imprisoned in Washington, DC's, main detention facility, the DC Jail.

A year earlier, Ray had been sentenced to sixty days for shoplifting. Twice he'd been arrested for drunk and disorderly conduct.

"Lawyer" was fifty-year-old Dovey J. Roundtree.

"They say you killed a lady."

What spiraled through Ray's mind is a mystery, and not many people cared.

Not about his mind.

Not about him.

Ray was a nobody in society's eyes.

No stocks and bonds, no real estate, no bank accounts, no car. Nothing of value.

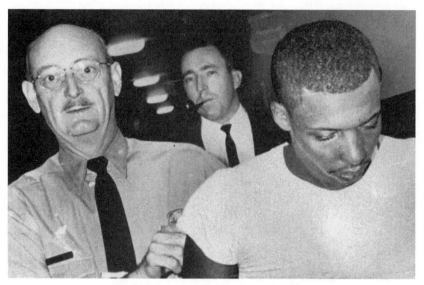

Raymond Crump Jr. on the day of the murder at DC's
Metropolitan Police Headquarters, 300 Indiana Avenue, NW.

When arrested on Monday, October 12, 1964, he had on him only a buck and a half.

The woman Ray was accused of killing on that chilly, clear DC day was definitely a somebody—a socialite, in fact.

White. Blonde. Beautiful.

"Mrs. Mary Pinchot Meyer, prominent Georgetown artist and a niece of a noted conservationist, was shot to death yesterday as she was walking on the C&O Canal towpath near Georgetown," reported DC's *Evening Star* on October 13.

That noted conservationist was the wealthy Gifford Pinchot, first chief of the US Forest Service and twice governor of Pennsylvania. His younger brother, Amos, Mary's father, had been an esteemed attorney (and also wealthy). Mary's mother, Ruth, an alumna of the elite, then all-woman Vassar College, was a former journalist.

The victim, forty-three, divorced, and the mother of two boys away at prep schools in New England, was a Vassar alumna too. So was her sister, Tony, at the time married to Ben Bradlee, *Newsweek* magazine's Washington Bureau chief.

What's more, the victim's celebrity friends included former First Lady Jacqueline Bouvier Kennedy, whose husband, John Fitzgerald Kennedy, had been close friends with Ben Bradlee. President Kennedy had been assassinated eleven months earlier in Dallas, Texas, shot as his open-top Lincoln limousine cruised past a grassy knoll in Dealey Plaza.

Henry Wiggins was an earwitness to the shooting of Mary Pinchot Meyer. This twenty-four-year-old Black employee of an Esso gas station and another guy were working on a car, a stalled Nash Rambler, across the road from the abandoned Chesapeake and Ohio Canal. At about 12:20 p.m. they heard screams.

"At first we didn't pay much attention," Wiggins told a reporter. "You know that area down there—it could have been some kids playing. Or it might have been a bunch of winos fighting. Then all of a sudden I heard a shot and I started across the road."

As he went, he heard another shot.

When Wiggins reached the low-rise stone wall separating the road from the footpath that hugs the C&O Canal, he saw a Black man standing over a white woman's body, a man who soon ran off.

Wiggins raced to his tow truck.

Within minutes, a crowd of cops—Park Police, Metropolitan Police—some on foot, others in scout cars, sirens wailing, were on the scene.

Wiggins was back too.

A manhunt ensued, and shortly after 1 p.m. a detective spotted Ray near the crime scene.

Soaking wet.

Tipsy.

Blood on his right hand.

He was questioned.

Cuffed.

Identified by Wiggins.

Hauled to the police department's headquarters.

Booked.

Placed in a lineup.

Identified by Wiggins again.

A week later Raymond Crump Jr. was indicted for first-degree murder.

At first, word was that Mary Pinchot Meyer's murder stemmed from a botched robbery.

"Robbery Motive Seen in Shooting of DC Artist," the *Washington Post* told its readers on October 13. But a day later the *Evening Star* reported, "Rape Weighed as Motive in Death of Mrs. Meyer." That same day a *Washington Post* front-page story explained the switch: the victim's pocketbook and wallet had been found in her studio, where an electric fan was still "blowing on a newly finished painting."

Robbery?

Rape?

Ray's mother, Martha Crump, believed in her bones that her son, the oldest of three, had *not* killed that white lady, let alone tried to rob or rape her. At her pastor's urging, Mrs.

Crump pleaded with Dovey J. Roundtree to take her son's case. Roundtree's reputation was legend in the Black community. Martha Crump's pastor called her a "righteous lawyer."

At first, Dovey doubted Ray's innocence. From what she had heard and read, the government's case against him was strong, very strong.

But at the end of their first meeting in the DC Jail on that late October day, Roundtree was convinced that Ray was many things—definitely none too bright—but no murderer. So she, long a champion and defender of nobodies—the poor, the shunted-aside, the brutalized, the degraded, the broken—was ready to fight like a tiger for Ray.

And she had this hanging over her head: if her defense failed, if a jury found Ray guilty of first-degree murder, he could spend the rest of his life in prison.

Or he could draw his last breath in a small chamber on the fourth floor of the DC Jail.

Strapped into its electric chair.

Riding the lightning.

THOSE POOR BROKEN FEET

DOVEY MAE JOHNSON ROUNDTREE came from fighting stock, was mentored and molded, inspired, pushed forward, blessed by warriors throughout her life. First and foremost was her maternal grandmother, Rachel Graham.

Born poor.

Born after the Civil War, in the early 1870s.

Born in the South during Reconstruction, when in the face of fierce and steaming racism, legions of courageous people, Black and white, strove through speeches, rallies, and, most important, through political and legal maneuvers to make America catch up to its creed.

In December 1865 chattel slavery had been abolished by the Thirteenth Amendment to the US Constitution. Four months later came the nation's first civil rights act. The Civil Rights Act of 1866 established that, except for Native Americans living on reservations, all people born in the United States were citizens of the nation with "full and equal benefit of all laws."

Republican Congressmen were responsible for this law at a

time when many abolitionists and civil rights activists made up the Republican Party.

But a law could be easily repealed. Not so with a constitutional amendment. Through Republican efforts, in 1868 came the Fourteenth Amendment. To birthright citizenship was added naturalized citizenship. What's more, the amendment banned states from denying *anyone* within their borders "life, liberty or property without due process of law" and "the equal protection of the laws."

Hope for a just America surged even more in February 1870 when Black men gained the right to the national vote through the Fifteenth Amendment.

Five years on, in 1875, when Dovey's Grandma Rachel was a toddler, came another civil rights act. This one declared that *all* people in the nation were entitled to equal treatment in hotels and restaurants, on railroad cars and such.

But in 1883, when Grandma Rachel was about ten, the US Supreme Court declared the 1875 Civil Rights Act unconstitutional.

And on May 18, 1896, in the case *Plessy v. Ferguson*, the Supreme Court ruled that segregation—Jim Crow—meaning separate railroad cars, water fountains, schools, parks for white and Black people—was all perfectly legal.

If these facilities were equal in quality.

That was a big "if." Separate-but-equal was generally nonexistent if white people had a say in the creation of and maintenance of those parks, those schools, those water fountains, those railroad cars. What Black people got was second-rate.

The backlash against progress didn't manifest itself just in legal decisions. Violence was a much-used tool.

Shootings.

Whippings.

Beheadings.

Hangings.

Burnings (of persons and property).

Torture and murder of Black men, women, and children, along with righteous white people, came at the hands of die-hard white supremacists. Many were members of the White Man's League, the Ku Klux Klan, and other paramilitary terrorist outfits.

DURING THESE DAYS OF freedom gained, freedom denied, Dovey Mae's Grandma Rachel was rendered a girl with broken feet.

"They were gnarled and twisted and horribly misshapen, with the bones sticking out in strange ways." Dovey Mae's first look at "those poor broken feet" scared her to death. And she never forgot the anguish that swept across her beloved grandmother's face when, several years later, she explained how her feet got that way.

Rachel was thirteen, living near Henrietta, North Carolina, where her pa worked on a farm, when the white man who managed that farm tried to rape her.

"I ran and fought every way I knew how. And I hurt him."

We don't know how she hurt that man, only how the brute hurt her.

With young Rachel in his clutches, he "stomped, hard as he could, on my feet—to keep me from runnin' for good, he told me.

But I kept runnin'. Wasn't nothing to do but fight him, hard as I could. He wasn't goin' to have his way with me."

The bones of her feet were never set right. So Grandma Rachel, a petite woman, walked "with a swaying awkwardness that late at night became a limp." At eventide, with a day's labor behind her—cooking, canning, making soap, making starch, scrubbing clothes, gardening, sweeping floors—Grandma Rachel tended to her paining feet with steaming hot foot soaks followed by a gentle rubdown with a homemade ointment of turpentine and mutton tallow.

DOVEY MAE WAS FIVE years old when she first laid eyes on Grandma Rachel's broken feet. This was about sixty miles east of Henrietta, in Charlotte, North Carolina, a cotton mill town nicknamed Queen City.

That's where Dovey Mae was born, on April 17, 1914, and where she lived, at 505 South Long Street, until shortly after a devastation on October 27, 1918.

Her papa, James Eliot Johnson, died.

Papa, twenty-six, was a casualty of the 1918–1919 influenza pandemic. It infected about a half-billion people, killing roughly 675,000 Americans and an estimated 25 million people worldwide.

Along with Dovey Mae, age four-and-a-half, Mr. Johnson left behind his wife, Lela, and three other daughters. The youngest were Rachel, just two months old, and Eunice, two years younger than Dovey Mae. Two years older than Dovey was Beatrice, known as Bea, the daughter of James and his first wife, who died before James and Lela married.

"I was too young to grasp the terrible sweep of the influenza epidemic," Dovey Mae later wrote. "I understood only that my tall handsome papa, who one moment had been riding me on the handlebars of his bicycle in the autumn sunshine, was gone, and my mother was crying."

GOD'S HOUSE

After Dovey's papa died, home was nearby at Grandma Rachel and Grandpa Clyde's house, 613 East Boundary Street. That was the parsonage of the church Grandpa pastored, East Stonewall African Methodist Episcopal Zion, a member of one of America's oldest historically Black denominations, the oldest being the African Methodist Episcopal Church (AME).

East Stonewall AME Zion was a family affair. Grandma Rachel baked the communion bread, made the communion wine, kept the altar linens pristine. Mama led the choir with her "rich alto." As for Grandpa, the Reverend Clyde Leonard Graham, he was a powerful preacher. His sermons made an everlasting impression on Dovey Mae—"a rich tapestry of Holy Scripture and political protest, all strung together in a way that shot through you like something electric."

That electrifying preacher, Grandma Rachel's second husband, was also a dutiful, generous family man. He had raised Dovey Mae's mama and her two brothers as if they were blood, just as Mama was doing with Bea.

———

GRANDMA RACHEL AND GRANDPA CLYDE's home, which now housed a family of seven, wasn't a large, sprawling place but a shotgun house: a narrow, rectangular one-story dwelling.

No halls. One room led into the next. (Think of a railroad car.) On hot, humid summer days, with front and back doors open, heavenly breezes could rush through it, bringing relief from the heat.

For the longest while folks said shotgun houses, once abundant in Charlotte and in other parts of the South, were so named because a shot fired from the front door could whiz right through the open back door. Now people say that this style of house originated in West Africa, that "shotgun" is a garbling of "togun" or "shogun," a West African word for "gathering place" or "God's House."

In Grandma and Grandpa's God's House money was often scarce: "We pieced out our existence in pennies, it seemed to me," remembered Dovey Mae.

Pennies, nickels, dimes, and dollars came from Grandpa's small neighborhood grocery store. From Grandma doing laundry for well-off white folks. From Mama cooking and cleaning in white folks' homes. Donations from parishioners helped, and as Dovey Mae and her sisters grew older they pitched in with earnings from this-and-that odd jobs. How much easier, lighter, life might have been had tall, handsome Papa lived. And not just on the financial front. His death "left a hole" in Dovey Mae's heart, a void that would be with her always.

Papa's heart for God remained with Dovey Mae too. Her father, operator of the printing press at the AME Zion Publishing House, had been in charge of Sunday school at the family church.

A section of Charlotte's Brooklyn neighborhood in the 1940s. The four houses to the right of the pole are shotgun houses.

One of Dovey Mae's prized possessions was his small black devotional. In it he had written: "By all let it be known that I, James Eliot Johnson, have loved the teaching of Sunday school."

Dovey Mae relished Mama's talk about how much she was like Papa: "I spoke like him, she told me often, used my hands in the way he did, had his ability to command the attention of a roomful of people."

THINGS FAR FROM GODLY stayed with Dovey too: stings, slaps, stabs to psyche and soul wrought by Jim Crow.

For her—child, teen, woman—segregation was detestable. Whether forced to take a back seat in a trolley car or enduring the stench of "garbage in the back-alley entrance to segregated movie theaters," she always "felt personally violated."

She'd never forget the spring day when she was six or seven and had the treat of going with Grandma Rachel into town to tend to some business. Grandma had a tight grip on her hand as they walked to the trolley stop. Then, when the trolley car pulled up, opened its doors, a joyful Dovey Mae broke free, bounded up the stairs, plopped down in an empty seat right behind the driver.

"Get that pickaninny out of here!" Mister Trolley Car Driver yelled. "You know she can't sit there."

Dovey Mae was also still a child on a fearsome night when shutters slammed shut, a kerosene lamp was hastily put out, and Dovey huddled in the darkness with her sisters crying. Outside, hoofbeats thundered and men howled, lashing their horses. Grandma paced with a grip on her broom.

Klansmen rode on by that night without harming Dovey Mae's home and family, but different Klansmen had done damage to Grandma Rachel when she was a young wife and mother. Her first husband, John Bryant, had gotten himself in their crosshairs for reasons that remained a mystery. To live, he fled, never heard from again.

JIM CROW AND WHITE terror didn't render Dovey Mae bitter, beat-down, broken. That was thanks to the prayer and praise song that pulsed through her home where, unlike money, love was never scarce. And there was Grandma's staunch proclamation that her children were "as good as anybody."

Soothing too was the yummy smell, yummy taste of Grandma's gingerbread and other baked goodies. With some summer days came pre-dawn forays into the woods for black-berries—"and Grandma knew how to find the ripest, the best."

Come any Sunday morning—the "grand procession."

With Mama and her sisters, Dovey Mae walked tall behind Grandpa Clyde and Grandma Rachel from the parsonage to their church. "Behind us marched the whole world—the dozens of families who made up Grandpa's flock, wending their way through the clay streets and alleyways of the neighborhood known as Brooklyn."

Long before Dovey Mae was born, when this largely Black neighborhood, this heart of Black Charlotte, was called Logtown, it earned high marks. The *Charlotte Observer* reported that a public health officer found the place "to be in a cleaner and healthier condition than any other part of the city." Its residents seemed "to vie with each other in keeping their premises free from all garbage and filth, and in improving and beautifying their yards."

Like godliness, like cleanliness, making the most of the mind was a must in Dovey Mae's home. Grandpa saw to it that the family had *The Book of Knowledge*, a richly illustrated children's encyclopedia that came in pieces: one volume a month.

Dovey Mae and her sisters were to go way beyond *The Book of Knowledge*. Mama, like Grandma, like Grandpa, wanted college in their future.

That was no ordinary ambition back then. In 1920, when Dovey Mae was six, a mere 6.3 percent of Black Americans (and 22 percent of white Americans) in their mid- to late twenties had a high school diploma. So it was no small thing when Dovey Mae's sister Bea headed off to Winston-Salem Teachers College (now Winston-Salem State University).

IN CHARLOTTE, THE PUBLIC school system didn't treat its young people equally. While white teens had a high school in 1908, Black teens didn't get one until 1923, when Dovey Mae

Brooklyn street scene, around 1915.

was nine. And she remembered her grade school, Myers Street Elementary, as a "broken-down old frame building."

Betty W. Barber, who attended Myers years after Dovey Mae (and later earned a PhD and became a college dean), agreed that as a facility the school left a lot to be desired. But Barber also spoke of an often overlooked truth about many schools for Black children when Jim Crow ruled: "The classrooms were crowded, the desks shabby, the books old with pages torn, but we were blessed with wonderful teachers. They were strong disciplinarians concerned not only with our education but with our overall well-being as children."

One of Charlotte's wonderful Black teachers was Edith (in some sources Edythe) Wimbish. She had Dovey Mae train her sights on the all-woman Spelman College in Wimbish's hometown of Atlanta, Georgia. There, in 1881, in the damp basement of Atlanta's first Black church, Friendship Baptist, two white missionaries, Sophia B. Packard and Sarah E. Giles, had opened the Atlanta Baptist Female Seminary with a student body of just eleven young Black women.

The school's prospects improved greatly when it attracted a benefactor in the Rockefellers, the powerful white family headed by oil magnate John D. Rockefeller Sr. After his donation of $5,000 in 1884 (roughly $120,000 in today's dollars), the school became Spelman Seminary (and later Spelman College) in honor of John D.'s wife, Laura Spelman Rockefeller, and her parents, Harvey and Lucy Spelman. They had been abolitionists.

Spelman! Spelman! Spelman!

That was Dovey Mae's high hope as she made her way through Charlotte's Second Ward High, where she was a member of the debating team, president of the Athletic Association, and an honor student, ranking second in her class for three years. There, she also took up the French horn and dreamed of becoming a doctor, at a time when only about ninety Black women in America had ever earned a medical degree.

But dream on Dovey Mae did!

She had many examples of dreaming big in Black Charlotte. As elsewhere in the nation, Queen City was the home of Black barrier-breakers, people who succeeded despite being perceived— and treated—as second-class citizens. In 1915, a year after Dovey Mae was born and fifty years after the abolition of slavery, Black Charlotte had, for example, three real estate companies, thirty-one restaurants, five blacksmith shops, three hotels, three insurance companies, twenty-four grocery stores, five drugstores. It also had two lawyers and twelve doctors.

One of those doctors was J. T. Williams, and he owned one of those drugstores. His real estate holdings also included a sublime house on South Brevard where other well-to-do Black families lived. South Brevard was also home to Black Charlotte's most prominent church: the stunning Gothic Revival Grace AME, which Dr. Williams had helped to get built.

The achievements of people like J. T. Williams surely inspired Dovey Mae.

But could she really leave Black Charlotte?

WINSTON-SALEM TEACHERS COLLEGE, a public school and so tuition-free, had taken Bea about 80 miles away from home. In contrast, Spelman, some 250 miles away, was a private school. And not cheap. Between entrance fee, tuition, room and board, textbooks, and other expenses, Spelman could cost about $300 a year. At the time, a full-time domestic worker who didn't live in, like Mama, may have earned about $10 a week (or about $500 a year).

Bea had gone off to college with some funds for living expenses thanks to money one of Grandma Rachel's brothers left her in his will. When Dovey Mae was in high school, there was no such legacy.

Then disaster struck.

Dovey Mae was fifteen when newspapers flashed headlines like this on October 24, 1929: "PANIC SEIZES STOCK MARKET."

And like this five days later: "STOCKS LOSE 10 BILLION IN DAY."

These headlines were harbingers of the Great Depression, the worst economic downturn the nation had yet seen, one that would last for ten grueling years. Thousands of banks would fail, wiping out customers' savings. Tens of thousands of other businesses, from factories to hardware stores, would fold, which meant millions of people lost their jobs. Without jobs, without any or much savings, tens of thousands of families lost their homes.

As joblessness, homelessness, hunger, and hopelessness rose, the suicide rate soared.

Dovey Mae's family was not spared the blows.

Grandma's laundry business lost customers. So did Grandpa's store, to the point that it closed. Luckily Mama still had work as a domestic.

Spelman?

When Dovey Mae graduated from high school in May 1931, Spelman seemed a doomed, dead dream.

But then . . .

3

WORTHY WISH

AMONG THE FAMILIES MAMA worked for were the Hurleys, Margaret and Bailey C., who lived on Crescent Avenue in an all-white part of Queen City. She was a homemaker. He was a district supervisor for the American Telegram and Telegraph Company.

Mama was chiefly a cook for the Hurleys. Dovey Mae worked for them, too, on weekends, mostly as nanny to the couple's little boy, Bailey Jr.

And just when Dovey Mae had probably given up on Spelman, Mr. Hurley got a job offer in, of all places, Atlanta. When he decided to take the job, Mrs. Hurley pressed Mama to work for them down there. She wanted Dovey Mae to come too.

Spelman would be within Dovey Mae's reach!

But there was a problem.

Grandma Rachel. She didn't want her daughter and granddaughter to be so far away.

For weeks, Dovey Mae sent up "my own silent prayers as I watched Grandma struggle and heard my mother's quiet, persistent arguments."

One: If Lela didn't pull up stakes with Dovey Mae and follow the Hurleys to Atlanta, what would she do for work?

Two: Dovey Mae's mentor, Edith Wimbish, had moved back to Atlanta. They'd have a friend in town.

Three: The Hurleys were "good people."

Grandma Rachel eventually gave the move her blessing. Leaving Dovey Mae's younger sisters in the care of their grandparents, in the fall of 1932 Dovey Mae and Mama packed their bags. They took with them a plan as well: while working for the Hurleys, they'd squirrel away every penny, nickel, dime, dollar they could to allow Dovey Mae to start at Spelman.

WHEN DOVEY MAE FIRST laid eyes on Spelman's twenty-acre campus, it took her breath away.

The red-brick "stately white-columned buildings."

The "lush green lawns ringed by dogwood and magnolias."

This was another world.

Spelman's crown jewel was Sisters Chapel, built in the late 1920s thanks to John D. Rockefeller Jr. and named in honor of his mother, Laura, and her sister, Lucy.

Students were required to assemble at the chapel for devotions every weekday morning, a preaching service every Sunday, and a midweek prayer meeting. Sisters Chapel was where faith—in God, in the progress of the race—was majestically on display at this school whose motto proclaimed "Our Whole School for Christ."

But it was nearly three years before Dovey Mae applied to Spelman College, some one thousand days of cooking, cleaning, serving, minding Bailey Jr., in the Hurley home about five miles northeast of Atlanta in Decatur.

Spelman's Sisters Chapel in 1927, the year that it was dedicated.

At one point Dovey Mae earned four dollars a week, Mama seven, with both of them probably sending pieces of their wages back to Queen City. Forty dollars was all Dovey Mae had toward college when she applied to Spelman in mid-May 1934.

"I [have] been obsessed with the thought of continuing my education," wrote twenty-year-old Dovey Mae Johnson in her application. "Every year have I hoped and prayed that my worthy wish would be possible but money held me back. Alas, I have found the only way to conquer such a difficulty was not in the praying and wishing but in the rising above the obstacle."

In response to the question "How do you expect to get the

remainder [of school costs]," she wrote "by obtaining work on campus."

Her worthy wish came true in what scholar-activist W. E. B. Du Bois called "the city of a hundred hills." Dovey Mae—who began to refer to herself more often as just "Dovey" around this time—was soon part of the dynamic intellectual hub, the Atlanta University Center Consortium, originally an alliance of three historically Black schools: Edith Wimbish's alma mater, Atlanta University (now Clark-Atlanta), Spelman, and its brother school Morehouse, which had also started out in the basement of Friendship Baptist church.

WHILE DOVEY HAD TO work and scrimp to get through college, not so for many of her peers. One classmate was Alice Carey Holmes. Her father, Hamilton Mayor Holmes Sr., was the first Black doctor in East Point, not far from Atlanta. Another classmate was Patricia Constance McWhorter. Patricia's father, Morehouse graduate Millard H. McWhorter, was the first Black doctor in Coweta County, Georgia. Patricia's mother, Anna, a Spelman alumna, had been an English teacher.

"Most of the stylishly dressed, beautifully spoken girls in my classes," Dovey said, had come from a world of "cotillions and coming-out parties and summers on Martha's Vineyard, a world so different from mine I could scarcely comprehend it."

It's hard to imagine when Dovey saw Spelman students stylishly dressed. The school had a dress code. "A student's wardrobe should include clothes and shoes suitable for out-of-door activities and for general wear in a moderate climate," stated the 1933–1934 catalog. "Elaborate or extensive wardrobes are not in keeping with the standards and ideals of Spelman College, and, if students bring them, their use is discouraged and may be prohibited."

Perhaps Dovey saw Spelman students in finery when they were leaving campus for winter, spring, or summer break. In any event, Dovey wasn't at Spelman to comprehend the Black elite, but to make the most of the excellent education the school offered. Surely buoying her up was Grandma Rachel's insistence that her children were "as good as anybody."

Margaret Hurley didn't agree. When Dovey was accepted at Spelman, and with Mama back in Queen City, Mrs. Hurley went from benefactor to beast.

On one occasion she mentioned to Dovey a young Black woman who had been a servant to one of her friends. "She's just doing fine now, isn't she? Without any old college." Another day, a friend of Mrs. Hurley flat-out called Dovey an "impudent little thing" as loud as she pleased.

Dovey the servant—absolutely acceptable.

Dovey seeking to rise in life—a prime vexation.

So much for the Hurleys being "good people."

STEELING HERSELF AGAINST DIGS and barbs, Dovey kept her head down, did her work—washing dishes, doing laundry, cleaning house, tending to Bailey Jr., serving tea.

Nights, tucked away in her bedroom, Dovey lost herself in her schoolwork.

Luckily, she had a refuge at 149 Fort Street. This was the home that Edith Wimbish, still a teacher, shared with her sister, Hattie (also a teacher), and their widowed mother, Maggie Baker Wimbish, principal of E. P. Johnson Night School.

Sunday dinner at 149 Fort Street—what a "feast," with its

"heaping portions" of food, its "elegant dining room." Those dinners, which Dovey attended regularly, it seems, were also feasts for the mind, the soul: "Mrs. Maggie Wimbish gathered Atlanta's most distinguished black citizens—lawyers, doctors, professors, educators."

Clerics too. One was Baptist minister James Madison Nabrit, whose mother, Margaret, had been one of Spelman's first students. His sister, also named Margaret and also a Spelman alumna, became the school's first Black faculty member and eventually a dean. Reverend Nabrit was a Morehouse graduate, as were his sons, one of whom would play a critical role in Dovey's life.

It was probably thanks to the Wimbishes that Reverend Nabrit had given Dovey a recommendation when she applied to Spelman. One question he had to answer was "What is your opinion of the applicant's moral character? (Honesty, dependability, earnestness of purpose, determination to do right?)."

"Very good," responded Reverend Nabrit. And at the end he wrote, "She comes highly recommended from her pastor and church at Charlotte, NC."

"She has the ability to lead" is the highlight of the recommendation furnished by Lula Norris, secretary of Charlotte's Black YWCA, where Dovey had been a Girl Reserve and a member of the Industrial Club.

Along with having folks outside of Spelman rooting for her, Dovey had a guiding light on campus in Mary Mae Neptune, a professor of English literature and faculty adviser to the student newspaper, the *Campus Mirror*.

In Dovey's eyes, Mary Mae Neptune was "as much a warrior with her Shakespeare text and her red pen as my grandmother

Mary Mae Neptune, a native of Belmont County, Ohio, in 1925. Neptune earned her bachelor's and master's degrees from Ohio Wesleyan University. Right before she joined Spelman's faculty in 1926, she taught English at Iowa Wesleyan College (now University) where she was also the dean of women.

was with her broom" and "without question a revolutionary, decades ahead of her time."

Neptune made her students face the racism in Shakespeare's *Othello*, the anti-Semitism in the bard's *The Merchant of Venice*. "She taught me how to think, helped me to become studious and to live unafraid. She turned on the light for me."

Neptune also encouraged Dovey to write for the *Campus Mirror*. Rising from contributor to news editor to associate editor in chief, Dovey covered on- and off-campus news, from Harvard University's celebration of its three-hundredth anniversary to the death of John D. Rockefeller Sr. and exhibits of Japanese woodcuts at Atlanta University. She covered guest lectures at Spelman and at other schools in the consortium.

In October 1936 she reported on the lecture of Dr. Rufus

The Campus Mirror Staff

THE CAMPUS MIRROR

The Students' Own Publication
"SERVICE IN UNITY"

THE CAMPUS MIRROR STAFF

Editor-in-Chief................................Ella Mae Jones
Associate Editors-in-Chief...............Frankie Smith
                                  Dovey Mae Johnson
Editors of News.......Dorothea Boston. Grace Days
Associate Editors of News................Alma Stone
                                 Gladys Holloway
Special Features................................Anatol Reeves
Asso. Ed. of Special Features.......Marjorie Greene
Sports and Jokes...........................Claretta Scott
Exchange Editor..............................Thelma Worrell
Social Editor....................................Gladys Ford
Music Editor..............................Franzetta Williams
Art Editor........................Calla Mae Rawlings

BUSINESS STAFF

Business Manager.......................Margaret Creagh
Secretary..Ollie Franklin
Treasurer...Jessie Hubbard
Circulation Manager...................Louise Gaillard
Advertising Managers................Clara Ivey Wilson
                                   Susie Taylor
Faculty Advisor................Miss M. Mae Neptune

SUBSCRIPTION RATES

75 Cents a Year, 10 cents a Copy, 40 cents a
Semester—Postage 2 cents a Copy

VOL. XIV   MAY-JUNE, 1938   No. 8

Editorial

"*A man's reach should exceed his grasp or what's a heaven for.*" In a few days we shall leave this center of learning to begin making practical application of the theories we have learned and the experiences we have had during the past four years, which is the first lap to our goal. The world, we know, is waiting for our entrance, not gladly as in yesteryears but with a degree of skepticism. Some used to wonder "Why the cool reception?" but judging from the relatively few achievements of students already graduated, we are greatly concerned about this matter of making the adjustment. Some say that schools have defeated their purposes, for, instead of teaching the student to adjust himself to surrounding conditions, he tries to make conditions adjust themselves to his ideas which have been chiefly problems solved from a text.

For us our mental processes have been strengthened and our fields of knowledge partially explored. In the class room, we have all shown some intelligence, although recently specialists have said that classroom activity is no index to our intelligence; on the campus, we have often had opportunities to enjoy, from our social benches, the beauty graciously bestowed by a Superior Being; and with buoyant, refreshing enthusiasm, we have entered into all extra-curricular activities.

We are grateful to our President, instructors, and interested friends for the excellent preparation which their fruitful experiences have brought us, and the patience they have had in imparting their knowledge to us.

Thinking on these things, this class of '38 marches *out*, never to be happy college students again but distinct individuals adventuring in various phases of life with the tools which they have moulded for themselves while in college. The world has flung to us a challenge and we accept with—"There is no chance, no destiny, no fate that can circumvent, hinder or control the firm resolve of a determined soul."

To Our Readers and Subscribers

It has been an enjoyable experience for the retiring staff and the contributing student body to give to our readers some information concerning the activities and thoughts of the students at Spelman.

And it is our sincere desire that the incoming staff will find cooperation as encouraging and stimulating as the retiring staff have found.

We wish you to know that we appreciate your deep interest in our growth.

Spelman Athletic Association Awards Letters

Dovey Johnson, '38

The Spelman Athletic Association took a step forward in encouraging physical education by reinitiating the custom of awarding letters for noteworthy athletic performance. This year the association awarded two letters; one to Minnie Head, a senior, and the other to Margaret Creagh, a junior. The awards were made by Susie Taylor, a member of the association, at assembly May 12. At this time announcement was made of the requirements of eligibility to receive a letter.

No mention of athletics for the past four years could fairly be made without some recognition being given Jessie Hubbard, who has maintained an unexcelled record in tennis, basketball, soccer, and baseball. During her four years here she has done much to awaken and inspire interest in sports.

Spelman Alumnae Receive Master's Degrees From Columbia University

Miss Millicent Dobbs, Spelman, 1932, and, before her leave of absence, a teacher in the Booker T. Washington High School in Atlanta, and her sister, Josephine Dobbs, Spelman, 1937, are the happy recipients of Master's Degrees, the first in Speech and the second in Home Economics, from Teachers College, Columbia University.

The Misses Dobbs, while studying in New York, have been the standard bearers of Spelman ideals in their many extra activities for the furtherance of finer Negro womanhood.

The Approaching End

Ruth Watson, '40

As the college year closes, our activities become more numerous and our days are apt to be filled with a fragmentary jumble of details—the old routine of dressing, rushing to breakfast, going to classes, completing laboratory work, studying for examination, wanting to sit on the campus, but realizing that it is growing dark and is almost time for bed again. The nearer the end comes, the closer crowds this accumulation of things-to-do-next until one begins to wish frantically that the end would hurry and come. However, this is only a sidelight on what really happens at this time of the academic year. Only yesterday I heard a freshman remark, "Recently, I have had so many lessons and other activities to do that I wonder if I'm me," and so it is with many of us, we are wondering "If I'm me."

Jones, a white professor of philosophy at Haverford College. He spoke on "The Challenge of the Closed Door."

In November 1936 she praised an address by theologian Howard Thurman, then at Howard University. In Sisters Chapel, Thurman warned students against being imitations of another people. "We must learn to understand and to appreciate our roots," he said. "We represent one of nature's interesting syntheses, since we have one part of our root in Africa and the other part in the New World."

Wrote Dovey: "The fact that we have become so expert at imitating other groups, and that we are ashamed of our African roots, Mr. Thurman described as insipid and disintegrating."

In the December 1936 *Campus Mirror*, Dovey wrote about a presentation at Sisters Chapel by Black singer and actress Etta Moten. Spelman students were "enraptured" by Moten's singing of three songs after her talk about three keys for success: "preparation," "initiative," and "the making of right contacts."

Having the right contacts had definitely been on Dovey's mind months earlier when she landed in jail.

From the May–June 1938 *Campus Mirror*. In the staff photo, Dovey is in the middle of the second row.

MIRACLE-MAKER

"Thief! You're a thief!"

That was Margaret Hurley one May day in 1936, hollering and carrying on something awful, accusing Dovey of stealing.

What?

Money?

Jewelry?

Food?

What?

Dovey couldn't make sense of it, didn't know what the woman was ranting about.

Thief!

What had she supposedly stolen?

Thief!

And it got worse.

Dovey was carted off to the Decatur jail.

Jail.

A scary place.

A nightmare place if you were Black. White guards were

known to beat Black inmates for no reason, known to prey upon women, young and all-the-way grown.

And jail was where no Spelman student was *ever* to end up. The white woman at the helm of Spelman, President Florence Read, made it clear that if a student found herself in trouble off campus, she shouldn't assume that Spelman would come to her rescue.

Entering the jailhouse, Dovey was "nearly numb with terror," but she had the presence of mind to give a guard Mary Mae Neptune's telephone number. "I knew only one white person bold enough to involve herself, and that was Miss Neptune."

Dovey made no mention in her memoir of giving any thought to reaching out to the Wimbishes, whose sphere, she well knew, included Black lawyers. Perhaps, at that time, in that place, distraught, in a panic, Dovey believed that only a white person could save her.

She waited.

Waited.

Thief!

Prayed.

Thief?

And—

"Throughout my life," she later reflected, "I have found that there is always somebody who would be the miracle-maker in your life if you but believe."

DUSK WAS DESCENDING WHEN a well-dressed white man, an attorney, arrived at the Decatur County Jail. He'd been dispatched by Professor Neptune and Spelman treasurer Phern

Rockefeller, a woman the *Atlanta Constitution* later praised for her "dedicated work in interracial and humanitarian activities."

Dovey told the lawyer most emphatically that she was not and had never been a thief.

After he left, Dovey, still unsure of her fate, kept on hoping, believing, praying, during what must have been the longest night of her life.

Spelman, a chance of a lifetime . . .

Slipping through her fingers?

And her family—the last thing Dovey wanted to do was bring shame upon them.

DAYBREAK CAME IN THE CITY of a hundred hills, and on the horizon, a greater miracle. That lawyer returned. This time when he left the jail, he took Dovey with him, took her back to Spelman.

Thanks to that lawyer, the charges of theft were gone with the wind, as were the Hurleys from Dovey's life. But so was her job, her room and board at the Hurleys' home.

If you but believe.

Professor Neptune and Phern Rockefeller fixed her up with housing on campus. Dovey came to her own rescue too. She took on as many jobs as she could get. She cleaned dorms, did research for Neptune, worked as a lab assistant in the biology department.

But it wasn't enough. There came a day when she faced the prospect of having to drop out of college. She owed the school several hundred dollars.

She found herself walking aimlessly around the Spelman campus, then standing before the faculty apartment building in which Professor Neptune lived. "I climbed the steps of the cement stoop of the apartment building, sat down, and began to cry."

Someone called out to her.

"What on earth are you doing here?" Professor Neptune asked.

If you but believe.

The next day in a meeting with Neptune and Phern Rockefeller, another miracle.

A scholarship had been found.

What's more, Professor Neptune, not a wealthy woman, agreed to pay off Dovey's debt to Spelman: a little over $300. Neptune also advanced Dovey the $13.32 needed to pay the first quarterly premium for a life insurance policy that made Neptune the beneficiary. If Dovey suddenly died, then Neptune would get the death benefit and so recoup the money she had spent paying off Dovey's debt (and the first insurance premium).

Dovey pledged to repay Neptune in pieces: at least five dollars monthly—or "oftener." She also agreed to keep up with the insurance policy's quarterly premium payments. (After paying Neptune back, Dovey would be free to make anyone she pleased the beneficiary of that life insurance policy.)

On June 8, 1938, in Sisters Chapel, Dovey Mae Johnson, double major in English and biology, received a bachelor's degree along with forty-seven other young women. And her family had been able to afford travel expenses for at least one member to be there, her sister Eunice.

That year's commencement speaker was the esteemed Dr. Frederick K. Stamm, pastor of the Clinton Avenue Community Church in Brooklyn, New York. "If young men and women are

Spelman College , Atlanta, Georgia , June 8, 1938

I, D ovey Mae Johnson, Spelman College class of 1938, residence 921 East Hill Street Charlotte, North Carolina , because of the loan made to me on June 8, 1938, by Miss M. Mae
Neptune, Professor of English at Spelman College, Atlanta, Georgia,
residence , R.R. 2, Barnesville, Ohio, do hereby promise to
repay this loan in monthly payments or oftener , of $5.00
or more each month that I am working. I am also legally bound
to make regular quarterly payments on life insurance with The
Equitable Life Assurance Society of the United States, 393 Seventh
Avenue , New York City, on which there is Collateral assignment / to said M.Mae Neptune in the sum of my indebtedness to said
      properly made
M. Mae Neptune for the following loan made by her to me while I
was a student at Spelman College :

   1. Payment of my full account to Spelman College made on
June 8, 1938 - 321.42

   2. Sums advanced to me in meeting the cost of taking
out my Life Assurance Policy , First Quarterly premium,
due , Oct. 14, 1938, paid by M.Mae Neptune. . . . . $ 13.32

   3. Sums advanced to me on my personal expenses by
M.Mae Neptune amounting to 21.51

                                            $ 356.25

                        Signed *Dovey Mae Johnson*

Witness *Phena R. chipilly Stanley*

(over)

Dovey's loan agreement with Neptune.

going into life to win, it is necessary for them to face the battle with some inner resources," he said, "and there is no place for fear in the life of one who works steadily."

Dovey Mae Johnson possessed in abundance the three inner resources Dr. Stamm stressed: Stamina. Sound thinking. Love.

And dreaming big had paid off for her.

5

NO

"NO," SAID THE FORMIDABLE Mary McLeod Bethune to Dovey M. Johnson. "There are things for you to do right here."

This was in July 1941, three years after Dovey graduated from college.

"Right here" was Washington, DC, which was about as segregated as any other Southern town.

Though eclipsed years back by Harlem, New York, as the "capital of Black America," Black DC was still a force, home to a host of living legends.

Carter G. Woodson, the second Black person to earn a PhD from Harvard (in history in 1912) and the "father" of Black history was one. Another was civil rights and women's rights activist Mary Church Terrell, a graduate of Oberlin College (1884), who in ten years' time would spearhead the campaign that led to the outlawing of Jim Crow in DC restaurants.

Washington, DC, was also home to the prestigious historically Black Howard University with its college of liberal arts, law school, pharmacy school, and medical school.

Dovey hadn't gone to DC in the summer of 1941 for Howard's medical school. After Spelman, with money tight, she set aside her dream of being a doctor. Instead, she took a teaching job in a place nothing like the intellectual hub she had enjoyed in Atlanta.

Dovey had put her stamina, sound thinking, and love to use at Finley High School in the rural town of Chester, South Carolina, some fifty miles south of Charlotte.

At Finley High, Dovey taught English and General Science. She counseled seniors on courses of study, on possible careers, on finding jobs, on pathways to college. For two summers, she made extra money training Black teachers at Piedmont Junior College in Rock Hill, South Carolina, about twenty-five miles from Chester, and where her little sister Rachel was attending Friendship College. (Her sister Eunice had opted for Shaw University in Raleigh, North Carolina.)

Dovey initially earned $68 a month at Finley High. For the teacher training, $100 a month. Bit by bit she was paying off her debt to Mary Mae Neptune. Month after month Dovey sent much of her money to Queen City. Dovey's family, long since living at 921 East Hill Street, really needed that money. Mama, still doing domestic work, was the chief breadwinner.

Grandpa Clyde, who years back had taken to drink, hadn't been the pastor of a church for a while. A 1934 city directory identified him, then in his late fifties, as doing some kind of menial labor, for it had him down as a "helper." Perhaps he was sweeping up in a barbershop or stocking the shelves of a grocery store.

Six years later, in early April 1940, in the space for his occupation, the US Census record had a blank. As it did for Grandma Rachel. Mama, forty-eight, was working as a "maid" for a private family, as were Eunice, twenty-three, and Rachel, twenty, both with three years of college. Like Dovey, they were all in mourning before April 1940 was out. Sixty-four-year-old Grandpa Clyde died on April 25. He had suffered a brain hemorrhage brought on by a serious kidney disease.

"Ill as he had been for so long, I found myself unprepared for his death. It was Grandpa who'd given me my love of books and an abiding hunger for things spiritual. He was the first minister I had known." And it was Grandpa who "had stepped forward to take the place of the father I'd barely known. Grief filled the house that summer, not in the desperate, wrenching way it had when my papa died, but with a stillness that slowed our days and blanketed everything in quiet."

Chester, South Carolina, proved too quiet for Dovey. And how long could Mama keep working herself to the bone?

In July 1941 Dovey went up to DC hoping to get a job in the defense industry.

WAR WAS RAGING IN EUROPE with the Axis powers, led by Nazi Germany, battling the Allied powers, led by Britain. America, not yet technically in the fight, was aiding the Allied powers as the "Arsenal of Democracy"—producing tanks, planes, munitions. And the doors of opportunity were opening to Black people in the defense industry where workers could earn from about thirty to maybe sixty dollars a week.

These opportunities were the result of Executive Order 8802, which President Franklin Delano Roosevelt (FDR) signed on June 25, 1941. Executive Order 8802 outlawed racial and ethnic discrimination in the defense industry. (Before that executive order, a survey showed that 50 percent of defense contractors would not hire Black people.)

With Executive Order 8802 came the Fair Employment Practice Committee (FEPC), tasked with investigating defense contractors who violated the president's order.

Executive Order 8802 and the FEPC didn't exactly spring from the goodness of FDR's heart. It was born of pressure from Black civil rights activists. One was Walter White, chief of the National Association for the Advancement of Colored People (NAACP). Another was A. Philip Randolph, a prominent labor leader. Randolph had threatened to lead at least 100,000 people in a march on Washington on July 1, 1941, if something wasn't done to prevent Black people from being locked out of defense industry jobs.

After FDR signed Executive Order 8802, Randolph called off the march.

MARY MCLEOD BETHUNE WAS just as tireless an advocate for her people as Walter White and A. Philip Randolph.

Back in 1904 she had started a school for Black girls in Daytona Beach, Florida, with $1.50—"We burned logs and used the charred splinters as pencils, and mashed elderberries for ink." Roughly twenty years later her school, with its motto "Enter to learn, depart to serve," was the coed Bethune-Cookman College (now University).

When Dovey went to DC in the summer of 1941, Bethune was in her fifth year as head of the Division of Negro Affairs in the National Youth Administration (NYA). The NYA was one of the many agencies in FDR's alphabet soup of initiatives to get America out of the economic depression, to give Americans a better life, a new deal.

The NYA sought to combat despair and juvenile delinquency

Mary McLeod Bethune, around 1911, with students from the school she founded, Daytona Educational and Industrial Training School, in Florida.

by providing young men and women, age sixteen to twenty-five, with jobs (such as clerical work) and job training (such as auto repair). As an NYA administrator, Bethune was determined to see that young Black people got a fair deal in accessing NYA-sponsored opportunities. (Dovey's job as a lab assistant at Spelman had been thanks to the NYA.)

When Dovey alighted from a train at DC's wondrous Beaux Arts–style Union Station in the summer of 1941, Bethune was also in her sixth year as president of the National Council of Negro Women, an umbrella organization of roughly thirty women's clubs—clubs devoted not to the likes of bridge parties and lah-di-dah afternoon teas, but to improving Black lives, especially those of women and children. At the time, 60 percent of Black women could find jobs only as domestic workers. These women, said one report, "often worked 12-hour days for pathetically low wages."

On top of heading an NYA division and the NCNW, Bethune was also a member of the Federal Council of Negro Affairs, better known as the Black Cabinet: FDR's top policy advisers on Black America, which numbered nearly 13 million, about 10 percent of the population.

DOVEY NEVER KNEW THE HOW, why, when of it, but she knew for a fact that Grandma Rachel and Mary McLeod Bethune were friends. When Dovey was ten or so, Bethune came to Queen City to speak at its Emancipation Day celebration and Grandma Rachel introduced her granddaughters to the great woman.

Straightaway young Dovey sensed in Bethune "something powerful, almost regal. Ebony-skinned and crowned with an enormous feathered hat that matched her silk suit, she spoke in a voice so rich, so cultivated, so filled with authority that it held me fast."

Years later, when Dovey decided to go to DC, Grandma Rachel insisted that she get in touch with Bethune. When she did, she was hoping that Bethune might be able to help her get a defense industry job. But Bethune told her that she had "something else in mind."

In the meantime, what Bethune needed Dovey to do "right here" was to be a research assistant, to scour newspapers, Black-owned, white-owned, for articles about Bethune's work, about Black setbacks and strides. Dovey did that work in a row house at 1812 Ninth Street, NW: Bethune's home and NCNW's headquarters.

"Every clip was logged into her files, as were the statistics she charged me with ferreting out and placing at her fingertips for the moment when she might need them in her fight for better schools, better housing, better lives for children."

Dovey watched Bethune "turn those cold numbers into tools, working them into letters to this or that official, citing them in phone conferences, packing them away in her briefcase for meetings at her NYA headquarters across town, slipping them into discussions with the colleagues who sought her out in [NCNW's] office for support and advice."

Dovey was left practically "speechless" on that fall day of 1941 when she first laid eyes on First Lady Eleanor Roosevelt in Bethune's headquarters. Like a scared mouse, Dovey promptly "retreated" to her corner of the office "in a state of awe."

In her crusade for social justice, Bethune had a powerful ally in Eleanor Roosevelt.

Spirited.

Forward-thinking.

One of the most progressive white women of the era.

Dovey soon discovered that the First Lady was not one to inspire fear. "No person," she recalled, "could remain ill at ease in the presence of a woman who arrived without an entourage and sailed past ceremony as she did. After our first introduction, she greeted me by name each time I saw her and unfailingly inquired for my welfare before sinking into one of the old armchairs and getting down to business" with Bethune.

It was months after Dovey settled in DC, bunking at the Phyllis Wheatley Y on Rhode Island Avenue, NW, about a five-minute walk from Bethune's headquarters, that she learned what Bethune's "something else" was.

NO GLAMOUR GIRLS NEED APPLY

WHEN WORLD WAR II erupted on the heels of Nazi Germany's invasion of Poland in 1939, Americans were caught up in a great debate.

Isolationists clamored for the United States to stay out of the fight.

Interventionists wanted the nation squarely in it, not just by supplying Allied forces with weapons of war, but also with boots on the ground, fighter planes and bombers in the air, torpedo boats and cruisers on the high seas.

A draft for military service for men ages twenty-one to thirty-five began in October 1940. Soon the question wasn't *if* the nation would enter the war but *when*. Nazi Germany, led by Adolf Hitler, had invaded Denmark and Norway, had blitzkrieged Belgium and Holland, had occupied France. Its Luftwaffe had pounded Britain with a four-month air assault. What's more, fascist Italy and the Empire of Japan had entered into a pact with Germany.

In this growing global conflict, when the United States stepped in big it would need all the resources that it could muster.

A few months before Dovey went to DC, in early May 1941,

one of the first women elected to Congress, Massachusetts representative Edith Nourse Rogers, sponsored a bill to create the Women's Army Auxiliary Corps (WAAC). This corps wouldn't be a part of the US Army, but attached to it.

WAACs were to serve as army support staff: to work at army bases, hospitals, and other military installations as accountants, bakers, clerks, cooks, cryptographers, truck and ambulance drivers, radio, teletype, and telephone operators. Women in such "behind-the-lines assignments" would free up men for combat duty.

Though no one dreamed of women serving in combat, many Americans were appalled by the very idea of the WAAC. Asked Michigan representative Clare Eugene Hoffman, "Who will do the cooking, the washing, the mending, the humble homey tasks to which every woman has devoted herself; who will nurture the children?"

Then came the morning of Sunday, December 7, 1941, when the Empire of Japan pulled off a spectacular air attack on the US naval base at Pearl Harbor on the island of Oahu, Hawaii. Within two hours, more than three hundred Japanese planes, dive bombers and torpedo bombers among them, destroyed or damaged eight battleships and nineteen other naval vessels, along with more than three hundred aircraft.

The attack left roughly one thousand Americans wounded and resulted in more than two thousand deaths. And it had America on high alert, especially in Dovey's temporary home, DC.

"Heavy Guard Thrown Around Capital's Most Vital Spots," reported the *Washington Post* on December 8, the day President Roosevelt addressed a joint session of Congress requesting a declaration of war against the Empire of Japan. In the Senate the vote was 82–0. In the House of Representatives the vote was 388–1.

That bill to create the WAAC was soon back in play. On March 12, 1942, after a three-hour debate, it passed in the House with a vote of 249–86.

New York congressman Andrew Somers was apoplectic. He lambasted the bill as the "silliest piece of legislation" he had ever seen. "A woman's army to defend the United States of America. Think of the humiliation. What has become of the manhood of America, that we have to call on our women to do what has ever been the duty of men?"

Two months after his rant, on May 14, 1942, Somers had to live with that "humiliation." The WAAC bill passed in the Senate (38–27). FDR promptly signed it into law.

THE WAAC ACT CALLED for up to 150,000 women volunteers. At the start 440 women were to be slated for Officer Candidate School. Of that number only forty could be Black.

The person tapped to head the Women's Army Auxiliary Corps was white: thirty-seven-year-old Oveta Culp Hobby, a former Texas First Lady.

Hobby had achieved great things in her own right. Before she became a Mrs., she had gone where few women had: to law school, in her case the University of Texas Law School at Austin. She later served as a parliamentarian (or adviser) in the Texas House of Representatives. Hobby had also worked as an assistant to Houston's city attorney.

Director Hobby's prospective WAACs had to be US citizens with no dependents under the age of fourteen. They had to be between the ages of twenty-one and forty-five, stand between five and six feet tall, and weigh at least a hundred pounds. WAAC candidates would have "to pass a physical examination and an intelligence test comparable to that required of an officer in the regular army," reported the *New York Times Magazine.*

One of Director Hobby's slogans was "No glamour girls need apply."

LIKE ELEANOR ROOSEVELT, Mary McLeod Bethune had been, as Dovey remembered, among the "grand lobbyists" for the WAAC bill. It "consumed" them "in the dark, terrifying months" after the attack on Pearl Harbor.

In her history of Black WAACs, Martha S. Putney laid out Bethune's position clearly: "Bethune saw in the WAAC an opportunity for black females not only to help the nation in its hour of need but also to share in the fruits of victory. She stressed the benefits of being in the service. She spoke in terms of democracy, equality, improved race relations, women's rights, and employment opportunities."

Bethune's vision was in keeping with Black America's Double V campaign.

Victory for democracy overseas.

Victory for democracy in the States.

Inevitably Bethune became very involved with Black WAACs. Denied the post of WAAC assistant director, she secured a position as a special assistant to the Secretary of War on the selection of Black officer candidates, known as the First Forty. All were "handpicked and approved" by her, stated Putney.

Yes, this was what Bethune had in mind for Dovey in the summer of 1941, anticipating that the WAAC bill would pass.

Before May 1942 was out, Dovey was back in Charlotte to hand in her application for Officer Candidate School. But when she visited the army recruitment center (located in the post office) she met with resistance. Mister Army Recruiter, a white man, refused to take Dovey's application. He claimed to know nothing about the WAAC. When she pleaded her cause, he ordered her to get out of his sight, threatened her with arrest.

Dovey, undaunted, went to Richmond, Virginia. Things were "more open" there, Bethune had said. And, fortunately, Dovey had family there: Mama's brother Ally, a movie projectionist, and his wife, Bessie, lived with their boy and girl in what seems to have been a rather nice home at 502 S. Harrison Street.

There was nothing nice about Richmond's recruiting center, also in a post office. There, a white Mister Recruiter took Dovey's telephone number but then never called her. During her second visit, a different Mister Recruiter "interrogated" her "at length" and "seemed stunned by my educational background." Finally, her persistence paid off.

On the Fourth of July 1942, the *Baltimore Afro-American* saluted her with the headline "Miss Dovey Johnson Passes WAAC Exams."

About a week later, in Richmond, twenty-eight-year-old Dovey Mae Johnson was one of five women sworn in as a WAAC officer candidate.

On July 14, Staunton, Virginia's *News-Leader* reported that Dovey and the four other women (all white) were soon to report to Iowa's Fort Des Moines where they'd be issued "uniforms and other equipment, including two girdles" and "train under strict military discipline." Dovey, five-foot-four and 123 pounds, probably wouldn't need a girdle.

Page 4

Waac NEWS
THE Armygals PUBLICATION

PUBLISHED WEEKLY BY THE SPECIAL SERVICE OFFICE
PROCESSED IN PUBLICATIONS OFFICE
FT. DES MOINES, IA.

The WAAC NEWS receives material supplied by Camp Newspaper Service, War Dept., 205 East 42nd Street, N.Y.C. Credited material may not be re-published without permission from the Camp Newspaper Service.

News Editor   T/5 Alice Amyx
Art Editor   T/5 Eleanor Robertson

Tradition Effaced

We women who hesitated—and there were a lot of us that did—before taking the oath that put us in the place of the man behind the gun, did so for one reason: How would we get along with so many DIFFERENT FEMALES? To think of being housed and regimented with so many personalities of different backgrounds, careers, religions, temperaments, etc. Sometimes it was bad enough with our own sister, our best girl friend——but strangers!

Yet we did it, and we love doing it. It's nothing we can explain, this getting along with countless female minds, unless we could ascribe it to the mutual patriotic spirit in each individual that gives accordance to the one sole purpose; to help free our allies and those people under the **heel** of our enemy who spiritually are allies with us—and to get it over with as quickly as possible.

There is, of course, a lot of griping over trifles which is characteristic of the human being, but nothing kills their cooperative, generous spirit.

We girls who work every afternoon came home on Friday evening, the night preceding formal inspection, and find our floors mysteriously scrubbed to a shining cleanliness. And no one admits doing it. One girl gets an emergency call that her mother is seriously ill, and she has no funds. Yet, what happens? A Waac gives her the money she's saved to pay for a course in a line of training that would have meant advancement to her. Another girl gets a telegram that her sister has died. She, too, is without funds. And what happens? A hat is passed around and the girl soon has money to go home. Then there was the girl who came back from a three day pass, and found her clothes all washed and neatly pressed.

Understand it? We don't try real hard. We just attribute it to that indefinable something we call generosity that bubbles over in the WAAC, soon to be known as the WAC.

Waac Portrait

1st O. Dovey Johnson, Recreational Officer for Special Services, until June 22 had been recruiting since November 6, 1942. All through the Southwest and Southeast, she traveled, working with 4th and 8th Service Commands.

1st O. Johnson was sworn in a year ago July 13 and entered the first Officers Training Class the following July 20.

Before going on recruiting, she was in Motor Transport nine weeks and in Public Relations three weeks.

In asking how many speeches she had made during her seven months of recruiting, 1st O. Johnson replied, "Approximately five-hundred."

Her greatest thrill, she says, was the speech she made June 19 at Majestic Theatre in Dallas, Texas. June 19 was emancipation day in Dallas.

1st O. Johnson taught English at Finley High School in Chester, South Carolina, and was copy writer and proofreader on the "Afro-American" newspaper.

Her one ambition she says is to fly. Airplane modeling has always been a hobby with her.

Cash Prizes!

The MacMillan Company is offering $2,500 for the best novel and $2,500 for the best work of non-fiction. There will also be (at the publisher's discretion) smaller awards, totaling $5,000, for other manuscripts or publishing proposals. All awards are outright payments and are in addition to the author's regular royalties.

A contestant must be either an American citizen serving in a branch of the armed forces of any of the United Nations, or anyone, citizen or otherwise, serving in a branch of the armed forces of the United States. Submissions should be made to the MacMillan Company, 60 Fifth Avenue, New York, N. Y.

★ ★ ★

Former farm girls, now Waacs at Camp Grant, Ill., volunteered to help get in the peas on farms near New Rochelle, Ill., when labor shortage threatened the crops. The girls drove machinery and took drinking water to men in the field. Joliet-Herald News.

A page from a WAAC newsletter featuring a piece on Dovey. In it, we learn that before she became a recruiter she was in motor transport (likely driving a truck) and in public relations. She is referred to here as a first officer, which is equivalent to captain.

ALL-IN

On Monday, July 20, 1942, Dovey M. Johnson, serial number A-308002, reported for duty at Fort Des Moines.

"I was dumped out—no other word will do—at the entrance to Fort Des Moines."

The vehicle that dumped out Dovey at the training camp gates was an army truck tasked all day with ferrying recruits from the train station. The driver had "shunted" Dovey, the only Black woman on that run, to the rear of the truck.

When Dovey emerged from it—

"Negroes on one side!" a white officer commanded. "White women on the other!"

Dovey soon learned that "white" included Asians and light-skinned Puerto Ricans.

Negroes on one side!

White women on the other!

Though stung, Dovey couldn't have been shocked. Like everyone else in America, she knew that Jim Crow ruled in the US armed forces.

———

FOR DOVEY AND OTHER Black women who arrived at Fort Des Moines on that July day, the presence of Mary McLeod Bethune was a godsend. Her encouragement, however, came with pressure.

"I know that you understand very clearly why you are here," she told Dovey. "You must see to it that the others do not forget. I'm counting on you to do that."

"That" was being a credit to the race, proving that they had what it took to lead, something countless women and men, children too, of African descent in America had been doing for more than three hundred years.

And thousands of Black Americans were beyond proud of the First Forty (actually the first thirty-nine because the fortieth never showed).

These Black WAAC officer candidates included teachers like Dovey, a waitress, a beautician, a musician, a housekeeper, a homemaker, an insurance agent, an office manager, a chiropodist. On August 1, the Black-owned *New York Age* trumpeted their presence at Fort Des Moines.

"Though a high school education is the minimum requirement for officer training," said the *Age*, "77 percent of the successful applicants had college backgrounds, and the majority of them received degrees." Some of those college degrees were from historically Black institutions such as Spelman, Howard, Prairie View in Texas, and Tuskegee in Alabama. Others were from majority-white schools such as Simmons College in Boston and the University of Southern California in Los Angeles.

The *New York Age* quoted Director Hobby as saying that as she reviewed the Black applications, she was "impressed by the integrity of their devotion to their country, and I was moved by the intensity of their desire to serve that country."

What some of these Black women said to the *New York Age* bore that out.

Cleopatra Daniels, a schoolteacher from Birmingham, Alabama, declared, "If we are to win the war, it must be won with the help and cooperation of all of us."

"I want to do my part to make America safe for my children and their children's children," stated Ruth Freeman, a graduate of Prairie View and a schoolteacher in Liberty, Texas.

Dovey seconded those emotions while being initiated into life army-style. She was all-in.

All-in while being outfitted with everything from pink bras and girdles and light-brown thick stockings to khakis (shirt, skirt, jacket).

All-in while learning to make a bed military-style with mitered corners and "so tight on the blanket fold that a quarter would bounce," remembered WAAC-mate Charity Adams Earley.

That bed was a cot with a flat, hard mattress. At the head, a tall locker. At the end, a footlocker. With that cot and the lockers came instructions on how to hang and pack things and the right way to shine government-issued brown leather oxfords.

Reveille at 6:30 a.m. Lights out at 9 p.m.

Between those hours there was training in close order drill along with classes in hygiene, first aid, map reading, military courtesy and customs, and other subjects. Physical training, including swimming, was another requirement.

"You are a member of the first Women's Army in the history

A training day at Fort Des Moines in 1943. The caption on the back of this photograph states: "Swinging along in perfect cadence," these Black WAACS "demonstrate their proficiency in infantry drill."

of the United States," stated the *WAC Field Manual*, published a year after Dovey reported to Des Moines. "You are one of the small percentage of women qualified in mind and body to perform a soldier's noncombat duties." According to the manual, "The demands of war are varied, endless, and merciless. To satisfy these demands, you must be fit."

The *WAC Field Manual* recognized that women in the corps had already passed "a rigid examination." But now the real army training would start. "Now you must build the strength and stamina, the control and coordination, to do a man's work any hour of the day, every day of the month."

This manual tells us what Dovey's physical training was probably like. It listed cadence exercises, from arm swings and flings to shoulder hunching and jumping jacks.

There were push-ups and sit-ups. There were full knee bends

with hands on knees and with hands on the floor. There was falling and crawling, two arm tugs, duck waddles, crab walks, crane walks, half swans.

The manual also included training in self-defense, against a left-hand grip, against a two-hand grip, against body holds and choke holds.

WHILE DOVEY WAS DEALING with the grind of basic training, she had Jim Crow cramping her life.

Negroes on one side!

White women on the other!

No living in the same barracks.

No sharing tables in the mess hall.

No Black officers would be permitted to kick back and relax in the one-and-only officers' club.

Dovey and the other would-be officers were not without recreational outlets. They could rent bikes at a place near the base and avail themselves of the tennis court on base and, at scheduled times, the swimming pool. But the pool had to be purified after Black women used it—at a time when the nation was fighting Nazi Germany with its calls for racial purity, its propaganda about the superiority of the Nordic race.

It was also at a time when President Roosevelt was maintaining that people the world over had the right to four freedoms: "freedom of speech and expression," "freedom of every person to worship God in his own way," "freedom from want," and "freedom from fear."

One WAAC slogan was "We Shall Not Fail Freedom."

Despite America failing true freedom at home, Dovey stuck it out.

On August 29, 1942, graduation day, she made history as

a member of the first class of officers in the Women's Army Auxiliary Corps. Of the thirty-nine Black officer candidates she was one of thirty-six that had passed muster.

Dovey had endured, she wrote, a "serious, challenging, and often strenuous experience." But it was also a bonding experience. "The Hup-two-three-four of infantry drill, the classroom lectures and tests, the thrill of being one of hundreds of women marching in step at a retreat parade, the sharing of company miseries caused by swollen feet and tetanus shots all crystalized to make a common denominator in experiences for many who but a few years ago had nothing in common but their sex."

And Lieutenant Dovey M. Johnson was still all-in after a slap in the face in downtown Des Moines at the Savery Hotel, where the army held special training sessions.

In downtown Des Moines there was no Jim Crow in public places. So while in town, Black and white WAACs exercised their right to go to the movies together and sit together in the Savery Hotel's dining hall.

"You darkies move those trays, and sit where you belong," barked a white male officer one day in that dining hall.

Lieutenant Dovey M. Johnson, along with Lieutenant Irma Jackson Cayton, whose husband, Horace, wrote for the *Pittsburgh Courier*, and eight other Black WAAC officers, sent a telegram to Mary McLeod Bethune about the incident in the Savery Hotel and other indignities they had been subjected to since arriving in Des Moines.

When word of this telegram reached Fort Des Moines (thanks to a snitch), Colonel Albert C. Morgan, acting post commandant, had Dovey and Irma report to his office.

Dovey Johnson and Mary McLeod Bethune at a
luncheon at Fort Des Moines around 1943.

He upbraided them as "agitators." That telegram to Bethune
was tantamount to an act of treason, he claimed. He asked them
to resign.

Did Dovey scurry like a frightened mouse into a corner of
the office?

"Colonel Morgan's scare tactics did not work," wrote
Martha S. Putney. Dovey and Irma "knew the definition of
'treason' and knew that what Colonel Morgan was talking
about was not it."

Remembered Dovey: "We might be agitators, I told him, but
we were not traitors. When we refused to submit our resignations,
as he demanded, he stared at us in stony silence for a moment,
then waved us out of his office."

Still Lieutenant Dovey M. Johnson was all-in.

All-in when she was sent out on the road as a WAAC recruiter and induction officer in Black communities, initially in the South.

All-in when doing her duty meant navigating Jim Crow —finding, for example, safe and decent places to grab a twenty-five-cent sandwich, a ten-cent cup of coffee.

Her uniform wasn't necessarily a shield. A Black person in uniform, male or female, was a prime vexation for many white people.

Dovey remained undaunted: "I believed in the war effort, in the critical role of women in that effort, and in the right of blacks to fight alongside whites—not later, not at some distant future date when America and the army walked out into the light and abandoned Jim Crow, but now."

When Dovey went out on the road in November 1942 with Tuskegee graduate Lieutenant Ruth Lucas, she knew that recruiting would not be easy. Not a single Black woman had applied for the WAAC Officer Candidate School since they arrived at Fort Des Moines four months earlier. The overall number of Black women enlistees was dismal: less than two hundred.

Segregation within the WAAC was one reason for the low numbers. An even greater turnoff was the nasty rumor that WAACs were really being groomed to be prostitutes for GI Joes.

Dovey sought to win Black women over at schools, at churches, NAACP meetings, YWCAs, community meetings, in people's homes. In Orangeburg, South Carolina, in mid-December 1942, she and Ruth addressed faculty and students at South Carolina State A&M, at Claflin College, and at Wilkinson High.

In January 1943, in Macon, Georgia, Dovey and Ruth spoke

one day at an AME church and on another set up their recruiting center in a post office.

In February they were in Florida, where the *Orlando Morning Sentinel* wrote: "Lt. Dovey M. Johnson, colored WAAC, will be in Orlando at the Army Recruiting Station, 204 Post Office Bldg, through Thursday for the purpose of interviewing colored girl applicants for the WAACS."

Later that month Dovey and Ruth were in Tampa, speaking at Black churches, at Gibbs High, and at a community center. In seeking Black WAACs, the duo also took to the airwaves of radio station WTSP. "NEGRO OFFICERS BEGIN WAAC RECRUITING" reads the caption of a photograph in the *Tampa Sunday Tribune* showing a confident, cheery-looking Dovey, flanked by Ruth Lucas and third officer Thelma M. Brown, in the midst of an interview with substitute schoolteacher Dillie Boyd Ivey.

WHATEVER CONFIDENCE, CHEER, SENSE of purpose Dovey had while in Florida was blunted one evening at a bus station in Miami. Dovey was on her way to another Florida town where she was to meet Ruth Lucas.

With the back of the bus filling up, Dovey took a seat in the front. She was feeling army strong in her uniform, feeling even a "sense of oneness" with white soldiers and sailors boarding that bus. That is, until Mister Bus Driver demanded that Dovey surrender her seat to a white soldier.

Dovey protested. "I am traveling on army business." She reached for her itinerary. "And I have orders to depart Miami by this bus."

Mister Bus Driver wasn't having it. He ordered Dovey off the bus and to the very back of the line.

Dovey acquiesced, perhaps figuring that by the time she got back on the bus she'd end up having to stand. But the outcome was worse than that.

With all the white soldiers and sailors on board, Mister Bus Driver shut the doors and pulled out of the bus station.

Lieutenant Dovey M. Johnson stood there in the darkness.

With her duffel bag.

With humiliation weighing her down.

With rage grabbing at her heels as she trudged to the near-empty bus terminal where she waited for another bus.

For more than an hour.

For more than two.

For more than three.

All-in?

OF COURAGE AND CONVICTION

"My job is to impress upon every Negro woman that her obligation to her country is just as real as the obligation of any other citizen," Dovey said to a reporter. This was in Dallas, Texas, in March 1943.

Dovey wrote to Florence Read, still Spelman's president, telling her that she found Dallas "beautifully planned." The city's downtown was "particularly attractive. Tall clean cut buildings—modernistically designed, provide an amazing skyline," but—"If only the heart of the people might soar heaven ward like the buildings!"

Dovey told Read that she had been called "n----er WAAC" numerous times and had been denied office space in the recruiting office because Blacks and whites weren't allowed to use the same restroom. Also, one day a cop stopped her and insisted on checking her credentials "to see if I had the right to wear a WAAC uniform."

In April, Dovey wrote to Read with good news: "Dear Pres. Read, Just a note to say I was promoted to Captain April 12!"

That summer Dovey and all the other WAACS got glorious

Dovey M. Johnson and Ruth Lucas during a visit to Spelman in the spring of 1943. The woman in the middle is Spelman's president, Florence Read. Ruth will one day become the Air Force's first Black woman colonel.

news. Come September they would no longer be WAACs but WACs: members of the Women's Army Corps.

This was no simple name change.

Thanks to the efforts of Representative Edith Nourse Rogers, the WAC would become, like the Army Nurse Corps, a branch of the US Army. Dovey and the other women doing that behind-the-lines work would be entitled to all the rights and benefits that men in the army had.

Before the conversion became official, in early September 1943, Dovey and other Black WAACs at Fort Des Moines were dealt a blow: There was to be an end to integrated training.

During a meeting headed by Commandant Colonel Frank U. McCoskrie about the particulars of a new Black regiment, a few Black women, including Dovey, expressed their objections to the plan. On her feet and with permission to speak, Dovey removed her captain's bars from her uniform, indicating that she was prepared to resign her commission or be discharged. "Sir, you are setting us back a hundred years."

Martha S. Putney, who joined the corps in 1943, wrote that Dovey "stated that if the lessons taught to her and other WAACs by the training films *Four Freedoms* and *Why We Are Fighting* were to have any meaning, then the regiment should not exist. It was an emotional speech, and Johnson practically preached to the group. When she finished, the meeting was summarily dismissed."

A few days after the meeting, that plan for more Jim Crow at Fort Des Moines was scrapped.

Putney added that other Black WAACs had offered their resignations and that Mary McLeod Bethune's NCNW had expressed its opposition to the plan.

CAPTAIN DOVEY M. JOHNSON returned to the road, keeping the faith in America, in Bethune's vision, in herself.

In the winter of 1943–1944 she was in Ohio. "I am interested only in women of courage and conviction," she told a reporter at the start of a recruiting drive that would take her, among other places, to Columbus, Akron, and Warren, with detours to inspect Black WACs posted in Indiana (at Camp Atterbury) and in Kentucky (at Camp Breckinridge and Fort Knox). What she found at those posts made her smile.

"Brown America may well be proud of the fine representation they now have in the WAC. I saw our women engaged in over fifty vital jobs," Dovey told a reporter. At Camp Atterbury, she met Black women who served, for example, as dental and physician assistants and drove ambulances—sometimes twelve hours a day.

In the spring of 1944, *Pittsburgh Courier* editor and columnist

Toki Schalk proudly reported on an event in Cincinnati sponsored by Alpha Kappa Alpha, a Black sorority. Dovey Johnson was, said Schalk, "without doubt one of this age's most forceful speakers."

Russian forces had trounced German troops on the Eastern Front by then.

American and British forces had beaten Axis forces in North Africa.

Then came D-Day—June 6, 1944—when some 160,000 Allied troops landed on the beaches of Normandy, France. This was the start of Operation Overlord, whose goal was to wrest control of Western Europe from Nazi hands.

Ten months later, on April 12, 1945, America was in mourning. President Roosevelt, the only person to serve as a US president for more than two terms, died of a massive stroke, leaving his vice president, Harry Truman, to see the war effort through.

A little over two weeks after President Roosevelt died, Nazi Germany's Adolf Hitler committed suicide. Within days, Nazi forces in Italy, then in Germany, Holland, and Denmark, surrendered. Four months later, in early August, the United States dropped atomic bombs on the Japanese cities of Hiroshima and Nagasaki.

"PEACE! It's Over," declared the *Charlotte Observer* on August 15, 1945.

Captain Dovey M. Johnson was soon homeward bound with a stop along the way in New York City, where her sister Bea lived with her husband, Gene.

On Broadway, the Big Apple's most famous boulevard,

Dovey had a fantastic time at one of what would be many postwar ticker-tape parades. "All around me, grown men wept openly and complete strangers hugged each other. I stood a-tiptoe in my starched dress uniform, cheering and waving a flag amidst a blizzard of ticker tape so thick it obscured the edges of the shops and theater marquees and office buildings that lined both sides of the street."

For a moment in time "black and white alike, it made no difference. . . . If every day could have been like the golden afternoon of that victory parade, when millions of people of every race cheered the arrival of peace . . ."

PEACE! It's Over.

An estimated 50 million to 80 million people, military and civilian—men, women, girls, boys—died in World War II.

From bombs, bullets, flamethrowers, armored tank shells.

In fires.

In below-zero cold.

Of hunger.

Of disease.

In POW camps.

In concentration camps.

PEACE! It's Over.

In America's fight for those "four freedoms," millions of Black Americans had seriously rallied 'round the flag.

More than 900,000 Black men served in the US Army, many consigned to noncombat duties stateside and overseas. Only one division of Black soldiers, the 92nd Infantry Division, saw combat in Europe.

The Army Air Corps had its first Black flyboys, the Tuskegee Airmen. Of the nearly one thousand pilots trained at Alabama's

Tuskegee Army Airfield, about half saw action overseas, proving their bravery by flying roughly 1,500 missions and more than 15,000 sorties in Europe and North Africa.

Roughly 167,000 Black men had served in the Navy, early on only as cooks or mess stewards.

About 18,000 Black men had served in the Marine Corps. Roughly 12,000 of these Leathernecks saw action in the Pacific, including on the Japanese island of Iwo Jima, site of one of the war's bloodiest battles, one stamped on American memories by the famous photograph of six white Marines raising a US flag on Mount Suribachi.

Black men, roughly 5,000, also served in the Coast Guard. Three became ship commanders.

Troops of American women had proved themselves ready and brave as well. Some 59,000 served in the Army Nurse Corps, which accepted only about 500 Black women. Still, that was better than the Navy Nurse Corps (with roughly 11,000 women), which didn't admit a Black woman (Phyllis Mae Dailey) until March 1945.

As for Dovey and other Black WACs, they numbered a little over 6,500 of the corps's more than 150,000 women.

WACs had paved the way for women to serve in other branches of the military, ones not very—or not at all—welcoming to Black women.

A mere 72 of roughly 90,000 WAVES (the Navy's Women Accepted for Volunteer Emergency Service) were Black.

Only five Black women were among the nearly 12,000 SPARs (the Coast Guard's Women's Reserve—the name derived from the Coast Guard's Latin motto *Semper Paratus*—"Always Ready").

Of the roughly 1,100 WASPs (Women's Air Force Service Pilots), a few were Asian and one was Native American but no Black women were accepted. The Marine Corps's Women's Reserve also barred Black women.

PEACE! It's Over.

But racial discrimination, surely, wasn't over in America. Neither was sexism. Still, so many Black people and so many women who served in the armed forces had a sense of new possibilities.

So what would thirty-one-year-old Captain Dovey Mae Johnson, a Black woman with serious leadership chops, do now?

Remain in the armed forces as her friend Ruth Lucas would do?

Return to teaching?

Work again for Mary McLeod Bethune?

9

HER LEGACY TO ME

EDITH WIMBISH STEERING HER to Spelman . . .

The Hurleys' move to Atlanta . . .

Mary Mae Neptune encouraging her, rescuing her . . .

Mary McLeod Bethune handpicking her for that "something else" . . .

Luck?

Or was there something about Dovey that compelled Life to pave the way for her, open doors, put her in the right place at the right time?

It was because of a chance meeting with A. Philip Randolph during the war that, after it, Captain Dovey M. Johnson became a warrior in a different sort of war.

CHARISMATIC ACTOR TURNED ACTIVIST A. Philip Randolph had as a young man taken on an upper-class British accent and had a penchant for "vouchsafe" and other quaint words. But behind his genteel ways was the heart of a street fighter.

Randolph, whose threat of a March on Washington had helped propel FDR to issue Executive Order 8802 and to create the Fair Employment Practice Committee, was in the forefront of

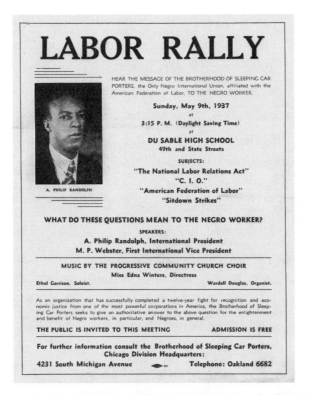

LABOR RALLY

HEAR THE MESSAGE OF THE BROTHERHOOD OF SLEEPING CAR PORTERS, the Only Negro International Union, affiliated with the American Federation of Labor, TO THE NEGRO WORKER.

Sunday, May 9th, 1937

at

3:15 P. M. (Daylight Saving Time)

at

DU SABLE HIGH SCHOOL
49th and State Streets

SUBJECTS:

"The National Labor Relations Act"
"C. I. O."
"American Federation of Labor"
"Sitdown Strikes"

A. PHILIP RANDOLPH

WHAT DO THESE QUESTIONS MEAN TO THE NEGRO WORKER?

SPEAKERS:
A. Philip Randolph, International President
M. P. Webster, First International Vice President

MUSIC BY THE PROGRESSIVE COMMUNITY CHURCH CHOIR
Miss Edna Winters, Directress

Ethel Garrison, Soloist.   Wardell Douglas, Organist.

As an organization that has successfully completed a twelve-year fight for recognition and economic justice from one of the most powerful corporations in America, the Brotherhood of Sleeping Car Porters seeks to give an authoritative answer to the above question for the enlightenment and benefit of Negro workers, in particular, and Negroes, in general.

THE PUBLIC IS INVITED TO THIS MEETING   ADMISSION IS FREE

For further information consult the Brotherhood of Sleeping Car Porters, Chicago Division Headquarters:

4231 South Michigan Avenue   Telephone: Oakland 6682

A flyer for a labor rally in Chicago in 1937. In 1925 Florida-born Asa Philip Randolph founded the Brotherhood of Sleeping Car Porters, a labor union dedicated to getting better working conditions and higher pay for the Black men and women who worked as porters and maids on railroad cars manufactured and operated by the Pullman Car Company, which once dominated the railroad car industry.

the fight to save that agency, which was set to shutter on June 30, 1946.

During the war, Black employment in the defense industry had nearly tripled, rising from 3 percent to 8 percent. Many of these Black hires were limited to the lowest paying jobs, as janitors and cafeteria workers, for example. But a job was a job. Without the FEPC, Black people might lose those jobs. Without a watchdog agency to investigate claims of discrimination, plants could not only fire, but also refuse to hire Black people.

The FEPC was also a watchdog on discrimination in federal government jobs. This opened the way for more Black women and men to become civil servants, from cleaners, clerks, and messengers to stenographers and even supervisors in, say, the Treasury Department. Without the FEPC, those doors might slam shut. By war's end, Black employment in the government had more than tripled, to some 200,000 jobs.

To save the FEPC, back in 1943, Randolph had launched the National Council for a Permanent Fair Employment Practice Committee. In letters, in articles, in speeches, Randolph was relentless.

"Where there is no freedom of opportunity and no economic security we cannot speak of democracy," he wrote to Du Bois during the war, urging him to join his council to save the FEPC. "That is the 'why' of our fight against the Axis; that is the 'why' of our insistence that the F.E.P.C. be made permanent by Congressional act."

Also during the war, before a Senate subcommittee on labor and education, Randolph billboarded the fact that with so many white men off to war there was a shortage of white skilled railroad workers. This shortage led to delays (including in troop transports) and to accidents because of botched work by inexperienced men.

But this shortage did not have to be. There were ample qualified Black railroad workers—from brakemen and switchmen to machinists and boilermakers—who were unemployed because of a catch-22. Many railroad companies refused to hire skilled workers who were not in a union. Many white-run unions refused to have Black members.

"There cannot be full employment unless there is fair employment," Randolph told that Senate subcommittee. He stressed, too, that racial prejudice and racial discrimination were two different things.

One was an emotion.

The other was a practice.

Instead of waiting for white people's emotions to change, Randolph was out to stop a discriminatory practice.

DOVEY FIRST MET RANDOLPH when she was seeking Black WACs in Kansas City, Missouri, at a gathering in the home of a fellow WAC. After Randolph watched Dovey hold forth in a recruiting pitch, he invited her to look him up if she was ever in New York City.

While visiting Bea, after celebrating at that ticker-tape parade, Dovey telephoned Randolph. The result was an appointment to see him in his offices at 217 West 125th Street, a three-story walk-up near the world-famous Apollo Theater. When Dovey left Randolph's office that autumn morning, she was thoroughly committed to his crusade, feeling as if she had "been fired from a cannon."

Before long, hup-two-three-four, Dovey was in Washington, DC, to get her assignment from the Black woman who ran Randolph's council: the whip-smart, savvy midwesterner Anna Arnold Hedgeman.

At Hedgeman's headquarters on F Street, NW, in DC, Dovey learned that she was to be the West Coast representative, to campaign for a permanent FEPC in California, Oregon, and the state of Washington, all home to major aircraft and ship manufacturers, employing thousands.

Before Dovey went west, she went home as planned. Neither Mama nor Grandma Rachel was thrilled about her taking a job that would put three thousand miles between her and them.

"Mama's face fell and Grandma grew quiet" on that early autumn day.

Dovey knew they would miss her terribly, as they'd missed her when she was at Spelman, when she taught in South Carolina, when she served as a WAC. Now, again, they would have to contend with sporadic visits. But Dovey assured them that she wouldn't be out on the West Coast *forever*. And of course, when Dovey left 921 East Hill Street, she left with their love.

After that, Dovey traveled farther south to fulfill a pledge.

"ALWAYS, SHE'D LIVED MODESTLY, sustained by her students and surrounded by her books. Even now the works of the writers she'd taught me to love—Shakespeare, Milton, Keats, Austen, Dickens—lined the walls of the tiny one-room apartment."

It was late October, 1945. Mary Mae Neptune, retired and in her seventies, was living in Decatur, Georgia. She served her guest tea.

"But as I surveyed the familiar volumes my gaze wandered to the threadbare furniture, the frayed draperies and worn rugs." Professor Neptune was living on a very small pension.

Mentor and mentee had kept in touch. Dovey had continued repaying that loan in pieces. A money order for two dollars here, ten dollars there, more during her military service when her monthly pay was $166 as a lieutenant, $200 as a captain.

Now Dovey was in Professor Neptune's home to pay off the balance she owed—plus a little extra.

"What on earth is this, Dovey Johnson?" asked a shocked

Mary Mae Neptune as Dovey placed bill after bill on a table for a grand total of $250.

Bill after bill after bill with Dovey "groping for some way to put into words the full weight of my indebtedness, the impossibility of ever repaying her legacy to me."

Dovey soon left that tiny apartment with its crowd of books, threadbare furniture, frayed draperies, worn rugs. When she did, she had Mary Mae Neptune's blessing on the FEPC work ahead of her.

WITH HER EXCELLENT PUBLIC relations and public speaking skills fine-tuned in the military, Field Representative Dovey M. Johnson sounded the alarm about the need for a permanent FEPC to Black people, white people, Latinos. In San Diego. In Los Angeles. In San Francisco. She worked with a range of civic and religious organizations. She raised funds for Randolph's National Council too.

Dovey described her work to Florence Read as "stimulating." Something desperately needed. "Somehow I have not been able to switch over to routine living. . . . I've got to be busy." After all those weeks and months of recruiting Black WACs, her new venture for the FEPC, talking to group after group, was perfect.

"California has a peculiar social chemistry," Dovey remarked in December 1945 to a group in the Bay Area community of Vallejo. By social chemistry Dovey meant California's racial and religious diversity. She urged the crowd to see the strength in that diversity and to recognize that when any one group "suffers discrimination, no other group is secure."

This was according to the *Vallejo Observer*, a Black-owned

biweekly. The newspaper also reported that Dovey "cited recent United States Employment Service figures which list 75 per cent of unemployed persons as members of minority groups while 50 per cent of available jobs are marked 'for white only.'" Dovey called on the crowd to write to their senators and representatives urging them to vote yes on a permanent FEPC.

But a bill for a broad-based, muscular FEPC was not to be. It would fail to clear Congress thanks to opposition from white southerners in the Senate.

Though the FEPC died, Dovey's work on the West Coast was not in vain. She did raise people's consciousness. What's more, had she never gone west, she might never have met that "soul on fire" who inspired her to blaze another trail.

SHATTER THE MONSTER

"THE ANSWER FOR BLACK PEOPLE, she told me in one of our first conversations, lay in the law. It was the law, misapplied, twisted, disingenuously interpreted, that had generated the monstrosity known as separate but equal. And it was the law just as surely, she argued, that could—that *would*—shatter the monster."

"She" was Pauli Murray, that "soul on fire," who in 1933 had earned a bachelor's degree in English from New York City's prestigious then all-woman Hunter College. Pauli had been one of only four Black students in a class of 250.

In 1944 she graduated from Howard University School of Law at the top of her class, the only woman in a class of seven.

Before Howard Law, Murray had applied to the graduate school of the University of North Carolina at Chapel Hill.

She was rejected because she was Black.

After Howard Law, she applied to Harvard Law—with a letter of recommendation from none other than President Roosevelt.

She was rejected because she was a woman.

Pauli Murray hadn't been naive. She knew the all-white

Pauli Murray in 1946. In December of that year, this native of Baltimore raised in Durham, North Carolina, received a Mademoiselle Merit Award, as one of the magazine's 10 picks for "Young Women of the Year." At the time she was practicing law in New York City. Murray, also a gifted writer, became the first Black person to earn a doctorate in law from Yale Law in 1965. The following year she was a cofounder of the National Organization for Women. In 1977, she became the Episcopal Church's first Black woman priest.

University of North Carolina and the all-male (and nearly all-white) Harvard Law would reject her. She wanted to make a case, a point, to have a paper trail of the injustice of Jim Crow *and* of what she termed Jane Crow, the subjugation of women to second-class citizenship.

Dovey had known Murray by reputation. What an absolute thrill it was to meet her in the fall of 1945 at a forum in Southern California where Dovey spoke on the FEPC. Murray, then at work on a master's in law from the University of California at Berkeley, was in the audience. After Dovey's speech the two got talking.

The answer for black people, she told me . . . lay in the law.

"As I studied her," Dovey wrote, "watched her quarterback discussions with her Berkeley colleagues, soaked up her cerebrations on the Constitution and the wrongs it could right if properly applied, I felt the power of an intellect that swallowed me up."

Dovey began reading all manner of things legal, from Pauli Murray's articles in the *California Law Review* to US Supreme Court opinions. Dovey grappled with the intricacies of the Constitution, of rulings, of laws.

"The more I processed Pauli's gospel—and a gospel it truly was—the more the law drew me like a magnet."

Once again there was Dovey with a big-deal dream. Black intellectual prowess was widely doubted outside the Black community—despite the Frederick Douglasses, the Du Boises, the Carter G. Woodsons, the Mary Church Terrells, the Mary McLeod Bethunes, the A. Philip Randolphs, the Pauli Murrays. What's more, in and outside the Black community, many people deemed lawyering men's work, believing that women—"the weaker sex"—lacked the mental muscle, the stamina to master the law.

In 1940, a year before Pauli entered Howard Law, America had roughly 173,000 male lawyers. Of that number about 1,000 were Black men. Of the nearly 4,200 female lawyers, a mere 39 were Black women. So Pauli Murray was indeed a rare bird and Dovey was prepared to be one too. She decided to attend Howard Law, then devote herself to shattering the monster.

Going to law school was financially feasible thanks to the Servicemen's Readjustment Act of 1944, better known as the GI Bill. Through it veterans honorably discharged who had served at least ninety days could get low-interest loans to begin businesses, low-interest mortgages for purchasing homes, and money for educational expenses. As a former WAC, Dovey could go to law school on the GI Bill.

The answer for black people, she told me . . . lay in the law.

The law wasn't the only magnet in Dovey's life while she was working out west to save the FEPC. There was also a man, Morehouse graduate William Andre "Bill" Roundtree. In her memoir Dovey wrote that, during her Spelman days, the two had chatted aboard trolley cars, gone to movies, enjoyed picnics and library study dates.

Light-brown-skinned Bill was, like Dovey's Papa, "so tall and so handsome." Like Dovey this native of Atlanta was not a member of the Black bourgeoisie. He came from a family of domestic workers and had been one himself. As a teen he was a servant in the home of a white assistant cashier at a bank. Bill was working as a houseman and yardman for the same employer when in 1942 he enlisted in the army, where he rose from private to lieutenant.

Though their romance had fizzled out after they graduated from college, during the war the two had kept in touch. After the war, a long-distance courtship ensued through phone calls.

As the law drew Dovey like a magnet, at first Bill cheered her on. Her plan to go to Howard Law became his plan too.

In December 1945, the couple met in Chicago to marry, she from her FEPC field work in Portland, Oregon, and he from Atlanta.

They married on Christmas Eve: Dovey in a powder-blue suit, Bill in his uniform. Their simple ceremony was held in the home of Baptist minister Ira M. Hendon and his wife, Belle. The

Reverend Hendon pastored the church to which Dovey's maid of honor and WAC mate Ruth Freeman belonged.

Married within just a few months of reconnecting?

Having not laid eyes on each other for years?

Dovey later chalked it up to "the madness of the postwar world, a time when the longing for normalcy eclipsed the common sense of otherwise sane souls."

AFTER THE WEDDING, DOVEY returned to her FEPC work. Bill was close by her side during the rest of her Oregon campaign.

But something was very wrong. "The more I talked of 'our' law school plans as we prepared to leave Portland, the quieter he grew."

After Dovey completed her work for the FEPC and the couple settled in Washington, DC, it became very clear to Dovey that something was very wrong. "Our days were filled with the pressing matter of securing jobs. But when we faced each other across the table in the evenings, our little efficiency apartment echoed in the way a home echoes when it is truly empty."

In the summer of 1946 Dovey and Bill faced a hard truth. Marrying *had* been madness, a mistake.

As for law school, it "had been my dream, not his, he said." Bill did not share her passion for a life devoted to the civil rights crusade. One day he told her that he planned to re-enlist in the army—"perhaps even go overseas again."

The two soon separated.

This time for good.

———

IN MID-SEPTEMBER 1946, DOVEY was no longer living in that efficiency apartment but in Room A205 in Wake Hall on 24th and Oklahoma, a government dorm for veterans. This was the address she gave on an application for a job as an administrative assistant with the Office of Price Administration, a job she did not get. However, a year later she got her wish to go to law school.

OF SACREDNESS

"Are you registering for your husband or your brother?"

That's what a clerk in the registrar's office at Howard University asked Dovey when she handed over the paperwork that would enable her to attend its law school on the GI Bill.

Remembered Dovey: "That a woman should have attained the rank of captain in the army seemed to confound her entirely, and her colleagues as well. One by one, they abandoned their posts at the counter and stepped over to scrutinize both me and my army papers, at which point the entire registration process ground to a halt."

Dovey finally cut through the nonsense. "Do it just like you do it for the male veterans."

In September 1947 Dovey became a student at Howard Law, a first-rate school at a university with the motto *Veritas et Utilitas*: Truth and Service.

Charles Hamilton Houston was the person who had made Howard Law first-rate.

This tough, tenacious, and physically imposing member of DC's Black elite was a graduate of Amherst College (magna cum laude and Phi Beta Kappa 1915) and of Harvard Law, where he became the first Black student elected to the editorial board of its scholarly journal, *Harvard Law Review*. At Harvard Charlie Houston earned a bachelor of laws (LLB) degree in 1922 and an SJD (the equivalent of a PhD in law) in 1923. He capped that with a year of civil law studies in Spain, at the University of Madrid.

Houston began transforming Howard Law in 1929 after he was appointed its vice dean. By the time he stepped down in 1935 to become the NAACP's general counsel, Houston had raised the standards for admission, developed a rigorous curriculum, and recruited the brightest minds he could find for his faculty.

Most important, Houston trained up a corps of law students to be crusaders, warriors against Jim Crow, believers like him that a lawyer was "either a social engineer"—a force for good—"or a parasite on society."

Houston and his troops, including future US Supreme Court justice Thurgood Marshall (class of 1933), took on Jim Crow in the workplace, in transportation, and, most of all, in education, always with a tight focus on the fact that "separate" schools and such were almost never "equal."

For example, Houston took up the cause of Donald Gaines Murray, an Amherst graduate. In 1935 Murray was denied admission to the University of Maryland's law school solely because of his race.

But where was Maryland's separate but equal law school for Black people? As a result of Houston's deft handling of the young man's lawsuit, Donald Gaines Murray was admitted to University of Maryland's law school.

For this victory and for his overall strategy for shattering the monster, Charles Hamilton Houston became known as "Mr. Civil Rights" and as "The Man Who Killed Jim Crow."

WHEN THIRTY-THREE-YEAR-OLD Dovey Mae Johnson Roundtree entered Howard Law in the fall of 1947, Houston was still waging legal attacks on Jim Crow, but he had stepped down as NAACP's general counsel for health reasons. He had handed the reins over to Thurgood Marshall, founder in 1940 of America's first civil rights law firm: the NAACP Legal Defense and Educational Fund—the LDF for short.

At Howard, Dovey witnessed some of Marshall's masterminding in the war on Jim Crow. She remembered him "and his band" of LDF attorneys practically taking over Howard's campus at one point. They "set up camp in the library, mined its materials and amassed more, and convened in our moot courtroom on the evenings preceding their oral arguments before the Supreme Court for 'dry runs' of the cases."

Weighing in was Professor James Madison Nabrit Jr., a graduate of Morehouse and of Northwestern University's law school and a civil rights attorney who had had a successful practice in Houston, Texas.

Professor Nabrit, whose father had given Dovey a glowing recommendation for Spelman, was without a doubt one of Charlie Houston's best recruits. And apparently a terror to first-year students.

"No one forgets the memorable and dramatic first meeting with Mr. James Madison Nabrit," wrote one of Dovey's classmates. Questions that freckled, ginger-haired, blue-eyed Nabrit lobbed at students "were baffling, his pace was inexorable." However, "as the days gathered themselves into weeks, we learned that no master could have a keener interest in his charges, no sage could stimulate the thinking processes more than this scholarly gentleman with the Texas drawl."

Dovey was forever indebted to fine minds at Howard Law, including George E. C. Hayes, "the venerable master of civil procedure," and labor law experts Joe Waddy and Howard Jenkins, but it was Nabrit, she said, "who made me a lawyer."

It was through Nabrit that she came to her "earliest understanding of the Constitution, of its perversion, and of its promise." She credited him with shaping not only her "approach to legal reasoning" but also her "vision of the law as a thing of sacredness."

Civil procedure.

Labor law.

Civil rights law.

Criminal law.

Constitutional law.

Heady, tough (and at times dry) stuff, requiring long hours of study in the library and in her little apartment in Southeast DC.

During her early days at Howard, there were moments when Dovey felt as if she was "drowning." This at a time when she was working two part-time jobs. What's more, Dovey was dealing with diabetes, which can cause fatigue and brain fog and which left her with some eyesight problems.

But Dovey received a lot of encouragement from members of the Howard Law family.

One of those people was attorney Ollie Mae Cooper. Dovey remembered her as a "mother hen and ally-in-chief to us women students." Cooper had graduated from Howard Law, magna cum laude, in 1921. "You can do it," Cooper told Dovey.

Fellow law student Julius Winfield Robertson was another source of inspiration and encouragement. Julius became a mentor and very good friend.

TOWERING, BOOMING-VOICED JULIUS ROBERTSON was the author of a 1944 pamphlet, *This Bird Must Fly*, a scathing attack on Jim Crow, calling for it to fly high and away, quick, fast, and in a hurry.

Like Dovey, Julius was a child of the South: born in Greensboro, Georgia, and raised in Knoxville, Tennessee. Like her, he had faced hard times. Forced to leave college during the Great Depression, Julius at one point served as a post commandant in Mississippi at a camp of the Civilian Conservation Corps, another of FDR's New Deal initiatives. After Julius moved to DC he became a civil servant, first as a messenger for the Department of Labor.

This big bear of a man was a husband and father of four when in 1945, at age twenty-eight, he entered Howard Law. In 1948, Julius graduated at the top of his class.

Two years later, on Friday, June 9, 1950, it was Dovey Mae Johnson Roundtree's turn to once again don cap and gown. Of the thirty-six students in Howard Law's class of 1950, she was one of only three women.

During her days at Howard Law Dovey had taken on more than just her coursework. We learn from her yearbook that in her second year she received a research award and was appointed to the *Howard Law Review*. As a senior, she was class vice president. She was also a member of a social and professional networking group, the Portia Club, and of Epsilon Sigma Iota Legal Sorority.

In that yearbook, opposite "Major Interest," some students

had listed "General Practice" or "Business and Labor Law" or "Criminal Law." For Dovey it was "Civil Rights."

As GRADUATION DAY NEARED, Dovey's surpassing joy was that Mama and Grandma Rachel would be there to witness her triumph. Dovey had scraped together enough money to send them round-trip Southern Railway tickets, ones stamped "Reserved Seat."

But when Dovey met Mama and Grandma Rachel at Union Station—no joy.

"Grandma was limping, and my mother, disheveled and agitated, walked alongside her, dragging the luggage and looking wildly about in all directions."

Grandma Rachel, who decades earlier had been rendered a girl with "those poor broken feet". . .

Grandma Rachel, who had "a swaying awkwardness" in her gait "that late at night became a limp" . . .

Grandma Rachel had stood during the entire train ride.

Mama too.

From Charlotte, North Carolina, to Concord, to Salisbury, to High Point, to Greensboro, to Reidsville, then on into Virginia, through Danville, Lynchburg, Monroe, Charlottesville, Alexandria, then into Union Station in DC.

A roughly ten-hour journey.

Grandma Rachel was near eighty. Mama in her fifties.

Those tickets stamped "Reserved Seat" meant absolutely nothing.

Grandma Rachel and Mama had to stand for all that time because the Jim Crow car was packed, not a seat to be had, and no one willing to stand in their stead.

They had to stand, too, because when they tried to sit in a half-empty car for white people, the conductor yelled them back into the coach for Black people.

Shortly before the train reached Union Station, Grandma Rachel "collapsed on the closed seat of the toilet in the bathroom at the front of the car, and stayed there," wrote Dovey.

WITH GRANDMA RACHEL AND MAMA in her apartment, Dovey examined those poor broken feet. "They were bruised and bleeding." They needed more than a steaming hot soak and massage. With trembling hands Dovey telephoned her doctor.

Spitting mad, Dovey was consumed with getting justice for her family.

"All through the whirlwind of graduation weekend, with Mama and Grandma rallying to cheer me as I marched proudly into Howard's Rankin Chapel to claim my diploma, my mind moved endlessly over the facts of their case and my chances of winning a lawsuit in their behalf against the Southern Railway."

In the end, with Grandma Rachel in no shape to go through a trial and begging Dovey to just leave the matter alone, Dovey acquiesced, accepting a settlement of a few hundred dollars on Mama and Grandma Rachel's behalf. This was in late 1951.

By then, Dovey had furthered her legal education by taking classes at Georgetown University, and in December 1950, Dovey had taken the grueling two-day bar examination. On December 17, the eve of day one, for inspiration she listened to a radio broadcast of the annual Spelman-Morehouse Christmas Carol Concert.

Two months later, on February 24, 1951, Dovey's name appeared in DC's *Evening Star* in an article headlined "14 Women

Included Among 295 Passing Bar Examinations." Of the 449 people who took the exam, 154 or nearly 35 percent failed to pass it.

Then, a week after her thirty-seventh birthday, on April 21, 1951, Dovey was sworn in as a member of the Washington, DC, bar.

Dovey J. Roundtree, Esquire, soon wrote to Florence Read, announcing that she had been "busy at it since" and had even earned "a fee or two." This was as a junior partner at a firm at 1931 Eleventh Street, NW, headed by three Black men: Lindsey W. Caine, Jesse W. Lewis, and her buddy Julius Robertson.

Dovey also told Read that she planned "to pull out of this organization within the next eight months" to establish a new firm with Julius.

A CALLING

EARLY DAYS WERE LEAN for the law firm of Robertson & Roundtree.

A basket of eggs.

A mess of collards.

That's how some clients paid for services, such as drafting wills and handling a small-claims court case, perhaps a tenant-landlord dispute in which the plaintiff wasn't suing for tens of thousands of dollars, but maybe a few thousand, even a few hundred.

Despite business being lean, one of the first things Dovey did was repay another debt to another Mary: Mary McLeod Bethune, then headquartered in a grand townhouse at 1318 Vermont, NW.

When Dovey went to that townhouse to repay her debt, she didn't give Bethune a stack of bills, but a pledge: for the rest of her life she would give the National Council of Negro Women free legal services. "It was, in my mind, the least I could do by way of paying her back. She'd brought me into an army that for all its discrimination had given me a voice and a role in shaping history."

DRAFTING WILLS AND UNTANGLING deceased people's estates were Robertson & Roundtree's bread and butter. "We took every case that came our way," remembered Dovey, "provided we could do so honestly, and worked it stem to stern, researching and cross-checking each other with enough fanaticism for a half dozen lawyers."

Their firm, with office space consisting of a room in one or another row house on Eleventh Street, NW, was "an almost round-the-clock operation." Julius worked at the post office nights and managed their practice by day. Dovey managed it in the evenings. By then, she worked days at the Department of Labor as an attorney-adviser.

During these lean days, Dovey and Julius were denied membership in the Bar Association of the District of Columbia (BADC) with its networking opportunities and its extraordinary law library housed in the district courthouse, space for which the BADC paid no rent. If Dovey, Julius, and any other Black lawyers wanted to use this library, they had to pay an eight-dollar annual fee. BADC, formed in 1871, opened its doors to white female attorneys in 1941. It would keep them shut to Black attorneys until 1958.

When Dovey and Julius did have business at the district courthouse, they had to leave the building if they needed a lunch break or if nature called. The courthouse bathrooms and cafeteria were whites-only.

In the face of obstacles and discrimination, Dovey and Julius remained committed. For them being a lawyer wasn't about fame and flash, wasn't about bringing in bundles of cash and acquiring things a lot of money can buy. Being a lawyer was "a calling."

Veritas et Utilitas.

A significant opportunity for Dovey and Julius to cleave to that calling, to be lawyers of truth and service, came on a September afternoon in 1952, a day on which DC was still in the grip of summer heat, with folks seeking relief with hand fans, electric fans, and long, tall glasses of ice water.

The case concerned the trampling of the rights of a WAC: Private First Class Sarah Louise Keys.

BACK IN JULY, TWENTY-TWO-YEAR-OLD Sarah Louise Keys, a receptionist and information clerk at Fort Dix, New Jersey, boarded a Safeway Trails bus in nearby Trenton. She was on leave and at the start of a roughly twenty-hour journey to Washington, North Carolina, where her family lived.

When that Safeway Trails bus pulled into the DC bus terminal, Sarah and the other passengers were transferred to a bus operated by Carolina Trailways for the rest of their journey farther south. Sarah opted for a seat near the front.

No problem.

But hours later, on the other side of midnight, that Carolina Trailways driver pulled into the bus terminal in Roanoke Rapids, North Carolina. A new Mister Bus Driver took over.

Problem.

While checking passengers' tickets, this white man ordered Sarah to the back of the bus so that a white Marine could have her seat. This was not only rude, but illegal, made so in 1946 after the ordeal another Black woman, Irene Morgan, had endured while traveling by bus.

En route home to Baltimore from Gloucester County, Virginia, Irene Morgan had refused the Greyhound bus driver's

Roanoke Rapids Bus Terminal, N. C.

A postcard showing a Carolina Trailways bus at the terminal in Roanoke Rapids, North Carolina, where Sarah Keys was humiliated, then arrested.

request that she surrender her seat to a white person. This Mister Bus Driver was operating under a 1930 Virginia law that empowered bus drivers to add to or subtract seats from the "colored" or white sections, make passengers change their seats, and give anyone who didn't cooperate the boot.

Irene Morgan was kicked off that Greyhound bus and placed under arrest. Thurgood Marshall's NAACP LDF took up her case.

In *Morgan v. Virginia*, the US Supreme Court determined that the 1930 Virginia law wasn't applicable. In a 6–1 decision the court ruled that segregation in commercial interstate buses ran afoul of the US Constitution's commerce clause. That clause gave the power to regulate commerce among states to *Congress*, not to states. In other words, a bus operating, say, only in Virginia could enforce Jim Crow seating, but a bus carrying passengers through more than one state could not.

Given Irene Morgan's victory, how was it that six years later another Mister Bus Driver could demand that Sarah Louise Keys surrender her seat?

Because there was massive, sustained white resistance to fairness, to justice, to obeying certain laws.

In July 1946, weeks after the *Morgan* decision, the NAACP's *Crisis* magazine printed a prescient article: "The US Supreme Court opinion in the Irene Morgan case . . . marks the beginning of the end of Jim Crow in this country. There will be resistance by whites in many areas. There will be demagogic statements by politicians and rabble-rousers. There will be timidity among many Negroes. Custom and habit, backed by state laws, have strongly conditioned both whites and blacks so that the overturn will not be sudden."

A Supreme Court ruling is one thing, enforcement another. If bus drivers, if CEOs of bus companies, if board members of those companies refused to obey a ruling like that in *Morgan v. Virginia* . . .

Shattering the monster was painstaking work on the part of thousands of people. Bus companies refusing to obey a US Supreme Court ruling had to be caught in the act. Lawsuits had to be filed. People had to put their lives on the line.

IN THE SUMMER OF 1952, Sarah Louise Keys took a stand in Roanoke Rapids, North Carolina. She took a stand against custom and habit, against timidity. She refused to surrender her seat.

In reaction, Mister Bus Driver ordered passengers onto another bus.

All except Sarah. She was left behind that night, about ninety miles from home. But getting home wasn't even an option. Sarah was arrested for disorderly conduct, carted off to jail.

No phone call.

No release until she paid a $25 fine the next day (equivalent to roughly $300 today).

Howard Law graduate and NAACP attorney Frank Reeves steered Sarah and her father, David, to Robertson & Roundtree.

David Keys, a Navy veteran, was an itinerant mason working in DC at the time. He was not a highly educated man, but he was smart and well-versed in *Morgan v. Virginia*. And it had been precisely to have his daughter spared hassles and humiliation that he had told her to buy a "through-line" ticket—that is, for straight-through service by Safeway Trails. No change in carrier. Now David Keys was determined to get justice for his daughter.

So was Dovey.

How could she not be after being yelled off that trolley car as a kid, after being kicked off that bus in Miami when she was a WAC, after what happened to Grandma Rachel and Mama when they took that train to attend her graduation from law school?

"That September afternoon of 1952 was the last day Julius and I passed like the proverbial 'ships in the night,'" recalled Dovey. Before that September afternoon, they spoke by phone, left notes for each other. Although neither could afford to quit their second jobs, they now found a way to set "aside hours at the edges, in the early mornings and late afternoons, to map out the basis of" their lawsuit on Sarah Louise Key's behalf.

Theirs was a full-on assault against the monster. They decided to sue both bus companies on four counts and seek $10,000 in damages on each count.

The first count was breach of contract involving Sarah's "through-line" ticket.

The second count was violation of the Interstate Commerce Act's ban on "undue and unreasonable prejudice." This was the Supreme Court's wording in its ruling in a 1950 lawsuit involving railroad dining cars.

The third count, wrote Dovey, was "for false arrest that had violated Sarah's right to equal treatment under the Fourteenth Amendment."

The fourth count was for "the mental anguish" Sarah had suffered from the time the bus driver in Roanoke Rapids ordered her out of her seat until she got out of jail the next day.

"The two lines connected in Washington, DC," Dovey explained. "Therein lay our argument for jurisdiction in the federal district court in the District of Columbia." Dovey and Julius served papers on both carriers on November 19, 1952, but met with no success. The suit against the southern carrier, Carolina Coach (doing business as Carolina Trailways), didn't stick because the company was incorporated in Virginia and headquartered in North Carolina, and so serving it papers in DC was "improper." As for the northern carrier, Safeway Trails, the company argued in a hearing before the US district court that it wasn't responsible for what happened to a passenger on another bus line. The court agreed and also ruled that the case was outside its jurisdiction. The case was dismissed on February 23, 1953.

But hope was in the air!

Around this same time the NAACP was working on a case challenging racial segregation in interstate railroad travel. This case, *NAACP v. St. Louis–San Francisco Railroad*, became combined with Robertson & Roundtree's *Keys v. Carolina Coach*. Their cases went not before the US Supreme Court but before the Interstate Commerce Commission, the federal agency charged at the time with regulating certain carriers engaged in transportation between states, including trains and buses.

AS OFTEN HAPPENS, THIS lawsuit took time. While the NAACP, Dovey, Julius, and Sarah Louise Keys and her father waited for a verdict, they eagerly followed another case that would send shock waves throughout the nation.

Brown v. Board of Education.

On May 17, 1954, the US Supreme Court handed down its decision in *Brown*, a consolidation of five lawsuits that shone the spotlight on the degradation endured by so many Black children attending public schools because of Jim Crow.

In a unanimous decision the Supreme Court declared that segregated public schooling was unconstitutional.

It had to end.

"Today, education is perhaps the most important function of state and local governments," wrote Chief Justice Earl Warren. Education, he said, was "the very foundation of good citizenship." But how could a child be expected to succeed in life if given a sub-par education? When it came to government-funded education, the doctrine of "separate but equal" had "no place," Warren declared. "Separate educational facilities are inherently unequal."

Public school desegregation in the South and in parts of the North would be a long-drawn-out and, at times, bloody affair, but the *Brown* decision was a watershed moment. As Charles

Johnson, president of Fisk University in Nashville, Tennessee, remarked shortly after the ruling, "If segregation is unconstitutional in educational institutions, it is no less so unconstitutional in other aspects of our national life."

On Friday, November 25, 1955, a year and a half after *Brown* and three years after Robertson & Roundtree took on Sarah Keys's case, the Interstate Commerce Commission ruled racial segregation unlawful on trains and buses traveling between states and in waiting rooms serving interstate transportation. "The disadvantages," said the ruling, "to a traveler who is assigned accommodations or facilities so designated as to imply his inherent inferiority solely because of his race must be regarded under present conditions as unreasonable."

"This is just the greatest thing for me and my people," Sarah Keys told the *New York Age* a few days later. By then she was no longer a WAC but a hairstylist in New York City. "It's a wonderful thing," Sarah added, "for the whole American people as well." In an interview with the *New York Times*, she thanked the NAACP and Robertson & Roundtree. Sarah said that Dovey and Julius "spent a great deal of their time and money on the case," as had she and her father.

Six days after the ICC ruling, veteran activist Rosa Parks made her famous stand in Montgomery, Alabama, sparking the 381-day Montgomery bus boycott, the hard-fought protest that greatly contributed to the end of the city's Jim Crow bus system and catapulted Baptist minister Dr. Martin Luther King Jr. onto the national stage.

By then, Julius had quit his job at the post office and Dovey hers with the Labor Department. Both were devoted to full-time practice.

Of course Dovey kept up with other protests, other lawsuits aimed at shattering the monster that not only humiliated and degraded Black Americans, from cleaners to prominent clerics and lawyers, but also harmed white Americans.

Jim Crow kept alive in so many a false sense of superiority.

It blinded legions to how hatred was soiling their souls.

It kept multitudes from catching hold of Dr. King's vision of the Beloved Community, of a day, as he would later say, when "nobody will shout 'White Power!'—when nobody will shout 'Black Power!'—but everybody will talk about God's power and human power."

ONE OF THOSE OTHER lawsuits in the fight for civil rights that Dovey followed was that of a young man from Selma, Alabama: Howard Law student Bruce Carver Boynton, the godson of the scientist and environmentalist George Washington Carver and the son of voting-rights activists Amelia and Samuel Boynton.

While heading home for the holidays one winter's night in 1958, Bruce Boynton, twenty-one, was jailed and fined ten dollars for trespassing.

This happened during a layover in Richmond, Virginia. Boynton had gone into the whites-only section of the restaurant in the Trailways bus station and ordered a cheeseburger and a cup of tea.

Boynton was an interstate passenger. His case, yet another one quarterbacked by Thurgood Marshall, went all the way to the US Supreme Court. On December 5, 1960, the court ruled that segregation had no place in interstate bus and train transportation. Period.

Not on the buses and trains.

Not in depot waiting rooms.

Not in depot restaurants.

The *Boynton* decision inspired the Freedom Riders, that incredibly brave band of young women and men, Black and white, who, beginning in the spring of 1961, tested *Morgan*, tested *Keys*, tested *Boynton*, by boarding interstate buses in the North. The buses were heading south, where the Freedom Riders faced rebel yells, Confederate flags, and wanton violence.

On September 23, 1961, the ICC did what it should have done years ago. After some arm-twisting by Attorney General Robert F. Kennedy (President John Fitzgerald Kennedy's younger brother), the ICC announced that the desegregation of bus and rail travel had to be obeyed. If not, the ICC would exercise its right to fine offending companies or revoke their licenses, put them out of business.

"Whites Only," "No Colored Allowed"—by November 1, 1961, all those kinds of signs had to go.

The airlines became the last travel industry to end Jim Crow. The Civil Aeronautics Act of 1938 had banned Delta, American, and other airlines from racial discrimination—in the air. But on the ground, Black travelers still had to put up with "White" and "Colored" spaces, from restaurants to restrooms, in airport terminals across the South, including in the nation's capital.

It took a different set of lawsuits and court orders to rid

airport terminals of Jim Crow. The last holdout was Shreveport, Louisiana's airport. It finally capitulated in the summer of 1963.

By then Attorney Dovey J. Roundtree had become, she said, "a different person, a different sort of lawyer, in fact, from the one who'd battled the ICC. I am not sure that I chose that path, so much as it chose me."

HURTING IN EVERY WAY

THE PATH THAT DOVEY CHOSE—or that chose her—did not lead to bigger, bolder civil rights cases that made front-page news. It led her to serve the voiceless, the powerless, Black people without money, without the inner resources that Sarah Louise Keys had because of her education, her military training, her father's steadfast support.

Dovey's path led her to the broken.

"To our doorstep came clients who were hurting in every way human beings can hurt—mothers fighting for their children, fathers fighting for their jobs, teenagers who'd been preyed upon by the adults charged with their care, husbands and wives in bitter child custody battles, victims of violent crimes."

There was twenty-one-year-old Barbara Vanison, left brain-damaged after her husband fractured her skull with a hatchet.

Barbara's husband, Maurice, twenty-five when he wielded that hatchet, had been a patient at the city-owned psychiatric hospital, St. Elizabeths, in Southeast DC. Maurice, who made no secret of wanting to do bodily harm to his wife (and to her mother as well), had been moved from a maximum security ward to a minimum security ward from which he escaped. St. Elizabeths hadn't bothered to notify the police that a dangerous man was on the loose. In 1957 Robertson & Roundtree sued the government for negligence and won for Barbara the hefty settlement of $25,000 (about $225,000 in today's dollars.)

Dovey and Julius had taken Barbara's case after other attorneys turned it down "as hopeless," said the *Evening Star*.

In September 1957 that same DC newspaper reported on a fifteen-year-old unwed mother with the mind of a child, who had thrown her newborn baby down an elevator shaft. This girl had been sent to a facility for children with mental disabilities in Laurel, Maryland, instead of jail "on a motion by Assistant Corporation Council Francis Murphy with the consent of the girl's lawyer." That lawyer was Dovey Roundtree.

Dovey had also served as the court-appointed lawyer for one of three boys (two were nine years old; one was ten) arrested for setting fires at their elementary school. "Attorney Dovey Roundtree," reported the *Evening Star* in early April 1958, "told the judge she intends to file motions soon questioning the circumstances" of her client's "arrest and the subsequent interrogation by police."

A few months later Dovey was the defense attorney in a case involving three boys arrested for break-ins. Cops had gone to the home of one, a thirteen-year-old, around five o'clock in the morning. They ordered him out of his bed, then hauled the child off to a police precinct for questioning without his parents. After the boy's alleged confession, he was sent to DC's Receiving Home for Children, a dilapidated detention center in Southeast DC. A few years earlier a group of concerned citizens who visited the place had been appalled by what they found—for one thing, "ninety-one children jammed into space designed for 43."

To our doorstep came clients who were hurting in every way human beings can hurt . . .

Then came the day when "our doorstep" ceased to be.

In early November 1961, while arguing a case in the district court, Julius fell ill, went home. The next day, he suffered a fatal heart attack. He was forty-five.

FORTY-SEVEN-YEAR-OLD DOVEY SOLDIERED ON in that calling to serve as legal advocate, counselor, and sometimes friend to the voiceless, the powerless, the resourceless, the broken. She did this work at a time when good seemed to have injustice by the tail.

September 30–October 1, 1962: in Oxford, Mississippi, segregationists battled with lawmen who included federal marshals President Kennedy had dispatched to uphold the right of twenty-nine-year-old Air Force veteran James Meredith to become the first Black student at the University of Mississippi. It was a right Meredith had won in a lawsuit handled by NAACP LDF attorneys.

November 20, 1962: President Kennedy issued Executive Order 11063, which banned discrimination in housing owned by the government, partially funded by the government, or built in part with federal funds.

August 28, 1963: About a quarter-million people attended the March on Washington for Jobs and Freedom, whose chief organizers included Dovey's mentors Anna Arnold Hedgeman and A. Philip Randolph and where Martin Luther King Jr. stirred millions around the world with his speech about a dream.

Back of King's dream of an America anchored in equality and harmony was a right-now dream of a potent civil rights bill aimed at changing the practices of white people whose hearts were hardened against Black people.

This legislation was "the order of the day at the great March on Washington last summer," King wrote in an article that appeared in January 1964 in the Black-owned *New York Amsterdam News*. King's piece was titled "A Look to 1964."

By then Kennedy had been assassinated. The Oval Office was now occupied by his vice president, Lyndon Baines Johnson. This Texan had a vision of a "Great Society" that demanded "an end to poverty and racial injustice," he declared during a speech in the spring of 1964.

That summer, on July 2, 1964, President Johnson signed the Civil Rights Act of 1964.

This statute was so much more muscular than the one enacted and then declared unconstitutional when Grandma Rachel was a child.

The Civil Rights Act of 1964 outlawed the use of people's race, color, sex, religion, or country of origin as a reason to discriminate against them.

It banned discrimination in public places and spaces—from parks to restaurants.

It created the Commission on Civil Rights to investigate violations of civil rights and the Equal Employment Opportunity Commission to review complaints of discrimination in the workplace.

What's more, universities and other entities receiving federal funding could have that funding cut off if they were found violating the law.

Later that summer, on August 20, 1964, Johnson signed the Economic Opportunity Act, the cornerstone of his "War on Poverty." Poverty was to be fought in a number of ways, including through government-funded job training by the agency known as Job Corps. From this act also arose VISTA (Volunteers in Service to America), later renamed AmeriCorps VISTA, with its opportunities for jobs (as tutors, for example) in poor rural and urban communities, from Appalachia to Bedford-Stuyvesant in Brooklyn.

ALONGSIDE THESE REASONS FOR great rejoicing were mingled for Dovey and like-minded souls too many occasions to weep and mourn.

Back on June 12, 1963, two months before the epic March on Washington, World War II veteran Medgar Evers, the NAACP's chief of Mississippi branches, was assassinated. White supremacists shot him outside his home in Jackson, Mississippi. His wife, Myrlie, and their three young children, Darrell, Reena, and James, rushed outside to see him bleeding on their front steps, watch him die.

Eighteen days after the March on Washington, on September 15, 1963, in Birmingham, Alabama, more than a dozen Black people were wounded and four girls, ages eleven to fourteen, killed when Klansmen dynamited the Sixteenth Street Baptist Church.

Reasons for Dovey and others to weep and mourn didn't end after the murder of Medgar Evers, didn't end after the bombing of the Sixteenth Street Baptist Church.

On August 4, 1964, between the time of President Johnson's signing of the Civil Rights Act and the Economic Opportunity

Act, the corpses of three civil rights workers were found in an earthen dam in Neshoba County, Mississippi. One Black, James Chaney. Two white, Andrew Goodman and Michael Schwerner.

Weeks earlier these three young men tried to get to the bottom of the torching of a Black church near that earthen dam. For that effort, they had been arrested on trumped-up charges, jailed, and handed over to Klansmen.

It was in this year of peril and promise, of triumphs and tragedies, that Dovey, undaunted, swung into action on behalf of hapless Raymond Crump Jr., imprisoned in the DC Jail.

14

INCAPABLE

"If anyone bothers you, I want to know about it right away. If you're frightened, and I'm not here, call out my name, as loud as you can, and tell 'em, 'My lawyer's on her way.'"

Dovey handed Ray her business card. This was during their first meeting in the DC Jail, where he had been kept in solitary confinement.

Dovey had picked up quick on the "disgust the white prison guards felt for Ray." She was worried sick that Ray might be psychologically and physically abused. She feared that any abuse might break Ray, who told her, "I don't know nothin'" and "I don't know why they got me," and "I didn't shoot nobody"—Ray who two years earlier had suffered a bad beating during a holdup. It left him prone to horrible headaches, even blackouts. And Dovey suspected that Ray's mind was also messed up from alcohol abuse.

Ray feared for his safety too. He told Dovey that after he was brought to police headquarters, the arresting officer had beat on him when he professed his innocence.

Prisoner #138013 cried as Dovey tried to explain things to him, as she sought to make sense of what he was doing near the

Chesapeake & Ohio Canal towpath when Mary Pinchot Meyer was murdered.

"Incapable." That's how Dovey summed up Ray.

"Incapable of clear communication, incapable of complex thought, incapable of grasping the full weight of his predicament," and incapable of the murder. "The crime just didn't fit him at all," she said in an interview years later.

But there Ray sat in prison blues in the DC Jail, having been indicted by a grand jury on October 19. David C. Acheson, US Attorney for the District of Columbia, signed off on the charge that Ray "purposely and with deliberate and premeditated malice, did shoot Mary Pinchot Meyer with a pistol, causing injuries from which the said Mary Pinchot Meyer did die."

"Purposely and with deliberate and premeditated malice" added up to the most serious of homicide charges, first-degree murder, punishable by death by electric chair in DC at the time.

Reporting on the grand jury's verdict the next day, the *Washington Post* said that Ray had been "found coatless and shivering behind rocks in the woods not far from the scene of the shooting." Cops had discovered a white jacket near the scene, which Ray's relatives said was similar to a jacket he owned.

The grand jury witnesses included US Army Lieutenant William Mitchell, who testified to jogging past the victim shortly before she was murdered and seeing a man trailing her down the towpath. The grand jury also heard from Esso employee Henry Wiggins, who had sped from the scene of the crime to the nearest

The success of the Soviet Union's space ship *Voskhod* (Sunrise), racial tensions in Britain, President Lyndon Johnson on the campaign trail and criticism of him by the Republican Party's presidential candidate are among the things the *Evening Star* thought worthy of front-page coverage, along with the murder of Mary Pinchot Meyer the day before.

Weather Forecast
District and Vicinity—Fair tonight, low 40 to 45. Fair and mild tomorrow. Today's high, 74, at 2 p.m.; low 40, at 7:15 a.m.
Full Report on Page B-4

The Evening Star

WITH SUNDAY MORNING EDITION

NIGHT FINAL

112th Year. No. 287. Copyright © 1964 The Evening Star Newspaper Co. *** WASHINGTON, D. C., TUESDAY, OCTOBER 13, 1964—48 PAGES Home Delivered: Phone LI. 3-5000 Daily and Sunday, per month, 2.25 10 Cents

Soviet Space Ship Lands

Laborer Is Charged In Slaying of Artist

Mrs. Meyer Shot to Death On Towpath

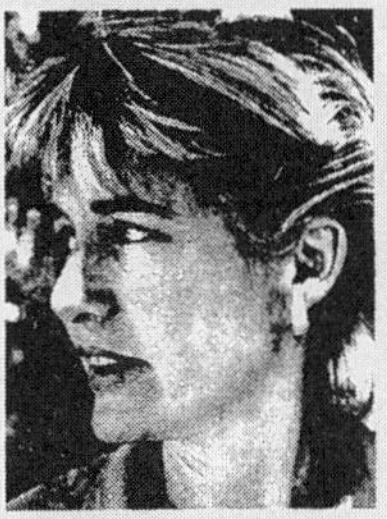

MRS. MARY PINCHOT MEYER

Mrs. Mary Pinchot Meyer, prominent Georgetown artist and a niece of a noted conservationist, was shot to death yesterday as she was walking on the C&O Canal towpath near Georgetown.

Washington police captured a suspect within an hour of the 12:46 p.m. shooting.

Mrs. Meyer, who would have been 44 tomorrow, was shot twice—in the left temple and in the chest.

Police said a tow-truck driver, parked on Canal Road, heard two shots and saw a man bending over her body. The driver and his partner on the truck heard her scream:

"Somebody help me."

Friends and relatives of Mrs. Meyer said the towpath between Key Bridge and Fletcher's Boathouse was one of her favorite walks, one she often had used with Mrs. John F. Kennedy, wife of the late President.

Mother of Two Sons

The blonde victim, who had two sons, was the divorced wife of Cord Meyer Jr., an author and government employe. Her uncle, Gifford Pinchot, was one of the nation's most renowned conservationists. A founder of the forestry profession, he headed the U.S. Forest Service under President Theodore Roosevelt and later served two terms as governor of Pennsylvania.

Mrs. Meyer's father, the late Amos Pinchot, was a founder of the Progressive party. Her mother resides in New York City.

In less than an hour police arrested the suspect, Raymond Crump Jr., 25, of the 1900 block of Stanton Terrace SE., soaking wet behind a rock in a wooded area beside the Potomac River near the slaying scene.

Crump, a laborer and father of five children, was brought before U.S. Commissioner Sam Wertleb and held without bond on a murder charge. A hearing was set for Oct. 23.

Motive Not Ascertained

Homicide Squad Capt. George R. Donahue said detectives investigating the slaying have reported that "to the best of their knowledge, she was carrying neither a wallet nor a purse."

Police refused to speculate on the nature of the struggle on the towpath. But detectives also declined to rule out the possibility that Mrs. Meyer may have been the target of an unsuccessful criminal assault.

Police were unable to identify Mrs. Meyer until several hours after the shooting. At first, the only clue to her identity was a glove found at the scene. The name Meyer was barely legible on the glove lining.

Seventh Precinct officers contacted all the Meyers in Georgetown, eventually reaching Mrs. Meyer's address at 1523 Thirty-fourth St. NW. They

See SLAYING, Page B-1

Pope Backs Liberals In Council Struggle

VATICAN CITY (AP)—Pope Paul VI has acted in favor of progressives at the Vatican Ecumenical Council in a critical struggle with conservatives, an official source said today.

The source—Dr. Gazton Cruzat, head of the press office of the Latin American Episcopate (Celam)—said the Pope had overruled conservative attempts to water down or block council action on the Jews, religious liberty, shared papal-episcopal power and modern world problems such as birth control.

Fifteen prominent cardinals, all progressive, petitioned the Pope on Sunday to intervene in what the Celam press office called "the gravest crisis since the council started."

List of Complaints

The progressives complained that leading conservatives:

Were seeking to have a draft declaration on the Jews reduced to a single paragraph.

Were trying to transfer the revision of a draft declaration on religious liberty from the largely progressive Christian unity secretariat to a special committee of mostly conservative cardinals.

Were moving to change a text on shared papal-episcopal power by deleting the word "full" from a reference that bishops had such "full and supreme power."

Were attempting to put off debate on the much awaited schema in the Roman Catholic church in the modern world.

On all four points, Dr. Cruzat said, the Pope agreed with the progressive viewpoint that there should be no deviations from the course followed so far by the council and its commissions.

"This is a great progressive victory," he added.

One of the 15 cardinals, Joseph Cardinal Frings of Cologne, Germany, had arranged a meeting with Pope Paul to urge his intervention. Cardinal Frings, apparently was selected as the progressives' representative at a meeting Sunday in Cardinal Frings' Rome residence.

There was speculation that the Pope had invited the petition from the progressives.

Pope John XXIII had faced a basic progressive-conservative clash from the very first week of the council in 1962. Cardinal Frings was one of the progressive leaders then who insisted that the 12 council commissions

See COUNCIL, Page A-4

700 Churchmen Hit Goldwater On Race Issue

Exploitation Laid To GOP Nominees By Episcopalians

ST. LOUIS (AP)—More than 700 Episcopalians, including 10 bishops, today accused the Republican presidential candidate and his running mate of a "transparent exploitation of racism among white citizens."

The statement was issued here concurrently with the triennial General Convention of the Protestant Episcopal Church.

It accused Sen. Barry Goldwater, the GOP nominee, and the party's vice presidential candidate, Rep. William Miller, of "manipulation of racism among white citizens."

Goldwater himself is an Episcopalian; Miller is a Roman Catholic.

Statement Is Issued

The statement said:

"They have sought to frighten citizens by equating the Negro struggle for freedom with crime and violence in the streets, while at the same time encouraging disrespect for law and order by their own expressed contempt for the federal judiciary especially for the U.S. Supreme Court."

The so-called "statement of conscience on racism in the presidential campaign" was issued here by William A. Stringfellow, a white New York attorney and prominent Episcopal layman, who has been active in church service projects in Harlem.

He said the statement was distributed to 1,100 Episcopal clergymen and laymen whom he felt "might share my concern about the racial crisis."

So far, Stringfellow said, 726 had signed the statement and returned it to him.

Offered as Protest

Many of them are among the approximately 8,000 Episcopalians here from across the country for the church's legislative convention. However, the document was not a part of official convention business.

Stringfellow said he did not consider it a proper subject for the convention agenda, but that the statement was being presented by Episcopal churchmen

See EPISCOPAL, Page A-4

THE FLESH AND THE SPIRIT

Johnson Creates a Style

By DAVID S. BRODER
Star Staff Writer

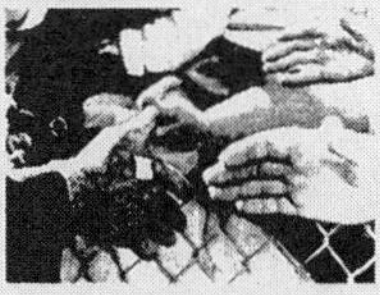

Johnson's bruised campaign hand in action.

President Johnson returned to Washington at 4:52 a.m. today from a week-long 10,000-mile tour of 15 states during which he set a new style in presidential campaigning and proved it works.

Johnson drew the biggest crowds of recent American political history as he stumped from North Carolina to California, from the shores of Lake Erie to the Gulf of Mexico, across the Midwest and through the Rockies.

Builds Momentum

To describe his week's work on this first frankly-political junket as "effective campaigning" is like calling Hurricane Hilda "a bit of a blow."

Johnson built momentum with every move. At the last of his countless stops he drew more than 25,000 persons to the Boise (Idaho) airport at 9 last night—double the crowd Republican nominee Barry Goldwater had in front of the State Capitol at mid-morning one day in September.

Hoarse-voiced but happy, he returned to his office with even the skeptics convinced that he has built a vast and enthusiastic personal following of his own. He is no longer just John Kennedy's suc-

See JOHNSON, Page A-6

Goldwater Hits 'Part-Time' Job

Assails Johnson On Sunday Tour

By CECIL HOLLAND
Star Staff Writer

TOPEKA, Kan. — Sen. Barry M. Goldwater accused President Johnson today of being "a part-time President" because of his "full-time politicking" and of making this week "a political travesty of the Lord's day."

The Republican nominee turned loose one of his hardest attacks on the President as he moved back into the Midwest for a week of campaigning. He will visit in the next five days 10 states having a total of 132 electoral votes.

"We face full-time responsibilities around the world, full-scale challenges," Goldwater said in remarks prepared for delivery here. "But not once do we hear of them from our part-time President.

"He gives us handshakes and handouts. He directs traffic and kisses babies rather than directing our foreign policy. He turns Sunday into a day of campaign chaos and the other days of the week into days of rest—so far

See GOLDWATER, Page A-6

Star Gets Early Tipoff On Landing of Voskhod

The Star was informed of the safe landing of Russia's three-man space ship today 25 minutes before the Soviet government announced the news to the rest of the world.

At 4:45 a.m. the newsroom telephone rang and Star Staff Writer Walter Gold was informed that "Moscow is calling."

It turned out to be Edward Baskakov of the newspaper Soviet Russia.

"We're calling The Star because you ran an editorial seven years ago that said you envied us for launching our first Sputnik," Baskakov said. "Now we want to know, do you still envy our accomplishments? Our space ship (Voskhod) landed about an hour ago. Are you still envious?"

"We wouldn't say we're envious, but we do congratulate you and your people for an outstanding accomplishment," Gold replied.

At that point, the radio-telephone transmission began to fade, and the 5,000-mile interview came to an end. When Gold asked the Associated Press for verification of the space ship landing, it was the first the wire service had heard of it except for rumor.

The "envious" editorial referred to by Baskakov was apparently one in the Oct. 6, 1957, Star, which commented on the shock with which the first Sputnik launching was received in the United States:

"So, even if grudgingly, we must take our hats off to the Russians," the editorial said. "They have done the job first, and it is undeniably a great achievement for which they deserve high praise."

BITTER 'BACKLASH'

Racial Issue Clouds Election in Britain

By GEORGE SHERMAN
European Correspondent of The Star

BIRMINGHAM, England — Sullen workers stood in little knots around factory gates, their cloth working caps in hand.

"What about their disgusting living habits?" shouted one.

"How can I raise my family next to them?" put in another.

"What will my property be worth if this continues?" said still another.

The "they" meant colored immigrants.

It was not Detroit, Chicago or even Alabama. But it might have been. It was Smethwick, an industrial suburb of Birmingham in the English Midlands, often called the "Detroit of Britain."

And the "white backlash" probably is as bitter in this little factory town as it is in any place in the United States.

Questions were being fired at a lonely candidate in an over-used raincoat who stood just across the road, pipe in one hand and makeshift microphone in the other.

It was a lunchtime factory meeting—British democracy at work.

No one seemed the least bit disturbed that this professorial gentleman with a cultured British accent was Patrick Gordon Walker, next foreign minister of Great Britain if he and the Labor party win Thursday's election.

Seven thousand colored immigrants have settled in Smethwick, among 61,000 whites who are jammed together in rundown rows of tenements next to railroad tracks, foundries and glass factories.

The term "colored" is more widely used than it is in the United States. It groups together Negroes from the West Indies and Indians and Pakistanis from Asia, plus many other immigrants from Commonwealth countries.

But all the trans-Atlantic symptoms of angry prejudice are in full force in Smethwick.

The town is almost totally working class, with a smattering of lower middle class.

It is also the second most densely populated area in Britain.

The road which leads up Cape Hill past Michell's Brewery from Birmingham — where modern glass office buildings are rising from Victorian ruins — goes through depressing, dirty, drafty rows of once-red or yellow brick shops and houses.

Into this industrial backwater Commonwealth immigrants flocked during the late 1950s and early 60s.

They were drawn by the new British prosperity and the freedom of entry from Commonwealth citizens. They took over menial jobs in foundries, hospitals and local buses. And they also leapfrogged along over-

See ENGLAND, Page A-4

'I Spied for GOP,' Says Democrat

By the Associated Press

A Democratic National Committee employe said today he was paid $1,000 to deliver copies of private Democratic messages and schedules to John Grenier, executive director of the Republican National Committee.

The charge was made in an affidavit dated Oct. 12 and signed by Louis Flax, a teletype operator working for the Democratic National Committee.

He said he acted with approval of Democratic party officials, after reporting to them he had been contacted.

Grenier, after reading the affidavit, declined to comment.

"I don't know anyone named Flax and I don't believe I'll comment on it," he said.

Earlier newsmen, called to the Democratic National Committee news and information offices by Wayne Phillips, assistant publicity director, listened in as Flax—using the alias of "Mr. Lewis"—called Grenier's office.

He was told by a woman who answered the phone that "we have been receiving the things if that was what you wanted to know."

Flax later said he delivered an envelope of copies of messages to Grenier's office. When newsmen entered his office, Grenier was seen inserting teletype copy into an envelope.

Phillips told newsmen that the Democrats had been mailing copies of their teletype messages—but with certain items deleted—to Grenier every day since Flax made his first delivery on Oct. 2.

3-Man Crew Had 16 Orbits In 24 Hours

Science Research Gains Claimed on Pioneering Flight

MOSCOW (AP)—The Soviet Union's three-man space ship, the world's first to carry more than one astronaut in orbit, landed safely today after completing 16 trips around the earth in 24 hours and 17 minutes, an official announcement said.

The program of scientific research, designed for 24 hours of flight, was accomplished in full, said the announcement.

It added that the doctor, scientist and engineer aboard the space ship Voskhod (Sunrise) conducted observations "directly in outer space."

The Soviet news agency Tass said all three men "are feeling well."

Foundation Declared Laid

A statement issued jointly by Premier Khrushchev's cabinet, the presidium of Parliament and the Communist party's Central Committee said the flight, totaling about 435,000 miles, laid "a firm foundation for lasting trips in cosmic space."

Tass correspondent Nikolai Zheleznov described the space-ship's return to earth in a dispatch from the flight control center.

He said the commander, Col. Vladimer Komarov, was ordered during the 17th orbit to end the flight. The pilot reported the switching on of instruments and braking facilities.

"Several minutes passed," the Tass dispatch continued. "The first to report to the ground the successful conclusion of the flight was Pilot Mikhailov.

"'I am seeing an object entering dense clouds,' he radioed to ground stations at 10:40.

Landing Area Ready

"Ground reports kept pouring in. In the preassigned landing area, numerous planes and helicopters were on patrol, ready to drop parachutists to meet the cosmonauts on the ground.

"At 10:57, 10 minutes after landing, the pilots reported: 'The object is visible on the ground, well visible, and the cosmonauts, three, beside it. They are walking about, walking briskly. Congratulations to all, to all.'

"The scientists, engineers and cosmonauts who were at the control post embraced and congratulated each other on another successful space flight.

"Radio operators reported from the landing spot: 'The cosmonauts were met by doctors and sporting commissioners. The cosmonauts are feeling well and are already sparring with correspondents.'"

Tass emphasized that only a 24-hour flight had been planned, but other indications caused speculation that the trip had ended far short of the originally scheduled time.

Answer Is Hidden

The announcement of the space ship's purpose, made after it was launched Monday from a "cosmodrome" 1,250 miles southeast of Moscow, said it would study medical reactions during "a long flight." How long was never stated.

The traditional Soviet silence on what the Russians are planning to do in space—contrasted with volumes of prepared in-

See SPACE, Page A-4

JAPANESE ART DISPLAYED HERE

AN EXHIBITION of 57 works by 18 Japanese artists is on display at the Corcoran Gallery of Art. For a complete list on current attractions at other galleries and for a better idea of how to enjoy yourself in the Capital, see the Tomorrow in Washington column on Page B-21.

Guide for Readers

"Emphasis on private enterprise is one of the aspects which struck me most as I studied the birth-to-death welfare system in this largest of the Scandinavian countries."

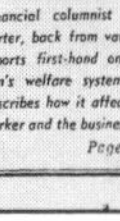

Financial columnist Sylvia Porter, back from vacation, reports first-hand on Sweden's welfare system, and describes how it affects the worker and the businessman.

Page A-25

'COPTER FORCES INCREASE

An increased force of helicopters sweeps over the Plain of Reeds near Saigon in conjunction with Vietnamese ground forces seeking out Viet Cong infiltrators who have been responsible for disastrous ambushes against government ground forces. Government forces found themselves in near-neckdeep water and enemy units escaped.—AP Wirephoto.

Esso station to call the cops, who soon picked him up and drove him back to the crime scene. Before the grand jury, Wiggins once again identified Ray as the man he had seen standing over the victim's body.

That grand jury indictment had come at the speed of light. Three days after the murder, on October 15, the US Attorney's Office was presenting its case against Ray before a grand jury. Assistant US Attorney Charles T. Duncan told the *Washington Post* that in a homicide case a prosecutor typically waits for the coroner's findings before moving on to the grand jury stage. However, the US Attorney's Office "is not bound by such procedure," said the *Post*. The newspaper also reported that the "disclosure of the prosecution's stepped-up timetable [on October 14] came as a simple, half-hour funeral service was held for Mrs. Meyer on what would have been her 44th birthday." The service was held in Washington Cathedral's Bethlehem Chapel. Some three hundred people attended.

ON OCTOBER 30, DOVEY appeared with Ray during his arraignment before US District Court Judge Luther W. Youngdahl. Ray entered a plea of not guilty. The trial date was set for the week of January 11, 1965.

Not wanting Ray to languish for two months in the DC jail—"an old stone building some compared to a dungeon," wrote Nina Burleigh in her book about Mary Pinchot Meyer, *A Very Private Woman*—Dovey sought to get Ray released on bond and found herself before Judge Burnita Shelton Matthews, who, in 1949, had become the first woman appointed to any district court. Matthews was no fan of Black people, according to George Peter Lamb, a Legal Aid lawyer assigned to Ray before Dovey stepped in. "Judge Matthews," said Lamb, "believed all blacks were guilty and the reason they were guilty was because they were indicted, and therefore they should plead guilty."

Regarding Ray as a "danger to the community," Judge Matthews denied bail.

Black guilt was uppermost in the minds of many white Washingtonians in majority-Black DC. But where so many Black people faced sub-par schooling, sub-standard housing, and lockout from decent jobs, was it any wonder that crime was on the rise?

"In June 1963 the *New York Times* ran a series of stories about the racial problems in Washington, DC," wrote Burleigh. "The first one opened with anecdotes about street violence instigated by black perpetrators: an Ohio tourist beaten and robbed by 'a band of fast-moving Negro girls'; an elderly clergyman beaten to death by four black youths for $1.29; two college girls from Pennsylvania raped by a gun-wielding black male. Violence was a symptom of the urban decay behind the postcard facade of the capital city."

Two months before the *New York Times* articles, Agnes Meyer (no relation to Mary Pinchot Meyer), whose husband owned the *Washington Post*, had warned of an "explosion" if the plight of the poor in DC wasn't addressed. This was in the wake of two race riots at sporting events.

Against this backdrop, many white people in DC were hard-pressed to believe Ray innocent. And many Black people in DC were no doubt hard-pressed to believe that he would get a fair trial.

In fighting for Ray, Dovey filed a writ of habeas corpus,

Latin for "you should have the body" (or the person) in court. She was asking for a hearing to determine if Ray was being illegally detained. For one thing, he claimed that he had been beaten while in police custody. But her main contention was that Ray never had a preliminary hearing, a day in court before a US Commissioner (now a magistrate judge) to establish that there was indeed a case to be made for holding Ray and proceeding to the grand jury stage. "I held that without a preliminary hearing, my client's detention was illegal."

On November 9, before US District Court Judge George L. Hart, Dovey got a hearing on her petition for a writ of habeas corpus. The US Attorney's office argued that a preliminary hearing was moot because Ray had already been indicted. The judge agreed. There is no law that says a defendant is absolutely, positively entitled to a preliminary hearing.

"Release Bid Is Refused in Slaying," the *Washington Post* told its readers the next day.

Dovey quickly filed an appeal.

A "shrewd move," wrote Peter Janney in his book about the murdered woman, *Mary's Mosaic*. Dovey "knew that the appeal wouldn't be decided for months, and the delay would afford her legal team much-needed time to prepare for trial. She also hoped that the media scrutiny focused on her client would abate in the intervening months."

Operating out of a row house at 1822 11th Street, NW, Dovey *was* her law firm, but she pulled in able minds to assist as need be. For Ray's case she had Purcell Moore, private investigator. There was also a cousin of Dovey's, Jerry Hunter, a Howard Law student. Along with legwork, he probably also helped out with some of the thinking, researching, and cross-checking—as was surely the case with Dovey's co-counsels, all Howard Law grads: Jerome Shuman and Alan V. Roberson, both in their late twenties, and George F. Knox Sr., in his forties.

No doubt with input from her team, on November 12 Dovey filed a motion for a psychiatric evaluation to determine if Ray was competent to stand trial and if he was in his right mind on the day of the murder. That motion was granted the following day, and on Monday, November 16, 1964, a deputy marshal transferred Ray from the DC Jail to St. Elizabeths Hospital, where he was to stay for no more than sixty days.

During these tense and challenging November days, Dovey, undaunted, was dealing with another hole in her heart.

MINISTER IN THE FAMILY

BACK ON NOVEMBER 1, around the break of dawn, Mama had telephoned with the news that Grandma Rachel, ninety-one, had died. Like Grandpa Clyde, she, too, had suffered from a kidney disorder.

On the day of the funeral, Dovey led the grand procession from that house on East Hill Street to the church Mama and Grandma Rachel then attended, Ebenezer Baptist. Dovey led the way because "I was the minister in the family, Mama said."

Mama wasn't speaking figuratively.

Back in 1959, when hospitalized for a hysterectomy caused by fibroids, Dovey had a lot of time to think. She was feeling that the law was "not enough" for her, that there was "something else" that she should be doing.

Another calling.

To serve humanity not only as a lawyer, but also as an ordained minister.

After her release from the hospital, Dovey went to Queen City to recuperate and to tell Mama and Grandpa Rachel about this second calling. Back in DC, Dovey began taking night classes at Howard's divinity school.

This was a Dovey with a law practice no longer lean but booming and a Dovey still battling diabetes. Because of it, she reached a point when she had to ask judges for permission to have with her in courtrooms a thermos of orange juice (to prevent her blood sugar from dropping dangerously low). Dovey was loath to do this for fear of appearing weak in the still male-dominated field of law. But she needed that orange juice—needed a shot of sugar. Otherwise she might pass out or, worse, fall into a diabetic coma.

Despite health problems, despite operating a one-woman law practice, Dovey remained undaunted. She carried on with her studies of what was for her Divine Law, something she'd been steeped in all her life.

Thanks to Grandpa Clyde, whose preaching had been "a rich tapestry of Holy Scripture and political protest, all strung together in a way that shot through you like something electric."

Thanks to Grandma Rachel, ever prayerful, who had baked the communion bread, made the communion wine, made pristine the altar linens.

Thanks to Mama leading the choir in her rich alto.

Thanks to Spelman with its motto "Our Whole School for Christ."

And back when Mama told little Dovey Mae how much she was like Papa, she had also told her that she would one day "live out his legacy, walk where he could not, do the things of which he'd only dreamed."

On November 30, 1961, Dovey was ordained as an itinerant deacon in the AME Church. Two years later as an AME itinerant elder. Once again Dovey was a pioneer. It wasn't until 1960 that the AME Church, founded in 1816, began ordaining women to itinerant orders, in which a person can be assigned to minister at different churches.

As a member of the ministerial staff at her church in Southeast DC, Allen Chapel AME, Dovey could preach, perform weddings, preside at funerals, baptize, teach Sunday school. So, yes, when Grandma Rachel was laid to rest, Dovey was indeed the minister in the family.

Beside her marched Mama, her sisters Rachel, Eunice, Bea, their husbands, other family. Behind them marched troops of neighbors. "The whole neighborhood echoed with the mighty sound of her home-going, and despite my sadness, my heart sang."

Grandma Rachel was not the first woman warrior Dovey lost. In 1955, Mary McLeod Bethune suffered a fatal heart attack. In January 1964, nine months before Grandma Rachel passed, Mary Mae Neptune, also ninety-one, died in a nursing home in Cambridge, Ohio, after "a long illness," an obituary said.

After Grandma Rachel's funeral, despite her sadness, Dovey returned to DC in fighting form for Ray Crump Jr., well aware that "a million eyes" were on his case, one of the biggest in DC's history.

NO WORDS. ONLY BREATHING.

ON JANUARY 13, 1965, day sixty of Ray's stay at St. Elizabeths, the hospital's superintendent, Dr. Dale C. Cameron, released the findings.

Ray was competent to stand trial. Psychiatrists also concluded that on the day of the murder he was not "suffering from a mental disease or defect."

Ray was transferred back to the DC Jail where he "deteriorated daily," remembered Dovey, where the "guards' hatred for him was so palpable."

Dovey visited Ray daily, praying with him, praying, too, that her and his mother's visits would keep him safe. Dovey was no doubt praying for herself, also, for strength in what was an uphill battle.

In preparing for Ray's defense, Dovey was being stymied by the district attorney's office.

"Four months after the murder itself," wrote Peter Janney, Dovey "still hadn't been able to get a clear statement from the government's lawyers, and therefore she wasn't sure whether a murder weapon had even been recovered." Assistant US Attorney Charles T. Duncan, a Black man in his early forties, who was, wrote Janney, "normally an ebullient man and quite friendly with Dovey," was now giving Dovey the brush-off.

"I've called you a couple of times," she said to Duncan when she ran into him in the courthouse one day.

"It's just a straight case," Duncan replied. "They caught him. He was down there."

"So were a lot of other people," said Dovey.

To get the information she needed, Dovey filed a motion asking for the names and addresses of all people who allegedly witnessed any of the facts charged in the indictment, who were at or near the scene of Ray's arrest, who were at or near the scene of the crime. She also asked for the "name, make, caliber and serial number" of the murder weapon, a list of items obtained from Ray's home or person, and a list of items "alleged to have been used by the Defendant in connection with the crime charged."

In return, Dovey received a long list of potential prosecution witnesses. She also learned that the US Attorney's Office had a zippered jacket, a sweatshirt, a sport shirt, a dark-colored plaid cap, a pair of corduroy pants, a pair of black shoes, and an open pack of cigarettes, hair specimens and a hair sample. The hair specimens were found on the cap and the jacket. The hair sample was taken from Ray in jail. This was something he had protested and something Dovey had tried and failed to prevent.

These items were "either obtained from the defendant or allegedly belonged to him," said the prosecution's written response to Dovey's request. "Allegedly" referred to items found near the crime scene: the cigarettes, cap, and jacket. The other clothing was taken from Ray in jail.

Two .38-caliber lead bullets also allegedly belonged to Ray.

EXHIBIT NUMBER	DESCRIPTION AND REMARKS	MARKED FOR IDENTIFICATION	RECEIVED Into EVIDENCE	WITNESS
1	Blue sweater	JUL 20 1965	JUL 27 1965	Worrell
2	Light Gray sweater	JUL 20 1965	JUL 27 1965	''
3	Heavy Gray sweater	JUL 20 1965	JUL 27 1965	''
4	Slacks	JUL 20 1965	JUL 27 1965	''
5	Shirt	JUL 20 1965	JUL 27 1965	''
6a	Tennis shoes	JUL 20 1965	JUL 27 1965	''
7	Blood Sample	JUL 20 1965		''
8	Bullet slug	JUL 20 1965	JUL 20 1965	Rayford
9	Bullet slug	JUL 20 1965	JUL 20 1965	Rayford
10	Glove	JUL 20 1965	JUL 27 1965	''
11	Glove	JUL 20 1965	JUL 27 1965	''
12	Topographic Map	JUL 20 1965	JUL 20 1965	Roscualle
13	Map showing exit to towpath	JUL 20 1965	JUL 20 1965	''
14	Cap	JUL 20 1965	JUL 22 1965	Wiggins
15	Jacket	JUL 20 1965	JUL 22 1965	''
16	Trousers	JUL 21 1965	JUL 22 1965	''
17	Shoes	JUL 21 1965	JUL 22 1965	''
18	Photograph of scene as seen by Wiggins	JUL 21 1965	JUL 21 1965	''
19	Statement of Wiggins	JUL 21 1965		
20	PD 251 re identification	JUL 21 1965		

Gout #1   CRIMINAL NO. 930-64   RAY CRUMP, JR.

Page one of the prosecution's exhibits.

But in the documents she received, Dovey learned that the US Attorney's Office didn't have the murder weapon.

An even bigger shock was the name and signature of the person listed below that of US Attorney David Acheson, an indication of the prosecutor she'd be up against at trial. It wouldn't be the "normally ebullient" and "friendly" Charles T. Duncan but rather Assistant US Attorney Alfred L. Hantman.

"Oh, brother! What are they doing to me!" Dovey said to herself.

"Tall, prepossessing, an imposing figure with bristling eyebrows and an extraordinary legal mind," according to Peter Janney, Hantman, white and forty-seven, "conveyed a formidable authority." Some remembered the former World War II Army

Air corpsman and George Washington University Law school graduate as "a screamer and a bully."

WHILE DOVEY WAITED FOR the Court of Appeals ruling on whether Ray had been illegally detained, she was absolutely consumed by this case that wasn't a paying one. Ray had no money. It seems that Ray's parents were able to provide some money, but not much. So not only was Dovey not getting paid for her time, but most of the expenses were coming out of her pocket, from court filing fees to her investigator's fees.

Dovey spent a lot of time on Ray's case. Time spent thinking and planning. Time spent drafting and filing motions. Time spent in court hearings on those motions. She also spent a lot of time exploring the crime scene and environs.

Jerry Hunter remembered that on "most Saturday afternoons, or whenever we got the chance we went to Georgetown and the canal. There wasn't a blade of grass we didn't know about."

After Dovey began exploring the area, she began getting telephone calls, often after midnight.

No words.

Only breathing.

The more she investigated the crime scene area, the more frequent the calls. Too, during those explorations Dovey felt eyes on her, sinister eyes, at times.

Dovey had few allies and sources of support within the white legal community. "My very presence, I knew, irritated and threatened many of the white judges and lawyers in the court-house, male and female alike." Many were still galled by her admission a few years earlier to the once all-white DC Women's

Bar Association, thanks to the valiant efforts of a future judge, Joyce Hens Green.

And these were still days of both promise and peril on the civil rights front.

On Sunday, March 7, 1965, scores of civil rights activists suffered the sting of tear gas, the agony of lashes from bullwhips, the pain of being trampled by sheriff's deputies and Alabama state troopers on horseback. This happened on the Edmund Pettus Bridge in Selma, Alabama, during a peaceful march to Montgomery, the state capital, in protest against the rampant suppression of the Black vote through such measures as literacy tests and violence.

As cries for justice continued, Dovey continued preparing her defense of Ray Crump Jr.

On June 15, 1965, the US Court of Appeals upheld, 2–1, the lower court's ruling on that business about the preliminary hearing.

A new trial date was set.

Dovey had thirty-four days to be ready.

VOIR DIRE

On Monday, July 19, 1965, jury selection for *United States v. Raymond Crump Jr.*, criminal case number 930-64, got underway where all DC felonies were tried back then: in the US District Court for the District of Columbia on Constitution Avenue.

The presiding judge was a white, fifty-nine-year-old World War II veteran named Howard Francis Corcoran, a graduate of Phillips Exeter Academy, Princeton, and Harvard Law.

At first Dovey didn't know what to make of Judge Corcoran, who had been practicing law since the 1930s, primarily as a corporate lawyer. Corcoran's public service included several years with the US Attorney's Office of the Southern District of New York. For one of those years he was acting US Attorney. But Corcoran was a brand-new judge, appointed by President Johnson just a few months before Ray's trial began.

In sizing up Corcoran, Dovey concluded that he had zero tolerance for "foolishness in his courtroom, from counsel or anyone else."

Next to size up were the prospective jurors via voir dire (French for "to see to speak" or "to speak the truth"), a hearing to establish the admissibility of evidence, to determine whether a person was qualified to take the witness stand as an expert witness—and also to reduce a large pool of potential jurors (in this case more than seventy-five people) to a small group of actual jurors.

When it comes to the jury, defense and prosecution lawyers usually begin by asking prospective jurors about their backgrounds, occupations, and attitudes, looking for clues as to whether Miss X, Mr. Y, or Mrs. Z would be a benefit or a detriment to the defense or prosecution side.

Did they harbor racial prejudice?

Did they distrust cops?

In this case, with capital punishment a possibility, both sides would have wanted to know how prospective jurors felt about the death penalty. Jurors may also have been asked how familiar they were with the C&O Canal towpath, if they fished in the part of the Potomac River that runs parallel to the canal, and whether they had ever been the victim of a crime, violent or otherwise.

In weeding out jurors, defense and prosecution were able to strike an unlimited number of jurors for "cause"—that is, for a specific reason. There was also the option of peremptory challenges, strikes that didn't require a reason. Here the limit was twenty.

AS QUESTIONS WERE ASKED and answered, as minutes ticked by, General Services Administration warehouse worker William M. Coston and IBM keypunch operator Cecelia L. Cyr were among those dismissed "for cause." The phrase "cap. pun." is scribbled after their names in a voir dire document.

One of Dovey's peremptory challenges was Cornelius V. Kelliher Jr., an administrative assistant at the CIA. Although

A page pertaining to jury selection. It shows some jurors were struck for cause and others for reasons that didn't have to be explained. "G" indicates a peremptory challenge made by the prosecution on behalf of the government. What looks like a triangle indicates one made by Dovey on behalf of the defendant.

Dovey didn't need to provide a reason for having him removed, it's easy to understand why she didn't want him on the jury. Scribbled after Kelliher's name was the fact that he had been attacked with a knife and his mother had been robbed, events which might prejudice him against someone accused of a violent crime. Also, Kelliher knew "by sight" a police officer who would be a prosecution witness.

There's no knowing what went through Ray's mind as he sat at the defense counsel table learning bits and pieces about the women and men who might sit in judgment of him, listening to people's views on the death penalty, then perhaps staring intently at the faces of the twelve main jurors and four alternates who were left when voir dire ended.

The main jury was composed of four white people and eight Black people, five men and seven women. They included Evelyn S. Carpenter, a clerk at the Treasury Department; Cecilia Chmielewski, a homemaker; Bessie E. Hawkins, a nurse's aide at St. Elizabeths Hospital; and Archie N. McEachern, a taxi driver with the Coast Line Cab Company.

The jury's spokesperson was Edward O. Savwoir, a Black program specialist at Job Corps.

After Savwoir and the other jurors were sworn in, Ray was sent back to the DC Jail.

"Jury Ready for Trial of Crump," the *Washington Post* announced the next day, reporting that two jurors had been struck because of bias. What they knew about the case had "influenced their judgment."

The *Post* didn't say what that judgment was.

SCARED TO DEATH

"THE GOVERNMENT'S PROOF AS you will hear it from the lips of the very many witnesses that appear from this witness stand will be clear, convincing, and should lead the jury to the honest conclusion by each of you that Raymond Crump Jr. deliberately, willfully and maliciously shot and killed Mary Pinchot Meyer," a woman "in the high noon of her lifetime when death struck suddenly and violently at about 12:25 p.m. on the afternoon of October 12, 1964."

This is from Assistant US Attorney Alfred Hantman's opening statement on Tuesday, July 20, 1965.

Hantman told the jury what Mary was wearing on the clear, chilly day that she was killed on the C&O Canal towpath—gray slacks, white shirt, two gray sweaters and over them a thicker blue Angora sweater. She also had on tan leather gloves, tennis shoes, and sunglasses.

What the victim didn't have with her was money or jewelry, "nor were there any other manifestations of wealth that could be seen by anybody who happened to be on the towpath at that time."

Hantman was driving home the point that Mary's murder wasn't the result of a robbery gone wrong: "We will show, ladies

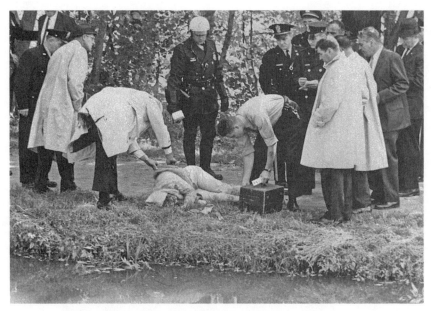

Police officers and detectives at the crime scene.

and gentlemen of the jury, that Mary Pinchot Meyer met with violence and death after a struggle with the defendant to escape his unprovoked attack upon her."

Ray, said Hantman, had approached Mary Pinchot Meyer from behind, "dragged her some 20 to 25 feet across the towpath towards an embankment which led down to the railroad tracks out of view of the people who happened to be traveling along Canal Road in their automobiles."

Mary Pinchot Meyer cried out, "God, somebody help," and continued to scream for about twenty seconds.

Then came the shot to the head with a .38-caliber revolver.

Still Mary put up a fierce fight, said the prosecutor.

"We will show you by clear and convincing evidence that Mary Pinchot Meyer immediately upon being shot grabbed her head. We will show you after she did that, she grabbed a tree."

Hantman promised to show that Ray tried to drag Mary from the tree. And Hantman was prepared to bring into the courtroom the blood-stained section of that tree.

And the struggle continued, said Hantman, alleging that Mary tore at Ray's jacket, ripped one of his pants pockets, desperately trying to escape, then—

Bang!

The shot to the right shoulder.

This bullet "coursed laterally through the body, severed the aorta which carries the blood to the heart and came out just underneath the skin over the heart area."

Hantman's "We will show . . .," "We will show . . .," "We will show . . ." went on and on, probably intended to persuade jurors that the evidence was overwhelming.

His opening statement is a little more than fifteen double-spaced typed pages.

And Hantman had more than forty-five exhibits lined up to show the jury. Besides the victim's clothing, among the items he wanted to enter into evidence were two bullet slugs, a blood sample, a map, slides of hair, slides of fibers, a photograph of a button, a statement from Henry Wiggins, and that blood-stained section of the tree.

What's more, Hantman had sixty-one witnesses lined up to testify. More than half were cops.

"I was completely overwhelmed by what he promised the jury he was going to present," Dovey told a journalist years later. "I was scared to death."

BEFORE THE PROSECUTOR'S OPENING STATEMENT, before the jurors took their seats in Criminal Courtroom 4, Dovey, her co-counsel George Knox, and Hantman stood before the bench for about fifteen minutes, going over some things with the judge (a "sidebar").

For one, Dovey chose to beat a dead horse. Declaring Ray's non-preliminary hearing "so prejudicial as to taint all proceedings," she motioned that a preliminary hearing be held forthwith or that the indictment be dismissed.

> Corcoran: You went to the Court of Appeals on that, didn't you?
> *Motion denied.*

Hantman had requests too. He wanted to post a large topographical map of the towpath area on the wall opposite the jury box. The map, he said, would be affixed to the wall with a type of tape that would not "mar" the courtroom walls and could be easily removed.

> Corcoran: I am not concerned about that.

He was, however, concerned about the size of the map, that it might be "so huge as to constitute prejudice." He told Hantman that he'd decide on the map after he saw it.

Eventually, the judge called for the jury to be brought in. By 10:30 that morning the twelve jurors and four alternates had taken their seats in the jury box. Corcoran explained to them how things were to work.

The attorneys would make opening statements outlining what they were out to prove and also closing statements. These statements, Corcoran stressed, "do not constitute evidence."

Furthermore, if in their closings, prosecution or defense mentioned something that did not "jibe with" the jurors' recollection, "it is your recollections which is to control you. You are to be the sole judges of the facts and the issues of fact in this case."

The judge also told the jury that the defendant didn't have to prove his innocence. Innocence was presumed. It was the prosecutor's job to prove guilt.

Beyond a reasonable doubt.

It was shortly after this that Hantman launched into his opening statement about all that he would *show*, and *show*, and *show*.

When he finished, he and Dovey were back at the bench. She wanted it on record that she found Hantman's statements "inflammatory and high prejudicial"—especially the bit about the blood-stained tree.

Corcoran: You have made your record.

Back in open court, it was time for Dovey's opening statement.

"The courtroom was quiet, expectant, as I rose." What Dovey said certainly surprised Hantman and likely stunned everyone else in the courtroom.

Dovey: If it please the Court, at this time we will reserve our opening statement on behalf of the defendant Raymond Crump.

Onlookers who didn't know Dovey's reputation may have thought that she was unprepared. Not so. "There are times, in trial, when it is best to hold one's peace," she later explained. "To reveal anything about the basis of my case to the prosecution placed me at great risk. I thought it best to tread lightly, and watch, and make my move when I saw an opening."

However, when the judge called for a fifteen-minute recess, she did not tread lightly. At the bench, she told Judge Corcoran that Hantman's opening statement was so prejudicial as to be grounds for a mistrial.

Corcoran: No, I don't think it is grounds for a mistrial.

AFTER THE RECESS, HANTMAN called his first witness.

Someone with clout and from the same social class as Judge Corcoran and Mary Pinchot Meyer.

Someone brusque and at times full of bravado.

THANK YOU, SIR

HANTMAN'S FIRST WITNESS WAS the person who had identified Mary's body in the DC Morgue, her brother-in-law Ben Bradlee, still *Newsweek* magazine's Washington bureau chief, but not for much longer. That week's issue announced that Bradlee was leaving *Newsweek* to become deputy manager of the *Washington Post*.

Journalist and author Zalin Grant reasoned that Hantman "scheduled Bradlee as the first witness, thinking in part, no doubt, that this well-regarded journalist and known friend of President Kennedy would make a good impression on the jury and help build his case."

Forty-three-year-old Benjamin Crowninshield Bradlee possessed prestige beyond that.

Raised in Boston, Bradlee was a Harvard graduate and ex-navy intelligence officer. His family tree included a wealthy New York lawyer, a fine artist, an ambassador to Britain, an editor of the high-society magazine *Vanity Fair*. And Bradlee was a descendant of counts, princes, and kings.

THROUGH HANTMAN'S DIRECT EXAMINATION of Ben Bradlee, jurors learned a series of bare-bones facts.

Bradlee's address.

Bradlee's occupation.

Bradlee's twelve and a half years with *Newsweek*.

Bradlee's relationship to Mary Pinchot Meyer.

Bradlee's identification of her body the morning after the murder.

There was also Bradlee's familiarity with Mary's habit of taking walks along the C&O Canal towpath, his knowledge that she was a painter, that her studio was a converted old garage, and that on the night of her murder he had discovered in that studio her pocketbook. "It contained a wallet, some cosmetics and pencils, things like that."

We don't know if Bradlee made a good impression on the jury. If he impressed or intimidated Dovey, it doesn't seem that she showed it in her cross-examination.

Dovey:	Mr. Bradlee, I have just one question.
Bradlee:	Yes, ma'am.
Dovey:	Do you have any personal, independent knowledge regarding the causes of the death of your sister-in-law? Do you know how she met her death? Do you know who caused it?
Bradlee:	Well, I saw a bullet hole in her head.
Dovey:	Do you know who caused this to be?
Bradlee:	No, I don't.
Dovey:	You have no other information regarding the occurrences leading up to her death?
Bradlee:	No, I do not.
Dovey:	Thank you, sir. I have no further questions, Your Honor.

In less than a minute Dovey had made Ben Bradlee irrelevant, an example of why George Peter Lamb, one of Ray's original Legal Aid attorneys, hailed her as "the world's greatest cross-examiner."

But all was not smooth sailing for Dovey J. Roundtree. Most frustrating of all: Ray had an alibi that she could not use.

When first questioned by police near the crime scene, Ray had said that he'd been fishing in the Potomac River, had slipped on some rocks, fell in. Thus the tears on his clothing. Thus the bleeding cut on his hand when a detective stopped him.

Where was his fishing gear?

Lost in the river, said Ray.

When cops searched the area where Ray said he'd been fishing, they found no fishing gear. After his arrest, armed with a search warrant, cops went to his home, an attached yellow-brick number in Southeast DC's Stanton Terrace public housing complex. In Ray's living room closet, cops found his fishing rod and tackle box.

Ray had lied to cover up an extramarital affair.

ON THE MORNING OF the murder, instead of going back to the job Brown Construction Company had him on (paving work at a hospital), Ray had met up with his girlfriend, Vivian. They picked up some booze, cigarettes, chips, then headed for a spot near the C&O Canal where Ray did sometimes fish.

After they "fooled around a little," Ray fell asleep, so deeply, he told Dovey, that he slid into the river. When he woke up, got himself out of the water, girlfriend was gone. Ray was making his way to a bus stop when a cop approached him.

But Ray refused to tell Dovey his girlfriend's last name.

With only a first name and skimpy description of Vivian, Dovey had her private investigator, Purcell Moore, turn the "city of Washington inside out" in search of this woman.

Moore succeeded. When Dovey telephoned Vivian—"hard, and tough, and angry"—she confirmed Ray's story but refused to testify in court, fearful that her husband would kill her if he found out about the affair.

Dovey was desperate for Vivian to testify because she didn't dare put Ray on the stand to retract his lie about fishing and tell the truth about what he was really doing on the day of the murder—not with Hantman as the prosecutor. Dovey feared that Ray, under a "barrage" of Hantman's questions during cross-examination, would "collapse, probably into tears."

So Dovey pressed Vivian to testify. After Dovey warned that if found guilty Ray could get the electric chair, Vivian agreed to provide an affidavit about her time with Ray on the morning of the murder. But that was no help. The court wouldn't accept Vivian's statement unless she testified in court to its veracity.

Vivian wouldn't budge. Like others in his life, Vivian abandoned Ray.

His wife, Helena, never visited him in the DC Jail, never attended the trial, not even on day one when Ray sat at the defense table between Dovey and co-counsel George Knox in a brand-new blue suit his mother had gotten for him. Ray was "shaking and reaching out to touch my hand every few minutes," remembered Dovey, "sensing, as I did, the press of the enormous crowd behind us."

That crowd included Ray's mother with about a dozen members of her church, newspaper and TV journalists, and what looked to Dovey "like a veritable sea of men in grey suits, along with two or three fashionably dressed white women." Dovey took those women to be friends of the victim.

Cicely Angleton, wife of CIA official James Angleton, was one of the victim's friends who attended the trial every day. She was "unnerved by the racial tension in the room," wrote Nina Burleigh.

Future high-profile defense attorney Robert S. Bennett also attended the trial every day, for he was Judge Corcoran's law clerk. "I sat next to the jury box, as if I was the thirteenth juror." Bennett recalled that throughout the trial Dovey had a "motherly warmth and her low-key, casual style concealed a very bright and aggressive advocate." In contrast, Hantman was "cold and arrogant at times and overreaching." What's more, Hantman did something Judge Corcoran told the then twenty-five-year-old Bennett to never ever do in a courtroom: chew gum. "It was disrespectful to the court and the jury." Hantman chewed gum "throughout the trial," said Bennett. "I am sure the jury noticed."

AFTER BRADLEE LEFT THE stand, Hantman called Georgetown pharmacist Harry Alexander Dalinsky, a friend of Ben Bradlee's who had also been friends with the victim.

> Hantman: Did there come a time when you saw Mary Pinchot Meyer in death?
> Dalinsky: Yes.
> Hantman: When and where did this happen, sir?
> Dovey: Excuse me, counsel. May we come to the bench, if Your Honor please?

Sidebar.

> **Dovey:**   I think it would be prejudicial to have this man testify about going to the Morgue and seeing the bullet wounds of this poor woman. We already have the identification made by the brother-in-law.
>
> *Overruled.*

In the end, Hantman didn't elicit any testimony about bullet wounds. All the jury learned was that Dalinsky had been at the DC Morgue with Ben Bradlee to identify the victim's body. As Dovey had no questions for him, the witness soon left the stand.

Hantman then called Randolph M. Worrell, a former technician at the DC Morgue.

Dovey had no questions for him. In preparation for the victim's autopsy, Worrell had removed her clothing. Hantman used Worrell to get before the jury the victim's sweaters, shirt, and other clothing, items Worrell said certainly looked like the clothing he had removed from the body.

> **Hantman:** Did you also at the same time, sir, remove from the body of Mary Pinchot Meyer a sample of her blood?
>
> **Worrell:**   Yes, I did.

When Hantman held up a test tube of blood, the judge called for a sidebar. Once before the bench, Hantman explained that he wanted to show that the blood in the test tube matched the blood found on the tree.

Hantman also said that the blood would support his theory that there had been a struggle, that Mary had been dragged, that her gloves had gotten bloody when she put her hands to her head after the first shot. As Hantman talked on about struggle and blood, his voice was loud enough for the jury to hear. Corcoran warned him to keep his voice down.

The judge had more questions for Hantman.

Corcoran:	And the purpose of showing the struggle is to show premeditation?
Hantman:	Yes, Your Honor.
Corcoran:	What do the articles of clothing add?
Hantman:	The articles of clothing merely show the gunshot wound—they not only show the gunshot wound but the proximity with which the shots were fired.

Dovey wasn't concerned about the clothing but she was very bothered by the blood.

Dovey:	If Your Honor please, he took me by surprise when he took this vial of blood out. I submit this is prejudicial.

Judge Corcoran didn't respond to Dovey. For the next few minutes there was more back and forth between Hantman and him.

But Dovey wasn't done.

Dovey:	About the blood that you have been shaking in front of the jury—
Hantman:	I haven't been shaking it in front of the jury. I just took it out to have it marked for identification, if Your Honor please.

Corcoran: All right. You held it up in front of the jury.

The judge warned Hantman against inflaming the jury. Dovey said that it was too late for that, that Hantman had already prejudiced the jury against Ray and he wouldn't get a fair trial. She motioned for a mistrial.

Corcoran: The motion is denied. Let's get on with the trial.

The test tube of blood was entered into evidence: the government's Exhibit 7. After Worrell confirmed that he'd delivered the vial of blood to the FBI, he was excused. Once again Dovey had no questions.

HANTMAN'S FOURTH WITNESS WAS deputy coroner Dr. Linwood L. Rayford, who had performed the autopsy on Mary Pinchot Meyer.

Dr. Rayford's testimony couldn't have been easy listening for the squeamish. He testified about Mary being "bloody about the head," and about finding on her body "superficial lacerations to the forehead, abrasions to the forehead, to the left knee and the left ankle," and "two circular wounds, about a quarter of an inch in diameter, both surrounded by darkened halos." In graphic detail, Rayford also testified about the path the bullets took in the victim's body.

Hantman brought forth two bullet slugs and the doctor identified them as the ones he had removed from Mary's body.

Dovey: We object to the admission of these two objects and request to be heard thereupon.

Another sidebar.

At the bench Dovey argued that no connection had been established between the bullets and her client. Admitting them into evidence would be "highly prejudicial."

Corcoran: I think the United States Attorney has a right to establish death and cause of death. These bullets have, obviously, been testified to as the cause of death. Whether they can be connected up later on is another point.

The bullets were entered into evidence and the jury learned from Dr. Rayford that those two "darkened halos" (dark circles around the wounds) were "suggestive of powder burns." The gun was fired at close range.

Through the rest of Hantman's direct examination of the deputy coroner, jurors, the press, Martha Crump, Ray, and others in Criminal Courtroom 4 heard more gory details. Hantman had just shown Dr. Rayford a pair of bloodstained tan gloves when Judge Corcoran interrupted. "Mr. Hantman, will you be much longer with this witness?"

It was about half past noon.

Learning that Hantman would be a bit longer, the judge ordered a recess until 1:45 p.m.

When court was back in session, counselors were soon back at the bench. Hantman described a line of questioning he wanted to pursue with Dr. Rayford about how the blood got on the victim's gloves and on the tree. Dovey renewed her protest against Hantman's line of questioning as "highly prejudicial," as bordering on "sensationalism." What's more, Hantman had a cart containing the blood-stained clothes and other exhibits right in front of the jury box. George Knox requested it be removed from the courtroom. Hantman insisted he would need it for upcoming witnesses.

Corcoran: Put it at the side of the jury box.

When Hantman resumed his direct examination of Dr. Rayford, the jury learned more details about Mary's wounds.

And this time, Dovey had questions for the witness.

In her cross-examination Dovey raised doubt as to how much of a fight the victim had been able to put up. She got the doctor to admit that the bruises could have come from falling as opposed to being dragged. On the matter of Mary being shot at close range, Dovey asked if it was likely that the shooter would have had "powder marks on his or her hands."

Rayford: Likely, yes.

Dovey would later make very good use of Dr. Rayford's response to her question about gunshot residue.

HANTMAN WASN'T DONE FOR the day. He had yet another witness, Joseph A. Ronsisvalle.

And Hantman got his wish to affix the topographical map to the courtroom wall. He also had copies in miniature for the judge, defense counsel, and jury.

The map, showing exits for the area of the towpath where the murder occured, was an official National Park Service map, and Ronsisvalle, a National Park Service employee, was there to firm up Hantman's theory that the killer couldn't have gotten out of the area because the police had sealed off all exits within four minutes of the "lookout"—that is, the be-on-the-lookout-for message radioed to police.

"With military precision, Hantman showed minute by minute the arrival time of police at each exit," remembered Robert Bennett.

Dovey didn't need a copy of the map. "I'd walked each of those exits dozens of times, with George and Jerry: the steps leading up to Water Street at Key Bridge, the steps at Chain Bridge, an underpass at Foundry Branch, another underpass at Fletcher's Boathouse."

In her cross-examination of Ronsisvalle, Dovey made him and that map irrelevant.

> **Dovey:** On this map, are there not places where a person walking on foot could leave the area of the towpath without using any of the fixed exits?
>
> **Ronsisvalle:** Yes.

"Fixed exits" were official exits as opposed to well-worn paths and short cuts not on the map.

Through Dovey's cross, jurors and spectators also learned that the witness wasn't personally all that familiar with the heavily wooded area. He had, in fact, never set foot on the towpath.

After Ronsisvalle left the witness stand, Hantman called his star witness, Henry Wiggins.

For Hantman, as Peter Janney put it, "Wiggins—a black man pointing the finger at another black man—seemed to be the ideal witness."

TO SIMPLICITY

WHEN HENRY WIGGINS TESTIFIED about what he had heard and seen nine months earlier, he said that he had a clear view of the man standing over the victim's body, that the man even looked up toward where he was standing, that he looked directly at the man, then ducked down behind the wall, bobbing up in a matter of seconds.

That's when he saw the man turn around and shove something into a jacket pocket. "It was dark, I believe, some kind of hand object." Then, said Wiggins, the man took off for the railroad tracks down below the towpath.

Wiggins also testified that the man he saw from a distance of about 120 feet had on a brimmed cap, a light-colored jacket, dark pants, dark shoes.

Hantman elicited testimony from Wiggins that let the jury know that for three years this witness had been a specialist in the Military Police Corps.

> **Hantman:** As part of your training, were you given any specialized training in the careful observation of people?

Dovey:	I object, if it please the Court.
Corcoran:	What is the ground of your objection?
Dovey:	The ground of my objection, if it please the Court, is he is now, I take it, trying to establish and make this witness a specialist in seeing and sighting objects and I submit that the military training and this line of questioning is all to make credible the testimony of this witness and I don't think he can do it in this manner through this witness.

Dovey was overruled and Hantman continued his line of questioning. In doing so, he handed Dovey ammunition she would later use.

Hantman asked Wiggins to describe the man.

Wiggins:	Well, I didn't get a very good look at his face but I did get a glance at it.

And?

The man was Black, medium build, weighed 180 to 185 pounds.

Hantman:	Were you able to determine how tall he was?
Wiggins:	Well, I couldn't make an exact estimate to that.

Hantman referred to the plaid cap and the light-colored jacket found near the crime scene along with the navy corduroy pants Ray had on when arrested.

It was going on 3:30 p.m.

Corcoran: May I ask you, Mr. Hantman, are you going to
 be long with this witness?

Hantman: Yes, Your Honor.

Court recessed.

THAT EVENING, AS ON every evening of the trial, Dovey kept company with herself on the screened-in back porch of her home across the Anacostia River, in the neighborhood bearing the river's name.

"Enshrouded in trees," the porch was "my sanctuary, my thinking place." Every case she had tried had been "mapped out on this porch, where complex matters invariably reduced themselves to simplicity."

WITH WIGGINS BACK ON the stand the next day, Hantman picked up where he left off. He asked the witness if he could identify the cap, jacket, and pants, along with the black wingtip shoes Ray had on when arrested.

Dovey objected. She pointed out, for example, that "there are zillions of pairs" of men's black shoes.

She lost, and in the end Wiggins testified that he first saw the shoes and the other clothing "when they was being worn by the defendant when he was standing over the victim at the scene."

Soon came one of the trial's most dramatic moments.

Hantman: Now, sir, can you look around the courtroom
 and identify for us the individual you say you
 saw standing over the body of Mary Meyer on
 the afternoon of October 12th, 1964?

Wiggins: Yes, sir.

It must have been a terrifying moment for Ray and one of great satisfaction for those in the courtroom who believed him guilty from day one.

For Hantman it wasn't enough for Wiggins to point out the person. He wanted him to leave the witness stand, go over to the defense table, and put a hand on the person's shoulder.

Dovey objected. Wiggins could very well make the identification from where he sat.

> **Hantman:** I submit the witness has a perfect right to come down and properly identify the individual, if he knows.

Corcoran asked Wiggins if he could identify the man from the witness stand.

> **Wiggins:** He is at the edge of that table there, sitting at the table there.

By then he was pointing.

The judge then told Hantman to stand behind the defendant to ensure a proper identification. But instead of doing exactly that, Hantman hammed it up.

First he stood behind George Knox.

> **Hantman:** Here?
> **Wiggins:** No, sir, at the far end.

Hantman stood behind Dovey's other co-counsel Alan Roberson.

Hantman: Here?

Wiggins: No, sir, the next person over.

Hantman then stood behind Ray.

Hantman: Here?

Wiggins: Yes, sir.

Hantman: May the record show, if Your Honor please, I am now standing directly behind the defendant Raymond Crump Jr.

Ray was probably shaking, maybe even reaching once again for Dovey's hand as tall, imposing Hantman with those bristling eyebrows stood behind him.

Corcoran: The record will so show. Proceed.

THROUGH THE REST OF Hantman's direct examination, jurors learned what Wiggins did after his duck and bob, from racing to his tow truck to returning to the scene with cops and identifying Ray from a distance of 15 to 30 feet and not wearing a cap or jacket.

In her cross-examination, Dovey challenged Wiggins's powers of observation, especially on the description he'd provided so that the police could issue that lookout.

Hadn't he testified that the man weighed about 185 pounds?

Hadn't he testified that he only got a glimpse of the man's face during that first sighting?

Did Wiggins recall telling anyone that the man was 5 feet 8 inches tall?

Wiggins:	Well, I believe I told one of the policemen which came down in the cruiser with me.
Dovey:	Would that be, then, an accurate estimate of what you saw, the man you saw weighed 185 and [was] five feet eight?
Wiggins:	That wouldn't be an accurate estimate, no, ma'am.
Dovey:	Well, now, are you telling us now you gave them information which was not accurate?

She was facing the jury.

Given the way Wiggins's next words tumbled, stumbled from his lips, he was clearly rattled.

Wiggins:	Well, this information which I gave them at that time which I was looking across the canal down on the subject there, would not be very accurate but as close as I can give—I give it them as close as I could remember.
Dovey:	And you gave them, though, what you thought you saw from across the canal?
Wiggins:	I tried to do my best.
Dovey:	All right. A hundred and eighty-five pounds; five foot eight.
Wiggins:	That's right.

THE *WASHINGTON POST* WOULD HEADLINE its coverage of that day's trial with "Witness Identifies Crump as Man He Saw With Murder Victim's Body."

The *Evening Star* would have "Witness Says Defendant

Stood Over Mrs. Meyer's Body." But this article pointed out what Dovey never said in her cross-examination but what she very much wanted the jury to pick up on: "Wiggins admitted," reported the *Evening Star,* "that he described Crump, who is noticeably short and slender, as being about 5 feet 8 inches and weighing 185 pounds."

When Ray was first questioned by police, a cop had asked for some identification and Ray had handed over his driver's license. It had him down as 5 feet 3½ inches tall and weighing 130 pounds.

The DC Jail had him logged in as 5 feet 5½ inches tall and weighing 145 pounds.

HAIR IS NOT LIKE FINGERPRINTS

HANTMAN CALLED SIX MORE witnesses that Wednesday.

There was Bill Branch, the guy Wiggins had been working with on that stalled Rambler, a man who gave muddled testimony on his movements after Wiggins ran over to the low-rise stone wall. And Branch was confused about whether he heard two shots or three.

The other witnesses were cops. One testified that once at the crime scene, he saw on the ground "signs of a scuffle," long drag marks behind the victim's body. Another officer admitted that by the time he got on the scene someone could have escaped through the exit he had been sent to guard.

If any courtroom spectators were daydreaming or about to doze off, they probably perked up when Officer Roderick Sylvis testified that when he was on the towpath he saw the head of a Black man pop out from the woods, then pop back in. He couldn't say for sure if the head had a cap. But he did say that his search for the person was in vain.

> **Dovey:** You can't, of your personal knowledge, say that the person whose head you saw is this defendant, Raymond Crump, can you?

Sylvis: No, ma'am.

On the witness stand Officer John Warner identified Ray as the man he had stopped after he had testified that he was told by Scout Car 71 to be on the lookout for a Black man wearing a light jacket and a dark hat and approximately 5 feet 10. He also testified to Ray's wet clothes, blood on his right hand, a tear on his pants, his fly unzipped, and to his story that he'd been fishing. Warner said he asked Ray to show him where he'd been fishing and that in doing so at one point Ray stopped. When Warner asked him how much farther, Ray said, "Just around the bend."

Dovey pursued this point in her cross-examination.

Dovey: Around the bend where the defendant indicated that he had been, did you know whether or not there were rocks there?
Warner: I don't know. I never looked there.
Dovey: You never went up there?
Warner: No, ma'am.

ON THURSDAY, JULY 22, day four of the trial, Hantman began as he had ended the day before.

With police officers.

To testify about finding a light-colored jacket, a pack of Pall Mall cigarettes about half full, a cap—a mind-numbing amount of minutia. More than once Hantman elicited testimony about Ray's fly being unzipped.

Under cross-examination, Lieutenant Arthur Weber said that he had been on the lookout for a "stocky" man about 5 feet 8 inches to 5 feet 10 inches tall.

Dovey also used her cross to reveal that no fingerprints had been found on that pack of Pall Malls. More important, that Ray's hands had never been tested for gunshot residue. Hantman had no proof that on the day of the murder Ray had fired a gun.

After Officer Weber noted that Ray's hands had been wet, Dovey rendered him a somewhat weak witness.

Did Weber know exactly how long Ray's hands had been in water?

He did not.

Couldn't a technician find gunshot residue under fingernails?

Weber: I don't think nitrates—I am not an expert.
Dovey: Oh, you are not an expert?
Weber: I am not an expert.

The most damaging testimony for the defense came from Elsie Perkins, Ray's next-door neighbor.

Perkins said that on the morning of the murder, she had seen Ray leave home not at his usual time (about 6:30 a.m.) but closer to 8 a.m. He was wearing a white T-shirt, a yellow sweatshirt, a jacket (beige or tan), and dark trousers.

Hantman: Did he have anything on his head?
Perkins: He had a cap, a kind of plaid cap.

When Hantman showed her Exhibit 14 and 15, the cap and the jacket, Perkins said she'd seen Ray wearing them before. Several times.

Perkins also testified that on the morning of the murder Ray had no fishing gear with him when he left home and that later that day while visiting Helena Crump she had seen that gear in their living room closet. She also said that, like her, Ray smoked Pall Malls.

Dovey used her cross to make the most of other things Elsie Perkins had not seen.

A bulge in a jacket pocket as if Ray was packing a .38-caliber pistol?

Perkins had seen no bulge.

Had she ever seen Ray with a gun?

No.

AROUND 3:20 P.M. JUDGE Corcoran told jurors that they would be excused until Monday. This was a concession to Dovey. That morning, she had asked him for a day's recess. "I am a one-woman office," she explained.

At the end of every day, the judge cautioned jurors against talking about the case. Now that they would have three days off, he doubled down on this warning. "There will be all kinds of news stories. You will probably hear news broadcasts, TV broadcasts, and you may have friends who may want to know what is going on. Please refrain from talking to anybody if you can avoid it." If anyone leaned on them for information, they were to contact the marshal's office. "Try to avoid any contact with the case even among yourselves," added Corcoran. "Forget it for the weekend."

In his coverage of the day's trial, *Evening Star* staff writer William Basham spent quite a bit of ink on Elsie Perkins's testimony in an article headlined "Meyer Witness Links Cap to Crump." He also reported that "some 40 policemen, Park police scuba divers, Navy deep sea divers and soldiers with mine detectors" had conducted a "thorough" search for that .38-caliber pistol, but no gun was ever found. That information had come from Detective Weber.

In addition, Basham reported that over the last two days "under cross examination by Mrs. Roundtree," most of the policemen who took the witness stand said they had been told to be on the lookout for a Black man who was about "five-feet-ten and weighed about 180 pounds. Crump is noticeably shorter and slender."

WHEN THE TRIAL RESUMED on Monday, July 26, and on the day after that, the jury heard from ten more prosecution witnesses.

Along with police officers, there was a National Park Service surveyor, the jogger William Mitchell, a police photographer brought in from his hospital bed, and three FBI special agents: a firearms expert; an expert on stains, including bloodstains; and an expert on hair and fibers. Also, having been unable to get into evidence that bloodstained section of the tree the victim had supposedly clung to, Hantman entered instead a photograph of it.

Hantman scored some victories with Mitchell. He testified that it was from a distance of two or three feet that he saw a Black man trailing the victim, a man who had on a cap with a brim, a light windbreaker, and dark pants. He estimated his weight to be 145 pounds. His height: "about my height." Mitchell was 5 feet 8 inches tall. When shown the cap, jacket, and pants, Mitchell said they were "similar" to those of the man he saw.

Was this man carrying a fishing rod?

"No, no fishing rod," replied Mitchell.

Allison C. Semmes, the FBI special agent on stains, testified that blood found on the victim's clothing was type O, as was the blood sample taken from her body in the morgue. Semmes couldn't say that there were bloodstains on the jacket that allegedly belonged to Ray, only "three very small diluted appearing stains" that "possibly consisted of blood." Dovey used her cross-examination to establish that no one else's blood had been found on any of the victim's clothing.

Spectators in Criminal Court 4 may well have thought at first that the defense suffered a major blow in the testimony of FBI Special Agent Paul Morgan Stombaugh, the hair and fibers expert. He explained that he had used a microscope to examine the hair found on the cap and jacket and the hair sample taken from Ray, looking for twenty-two different characteristics. He found that the hair on the cap and jacket matched the hair sample from Ray. He concluded that all the hair came from the same person or from two different people whose hair was identical on the microscopic level. However, in his opinion, the latter was a remote possibility.

Dovey didn't have the money to bring in a hair expert, but she had done her homework. In her cross-examination, she read a passage from a book on criminal investigations by a former FBI investigator who wrote, "At best an expert can say that two specimens of hair are similar." An expert could not say that "they are identical."

Stombaugh's testimony failed to prove that the cap and jacket belonged to Ray.

Dovey: In other words, hair is not like fingerprints?

Stombaugh: No. Hair changes characteristics. Fingerprints do not.

After the witness was excused, Hantman addressed Judge Corcoran. "Your Honor please, that is the Government's case. And the Government rests."

The next day, Dovey mounted her defense. Finally, the jury would hear her opening statement.

22

EXHIBIT A

DOVEY'S DEFENSE WAS ROOTED in her first impression of Ray on that late October day in 1964.

Incapable.

The crime simply didn't fit the man.

What would she *show* and *show* and *show*?

In her opening statement Dovey told jurors that despite the prosecution's "great quantity of evidence" they simply couldn't find proof that Ray was the person "who fired the gun on that fatal afternoon causing the death of Mrs. Meyer."

Dovey would also show her client to be a "person of peace and good order in the community wherein he lives."

She anticipated jurors wondering, *So what?*

"Evidence of good character may be sufficient alone without anything else to raise a reasonable doubt," she said, "and having raised reasonable doubt in your minds, then you may not convict Raymond Crump Jr. as charged of murder in the first degree."

Against Hantman's more than forty-five exhibits Dovey would present just one.

"No one said, 'This is Exhibit A'" but, she said, the jury had seen this evidence every day of the trial.

Ray was Dovey's Exhibit A.

"And I urge you, ask you, as we go forward, to look at Raymond Crump Jr. and then you weigh him besides the evidence that you have before you these long, tedious days of the trial."

In contrast to Hantman's fifteen-plus-page opening statement, Dovey's runs just a little over two pages.

Next Dovey called her witnesses.

HOMEMAKER LOUISE WESTER WAS the Sunday school superintendent at Ray's church, Second Baptist Southwest. She had known Ray for about twelve years.

Roach Young (occupation not recorded) also attended the same church. He had known Ray for about thirteen years.

The Reverend Jesse A. Brown, pastor of Second Baptist Southwest, had known Ray for about eighteen years.

All three testified that Ray was known to be not a violent person, but rather peaceful, calm, quiet.

After the Reverend Brown left the witness stand, Dovey addressed Judge Corcoran: "At this time, if it please the Court, the defendant rests."

Dovey had begun her opening statement around 10:40 a.m. When she rested it was about 10:55.

"There wasn't a sound in the courtroom, except Mr. Hantman's chair scraping as he stood up and looked at me, and then at Judge Corcoran, in pure astonishment."

After the jury was ushered out, Dovey and Hantman stood at the bench.

Hantman: If Your Honor please, I am caught completely flatfooted at this moment because I never

anticipated in my wildest dream that counsel
would rest her case without—

For one, he thought she'd be calling more witnesses.

Typically, before closing arguments the defense and prosecution confer on the instructions to be given to the jury. Hantman
didn't have his paperwork ready. But he'd have to get it done
within a few hours. Corcoran, also taken back by the brevity
of Dovey's defense, wanted Dovey and Hantman to give their
closing statements that afternoon. "I hate to keep this jury sitting
around," he told them. "They are getting impatient, I can see."

Corcoran had the jurors brought back in, told them that
they'd hear closing arguments around 2:30 p.m., then excused
them.

ADLER HEELS

IN THE TRIAL TRANSCRIPT, Assistant US Attorney Alfred Hantman's closing statement begins on page 903 and ends on page 926.

Between his start and finish Hantman reminded the jury of the charge against Ray, that he "purposely and with deliberate and premeditated malice did shoot Mary Pinchot Meyer with a pistol causing injuries as a result of which Mrs. Meyer died."

He reminded them of the vial of blood.

The bullets.

The dark circles around the victim's wounds.

The blood-stained tan gloves.

The abrasions and lacerations on the corpse.

The map.

Henry Wiggins's testimony that he had seen Ray standing over the body, then shoving something into a jacket pocket.

Elsie Perkins's testimony about what Ray was wearing on the morning of the murder.

FBI Special Agent Stombaugh's testimony on Ray's hair sample being a match for hair found on the jacket and the cap.

"Can there be any doubt that this jacket and this cap are the articles of clothing owned by and worn by Crump on October 12th 1964?" Hantman asked as he exhibited the clothing once again.

There was a lot more Hantman wanted jurors to remember, from testimony by police about arriving on the scene and one officer seeing a Black man's head pop out of a wooded area to Ray having been found soaking wet and his claim that he'd been fishing.

"Tie this up," said Hantman. "Tie this up with the testimony of Mrs. Perkins. When she saw the defendant leave his home that morning he wasn't carrying anything."

"Tie that up," said Hantmen, "with the testimony of Mr. Mitchell," the jogger who said he had seen a Black man in a cap and light windbreaker trailing the victim.

Hantman also reminded the jury that when first approached by police, Ray, besides being wet, had a cut on his hand.

And that his fly was unzipped.

Hantman once more reminded the jury of blood—on the tree, on the victim's clothes. He asserted that "in all probability" the three small stains that the FBI agent found on the jacket that allegedly belonged to Ray were bloodstains. "They were Mary Meyer's blood that spattered when she was shot."

When done, he thanked the jury.

It was about 3:30 p.m.

After a ten-minute recess, Dovey gave her closing statement.

SHE FIRST THANKED THE jury for its "attentiveness," its "seriousness," and apologized if at any point she seemed "overly aggressive and pushy," if she seemed in any way to be discour-

On the day after the murder, police officers, along with bystanders, watch as the Park Police's Private C. G. Vermillion prepares to dive into the C&O Canal in search of the gun.

teous to Judge Corcoran or to Mr. Hantman. "But," she added, "my business here has been the business of a man's life laid on the line with circumstantial evidence."

Like Hantman, she, too, wanted jurors to remember what Wiggins and Mitchell had said about the suspect's height and weight.

Was Ray 5 feet 8 inches tall?

Did Ray weigh 185 pounds?

Dovey continued to sow seeds of doubt.

Could someone have escaped the area before or after police arrived on the scene?

Where is the gun?

How did the prosecution explain the absence of any of the victim's blood on clothing that allegedly belonged to Ray?

Had a strand of Ray's hair been found on Mary's body?

How could there have been no transfer of blood or hair if, as the prosecution claimed, there had been a great struggle?

She reminded the jury of what her character witnesses had said about Ray.

"Lawyer" was almost done.

As on other days in Criminal Courtroom 4, Ray didn't just have Dovey with the law degree, Dovey who had taken classes at Georgetown Law, Dovey who had been practicing law for fourteen years fighting like a tiger for his life.

The other Dovey was there too: the granddaughter of a once electrifying preacher, the granddaughter of a woman who had prayer and praise song pulsing through her home, the daughter of a Sunday school superintendent, the daughter of a woman who led a choir, the girl who grew up in a "God's House," the woman who became an AME minister.

"I leave this little man in your hands."

Both Doveys were bringing it home.

"And I say to you fairly and truly, if you can find that he is five feet and eight inches tall, that he weighs 185 pounds, irrespective of what he wore that day—if you can find—I cannot from this evidence—and I say you must have a substantial and a reasonable doubt in your minds, and until the Government proves its case beyond such doubt, then you must bring back a verdict of not guilty."

HANTMAN WASN'T DONE. As was his right, he made a rebuttal argument.

"Circumstantial evidence is equally competent, equally forceful, equally as admissible with direct evidence," he said. He reminded the jury that Wiggins had been a specialist in the Military Police Corps and made it sound as if Wiggins had only said the man "looked" to be about 185 pounds.

Hantman even said that he didn't think a difference of 35 or 40 pounds was all that significant, restating that once in custody Ray had been found to be 5 feet 5 ½ inches tall and to weigh 145 pounds. He put his Exhibit 17, Ray's black shoes, on the lectern in front of the jury box.

> **Hantman:** Look at the heels on these shoes. They are practically Adler-heel shoes. There are at least, as I look at it, and you will have to make up your own mind, two inches of heel on that pair of shoes. These are the shoes the defendant was wearing.

(Adler was a shoe company famous for its "elevator shoes," ones constructed to make men look taller.)

Hantman told the jury that Mitchell had said the man he saw was 5 feet 8 inches tall and weighed 145 pounds.

Hantman went on to stress the rapid arrival of police on the scene. He claimed that Ray had ditched his cap and jacket because he knew Henry Wiggins had seen him. Hantman also told the jury that the .38-caliber pistol might very well still be in the area of the C&O Canal towpath.

Hantman talked again about blood, including that blood on the tree.

He sought to make Dovey's character witnesses irrelevant. "Does it mean that if a person has peace and a good character he has a license to commit crime?"

Hantman circled back to Ray's lie about fishing.

"The evidence is clear," said Hantman in winding down. "The evidence is convincing. I submit to you, ladies and gentleman, the evidence is overwhelming."

He urged jurors to think with their *heads*, not with their *hearts*. If they did that, they could come to no other conclusion but that Ray Crump Jr. was guilty.

It was going on 5 p.m. Jury deliberation would begin the next day.

IF JUSTICE IS TO BE DONE

On Thursday, July 29, 1965, Judge Corcoran delivered his charge to the jury.

First, Corcoran thanked the jurors for their service. He acknowledged that jury duty "is never easy, for it is never easy to sit in judgment on your fellowman." But jury duty "is always important. If justice is to be done, the burden must be borne."

Judge Corcoran asked the jury to do its duty with "all care and deliberation" and "free from passion, free from bias, free from prejudice." Focus on the evidence, he said.

On the verdict, which had to be unanimous, the jury had five options.

Guilty of first-degree murder: punishable by death.

Guilty of first-degree murder: punishable by life imprisonment.

Guilty of first-degree murder but unable to agree unanimously on the punishment (in which case the judge would determine the sentence).

Guilty of second-degree murder (killing with malice but without premeditation): punishable by up to life in prison.

The fifth possibility: Not guilty.

By 11:00 a.m. Treasury clerk Evelyn S. Carpenter, homemaker Cecilia Chmielewski, St. Elizabeths Hospital nurse's aide Bessie E. Hawkins, cab driver Archie N. McEachern, Job Corps program specialist Edward O. Savwoir, and the other seven jurors were escorted to the jury room to commence deliberations. The four alternates had been discharged.

Four hours later, with the jury still deliberating and Ray at the defendant's table with his counsel, Judge Corcoran returned to the bench and asked Dovey and Hantman to approach.

He had a note from the jury foreperson Edward Savwoir.

"Your Honor,

(1) Did the police officers go with defendant Crump to the spot or rock which he said he was fishing and from which he said he fell? If so, at what time on what date?

(2) May we please have all photos admitted as evidence as well as the small map of the area that was distributed to us previously?

(3) May we know if defendant Ray Crump is left or right-handed?"

The photos the jury wanted to see included several of the crime scene and the photo of the tree.

Judge Corcoran informed Dovey and Hantman that he proposed to respond thus:

"(1) Your recollection of the evidence controls."

(2) Photos and map herewith.

(3) Your recollection of the evidence controls." (By "your recollection of the evidence controls," Corcoran meant that the jurors must rely on their memories.)

With no objections to his proposed response, the judge recessed the court.

AT 10:30 P.M., JUDGE CORCORAN was back in the courtroom.

Another note from the jury.

"After 8 ½ hours we have 8 jurors who have reached a decision and 4 who have not. Do you consider this jury deadlocked?"

With no objection from the prosecution or defense, Judge Corcoran replied, no, he didn't think the jury "hopelessly deadlocked."

He did, however, think it was time for the jury to retire for the night. "You will resume your deliberations in the morning," the judge wrote to the jury, advising them that they'd be "comfortably taken care of tonight," meaning they'd be given lodging and meals and kept from the outside world. Judge Corcoran also told them not to mention the "numerical standing of the jury" in future.

The next morning the *Washington Post* reported that Ray's mother, Martha, had been waiting for the verdict in a corridor of the courthouse the whole time.

25

WEPT

PAGE 995 OF THE trial transcript tells us that on Friday, July 30, 1965, at about 11:40 a.m., after about eleven hours of deliberations, the jurors took their seats in Criminal Courtroom 4.

Deputy Clerk: Will the forman please rise.

Edward Savwoir stood up.

Deputy Clerk: Mr. Foreman, has the jury agreed upon its verdict?
Savwoir: It has.
Deputy Clerk: May we have the verdict, please?

Edward Savwoir handed the verdict form to the deputy clerk, who in turn handed it to Judge Corcoran. The transcript is silent on exactly what happened next. Presumably Judge Corcoran looked over the verdict form, found nothing irregular, then handed it back to the deputy clerk.

Deputy Clerk: Will the jury please rise.

The jury stood up.

Deputy Clerk: Members of the jury, we have your verdict which states that you find the defendant Ray Crump Jr. not guilty, and this is your verdict so say you each and all?

Yes.

Judge Corcoran discharged the jury, then addressed the defendant. "Raymond Crump, you are a free man."

"Ray's mother cried out," recalled Dovey forty years later, "and so did her minister and her friends from church."

Dovey and Ray hugged.

Soon, they were out of Criminal Courtroom 4, out of the US District Court for the District of Columbia, out onto Constitution Avenue.

Dovey asked, "Is there anywhere you want to go, Ray?"

Ray replied, "I wants to go home."

THE NEXT DAY THE *Washington Post* reported that Ray "swayed forward against the counsel table, closed his eyes and seemed to be near fainting when the verdict was read by a court clerk."

A South Carolina paper said he "wept."

CODA

WHEN *WASHINGTON POST* STAFF WRITER William Chapman reported on the outcome of the trial on July 31 under the front-page headline "Crump Free in Murder on Towpath," he, like writers for the *Evening Star,* the Philadelphia *Inquirer,* Virginia's *Danville Register,* the *Orlando Sentinel,* and other newspapers, included foreperson Edward O. Savwoir's statement on the verdict: "There were many missing links . . . we just didn't get the man at the scene."

About a week and a half later, Ray wrote to Dovey from Mount Gilead, North Carolina, about sixty miles east of Queen City and about seven miles east of Norwood, North Carolina, where he'd been born.

"Just a few line to say hello and thank very much." Ray reported that "at the present time I am during alright and so for I had no trouble and thing are looking good for me right now."

He asked Dovey to gather his personal effects still with the Metropolitan Police Department and to send them to his mother so that she could send them to him. Those items included his driver's license, a lighter, a picture, and a buck and a half.

But Ray Crump Jr. didn't do "alright" after those nine months in the DC Jail. Before the trial, his rap sheet had two drunken and disorderly charges and one shoplifting charge. Over the years after his acquittal, Ray was arrested more than twenty times, in DC, in Maryland, in Virginia, in North Carolina, and on far more serious charges.

Assault with a deadly weapon more than once.

Arson more than once.

Gun possession.

Rape.

The victims of these crimes included his second wife, Lois; a girlfriend; and a guy with whom he had a beef over money.

He lived quite a long time, notwithstanding his troubles. Raymond Crump Jr. died on June 4, 2005, at the age of sixty-six.

Dovey was forever "heartsick" over what she deemed the shattering of Raymond Crump Jr. "He was not a remotely violent man when he was jailed for Mary Meyer's murder in 1964, but he became one afterward."

In February 1976, the *Washington Post* reported on a *National Enquirer* piece alleging that when President Kennedy was assassinated he and Mary Pinchot Meyer had been having an affair and that she had kept a diary that ended up in the hands of CIA official James Angleton, who supposedly destroyed it.

Many people, including Robert Bennett, Judge Corcoran's law clerk at the time of the trial, maintained that justice had not been done in Corcoran's court, that Ray was the killer. Others believed that Ray was a scapegoat, that Mary Pinchot Meyer was a woman who knew too much about Kennedy's assassination. Such people pointed out that Meyer had been shot execution-style.

Some people have also made much of the fact that Mary Pinchot Meyer's ex-husband Cord Meyer was a CIA official, who was, wrote Dovey, presented in the press at the time as an "author and lecturer." Some newspapers did describe him that way, but two days after the murder the *New York Times*, with its huge readership, stated that Cord Meyer was working for the CIA in New York City.

Certainly the causes of acquittals and convictions are often the subject of debate.

Was Ray acquitted because eight of the twelve jurors were Black?

The David (Dovey) and Goliath (Hantman) optics may also have been a factor.

Did Dovey win the day because of her simplicity, motherliness, and skillful cross-examinations?

Or had the sometimes cold, arrogant, gum-chewing Hantman been his own worst enemy? Robert Bennett concluded that Hantman had overtried his case. Hantman "took a vacuum cleaner approach to presenting evidence. He put it all in no matter how insignificant, and this diluted the impact of his strong evidence."

Looking back on Ray's acquittal, Dovey stated that at least she had made it "impossible for the matter of Mary Pinchot's murder to be sealed off and forgotten, as the government so clearly wanted to do," and "to the extent that my efforts in defending Raymond opened the path for researchers seeking to know more about the troubling circumstances surrounding her death, I am gratified."

What is not in doubt is that Ray's acquittal brought Dovey "the kind of success of which many lawyers dream. If success is defined as volume of cases, notoriety in the press, and respect in the legal community, then it can fairly be said that in the wake of the Crump case, I achieved it."

Dovey's success contributed to changing notions about the capabilities of Black lawyers, women lawyers. Dovey is part of the reason why Black women lawyers are no longer rare birds.

AFTER RAY'S CASE, JUDGES appointed Dovey to some of the toughest murder cases and she was proud to win acquittal "for other men who, like Ray, had no chance at all."

Dovey's success and reputation even led to a nomination for a judgeship. In March 1969, the Bar Association of the District of Columbia, the organization that denied Black lawyers membership when she began practicing law, wrote to Attorney General John N. Mitchell endorsing Dovey and three other attorneys to fill two vacancies on the US District Court for the District of Columbia.

The Attorney General soon received a stream of letters of recommendation on Dovey's behalf, including from Florence Read (long since retired from Spelman) and civil rights activist Dorothy I. Height, another protégé of Mary McLeod Bethune. Height was then president of the National Council of Negro Women, for which Dovey was general counsel and still serving the organization at no charge.

Dovey J. Roundtree, Esquire, didn't get that judgeship, but her work continued to be noticed and applauded.

While enjoying success and awards, Dovey remained rooted and grounded in *Veritas et Utilitas*. She became an Edith Wimbish, a Mary Mae Neptune, a Mary McLeod Bethune, a Professor Nabrit. She opened her office to young attorneys "for seminars, coached, and trained and mentored them." It did her heart good to hear from law students how much they had been "inspired by what they witnessed in that fourth-floor courtroom in the last two weeks of July 1965."

In the 1970s, then at the helm of Roundtree, Knox, Hunter & Parker, Dovey moved into family law, becoming an advocate for children. "More and more, as I labored at the bar and in the pulpit and in the privacy of the counseling room," she explained in her memoir, *Mighty Justice*, "I confronted shattered children, children caught between warring parents, children who'd borne witness to the most horrific crimes, children neglected and shunted aside, children preyed upon by those entrusted with their care." She added that her law practice and her ministry at Allen Chapel AME "tightly bound from the beginning, became almost indistinguishable, one from another."

Dovey the riveting public speaker stayed active too. Invitations came from churches in and outside DC, from college and universities, from organizations as different as the DC's Cosmetologist Association and the city's Tots and Teens chapter. In late August 1992, the Carlisle, Pennsylvania, *Sentinel* announced that Dovey, age seventy-eight, was to be among the speakers at an upcoming conference at the US Army Military History Institute at Carlisle Barracks. The theme of this conference was Black service in the US armed forces during World War II. Dovey's session was titled "Looking Back But Forward."

Four years later Dovey the lawyer retired and went back to

Dovey Johnson Roundtree in 1995. Her numerous awards included a "Lawyer of the Year" award from Howard Law, a Spirit of Spelman College Founder's Day Award, an American Bar Association Margaret Brent Women Lawyers of Achievement Award, and an Award of Excellence from the Charlotte, North Carolina, chapter of the Thurgood Marshall Scholarship Fund. "I've come to the conclusion that there's not much in life except helping people, and both law and religion do that," she told the *Washington Afro-American* in 1965.

Queen City, where she eventually lost her eyesight due to complications of diabetes.

But Dovey didn't lose her vision. In her waning days, surely she hoped, dreamed, prayed that troops of young people in future generations would find in her story strength for their journeys and enough stamina, sound thinking, and love to devote at least some of their time, talent, and treasure to mending brokenness in their world.

Dovey Mae Johnson Roundtree passed away on May 21, 2018, several weeks after her 104th birthday.

ACKNOWLEDGMENTS

I am so grateful to my editor, Simon Boughton, for your careful reading of drafts, your astute, fine thinking, and your excellent direction. Gratitude is also due to others in the Norton family: Assistant Editor Kristin Allard, Project Editor Dassi Zeidel, Copy Editor Laurie Lieb, Production Manager Julia Druskin, Designer Steve Attardo, and cover artist Monique Aimee.

I am also grateful to many people outside the Norton family, people who responded so promptly and generously to my inquiries and provided invaluable information and/or priceless material.

At Spelman College Archives: Kassandra Ware, truly "another light."

At the US District Court for the District of Columbia: Bryant Johnson.

At the National Archives and Records Administration: Damani K. Davis, Mena-Keona S. Nokes-Drake, Stanley Coln, Tracy Coates, and Nakisha Smith.

At the National Archives for Black Women's History: Kenneth J. Chandler.

At the Robinson-Spangler Carolina Room, Charlotte Mecklenburg Library: Robert Stocker and Shelia Bumgarner.

Thank you, David DiLapi, CPA, for helping me decipher the Dovey Johnson Roundtree–Mary Mae Neptune loan agreement.

Thank you, attorneys Stephen J. Pollak, John V. Geise, and William John O'Malley Jr., for your generous responses to questions about the law.

Thank you to my sister Nelta for reading the manuscript and assisting with research.

And thank you to my agent, Jennifer Lyons, for all that you continually do.

NOTES

For complete citations of books heavily consulted, please see Selected Sources.

Abbreviations

DJR Alumna File, Spelman: Dovey J. Roundtree Spelman Alumna File, Spelman College Archives, Atlanta, Georgia.

DJR Papers, NABWH: Dovey Johnson Roundtree Papers, NABWH_005, National Archives of Black Women's History, Mary McLeod Bethune Council House, Washington, DC.

Crump: United States v. Raymond Crump Jr., Criminal No. 930–64, US District Court for the District of Columbia.

Prologue

1 **"Lawyer . . . ?":** Roundtree and McCabe, *Mighty Justice*, p. 192.

1 **Ray's priors:** "Laborer Is Charged in Slaying of Artist," *Evening Star*, October 13, 1964, p. B1; Janney, *Mary's Mosaic*, p. 95.

1 **"They say you killed . . .":** Roundtree and McCabe, *Mighty Justice*, p. 192.

2 **Ray's lack of assets and his dollar and a half:** "Affidavit in Support of Application to Proceed Without Prepayment of Costs," October 20, 1964, *Crump*, Folder 1, pdf pp. 44–45.

2 **"Mrs. Mary Pinchot Meyer . . .":** "Laborer Is Charged in Slaying," p. A1.

3 **"At first we didn't . . . started across the road":** "Laborer Is Charged in Slaying," p. B1.

4 **"Robbery Motive Seen . . ."**: headline to article by Alfred E. Lewis, *Washington Post*, October 13, 1964, p. A1.

4 **"Rape Weighed as Motive . . ."**: headline, *Evening Star*, October 14, 1964, p. B1.

4 **"blowing on a newly . . ."**: "Gun Hunted in Artist's Canal Death," *Washington Post*, October 14, 1964, p. A1.

5 **"righteous lawyer"**: Janney, *Mary's Mosaic*, p. 90.

1: Those Poor Broken Feet

7 **Grandma Rachel's birth:** Her death certificate gives December 30, 1872 ("North Carolina, Death Certificates, 1909–1976," digital image s.v. "Rachel M. Graham," *Ancestry.com*). Her Social Security application gives December 30, 1871 ("US, Social Security Applications and Claims Index, 1936-2007," digital image s.v. "Rachel Millis Graham," *Ancestry.com*).

9 **"They were gnarled . . . poor broken feet"**: Roundtree and McCabe, *Mighty Justice*, p. 3.

10 **"I ran and fought . . . his way with me"**: Roundtree and McCabe, *Mighty Justice*, p. 4.

10 **"with a swaying awkwardness . . ."**: Roundtree and McCabe, *Mighty Justice*, p. 5.

10 **Dovey's residence and her father's death:** "Standard Certificate of Death," North Carolina State Board of Health and Bureau of Vital Statistics, digital image s.v. "James Johnson," *Ancestry.com*.

11 **"I was too young . . . my mother was crying"**: Roundtree and McCabe, *Mighty Justice*, p. 6.

2: God's House

12 **"rich alto"**: Roundtree and McCabe, *Mighty Justice*, p. 17.

12 **"a rich tapestry . . ."**: Roundtree and McCabe, *Mighty Justice*, pp. 14–15.

13 **shogun houses:** "Shotgun Houses," *Encyclopedia of African American Society*, ed. Gerald D. Jaynes, vol. 2 (Thousand Oaks, CA: Sage, 2005), p. 744; "Shotgun Houses," Data Center, http://www.datacenterresearch.org/pre-katrina/tertiary/shotgun.html. Last accessed February 24, 2020.

13 **"We pieced out. . .":** Roundtree and McCabe, *Mighty Justice*, p. 15.

13 **Grandpa's store:** 700 S. Plum as per *Charlotte, North Carolina City Directory*, compiled by Ernest H. Miller (Charlotte, NC: Piedmont Directory Co., 1917), p. 249. In a 1993 interview Dovey's sister Eunice remembered that Grandpa also managed a business for a white man. Hagans, Zenobia Gray, and Eunice Johnson Brown interview, Behind the Veil Oral History Project: Documenting African-American Life in the Jim Crow South, https://repository.duke.edu/dc/behindtheveil /btvnc02024. Last accessed March 15, 2020.

13 **"left a hole":** Roundtree and McCabe, *Mighty Justice*, p. 7.

14 **James Johnson's employment:** He was identified as a "common laborer" on his death certificate, but the *Charlotte, North Carolina City Directory*, compiled by Ernest H. Miller (Charlotte: Piedmont Directory Co., 1918), p. 334, listed him as a pressman for the AME Zion Publishing House.

14 **"By all let it be known . . .":** Roundtree and McCabe, *Mighty Justice*, p. 18.

14 **"I spoke like him . . .":** Roundtree and McCabe, *Mighty Justice*, p. 17.

14 **"garbage . . . personally violated":** Roundtree and McCabe, *Mighty Justice*, p. 11.

15 **"Get that . . . there":** Roundtree and McCabe, *Mighty Justice*, p. 9.

15 **KKK incidents:** Roundtree and McCabe, *Mighty Justice*, p. 13, p. 5.

15 **"and Grandma knew . . .":** Roundtree and McCabe, *Mighty Justice*, p. 7.

15 **"as good as anybody":** Roundtree and McCabe, *Mighty Justice*, p. 11.

15 **"grand procession . . . known as Brooklyn":** Roundtree and McCabe, *Mighty Justice*, p. 8.

16 **"to be in a cleaner . . . beautifying their yards":** "The Cleanest Portion of the City," *Charlotte Observer*, May 31, 1878, p. 3.

16 **Statistics on college attendance in 1920:** Digest of Education Statistics, Table 104.20, National Center for Education Statistics, https://nces.ed.gov/programs/digest/d13/tables/dt13_104.20.asp. Last accessed February 24, 2020.

17 **"broken-down old frame building":** Roundtree and McCabe, *Mighty Justice*, p. 18.

17 **"The classrooms were crowded . . .":** Betty W. Barber "Struggle, Commitment, and Determination: An African-American Woman's Journey to Self-Development," in *The Emergence of Women into the 21st Century*, edited by Patricia L. Munhall and Virginia M. Fitzsimons (New York: NLN Press, 1995), p. 378.

18 **Dovey's high school activities:** "Application for Admission," May 16, 1934, DJR Alumna File, Spelman, Folder 1934a, pdf p. 3. Dovey mentioned her study of the French horn on p. 19 of her autobiography, *Mighty Justice*.

18 **Black women with medical degrees:** Thomas J. Ward Jr., *Black Physicians in the Jim Crow South* (Fayetteville: University of Arkansas Press, 2003), p. 53.

18 **Black businesses in Charlotte in 1915:** C. H. Watson, ed., *Colored Charlotte: Published in Connection with the Fiftieth Anniversary of the Freedom of the Negro in the County of Mecklenburg and the City of Charlotte, North Carolina* (Charlotte: AME Zion Job Print, 1915), p. 6.

19 **Cost of Spelman:** "Expenses," *Catalog of Spelman College 1928–1929*, April 1929, pp 43–44.

19 **Earnings of domestic workers:** Elizabeth Ross Haynes, "Negroes in Domestic Service in the United States," *Journal of Negro History* 8, no. 4 (October 1923): 404.

19 **"PANIC SEIZES STOCK MARKET":** *Hutchinson (Kansas) News*, October 24, 1929, p. 1, https://newspaperarchive.com/hutchinson-news-oct-24-1929-p-1/. Last accessed March 12, 2020.

19 **"STOCKS LOSE 10 BILLION IN DAY":** *Klamath News*, October 29, 1929, p. 1.

3: Worthy Wish

21 **Hurley residence and Mr. Hurley's job:** 1930 United States Federal Census, Charlotte, Mecklenburg, North Carolina; "US City Directories, 1822–1995," digital images s.v. "Bailey C. Hurley," *Ancestry.com*.

21 **"my own silent prayers . . .":** Roundtree and McCabe, *Mighty Justice*, p. 20.

22 **"good people":** Roundtree and McCabe, *Mighty Justice*, p. 20.

22 **"stately . . . dogwood and magnolias":** Roundtree and McCabe, *Mighty Justice*, p. 21.

22 **Dovey and Mama's weekly earnings:** Notes, September 20, 1934, DJR Alumna File, Spelman, Folder 1934a, pdf p. 16.

22 **Forty dollars and "I [have] been obsessed . . . the obstacle":** "Application for Admission," May 16, 1934, DJR Alumna File, Spelman, Folder 1934a, pdf pp. 2, 3.

23 **"How do you expect . . . work on campus":** "Application for Admission," PDF p. 2.

24 **"city of a hundred hills":** W. E. B. Du Bois, *The Souls of Black Folk: Essays and Sketches*, 2nd edition. Chicago: A. C. McClurg & Co., 1903, p. 75.

24 **"Most of the stylishly . . . comprehend it":** Roundtree and McCabe, *Mighty Justice*, p. 28.

24 **"A student's wardrobe . . . prohibited":** "Dress," *Catalog of Spelman College 1933–34*, April 1934, pp. 66–67.

25 **"She's just doing fine . . . impudent little thing":** Roundtree and McCabe, *Mighty Justice*, p. 22.

25 **Wimbish family:** 1930 United States Federal Census, Atlanta, Fulton, Georgia, digital image s.v. "Edith Wimbish," *Ancestry.com*. Edith's father Christopher Columbus Wimbish Sr., deceased, had been a customs collector. One of her brothers, Christopher Columbus Wimbish Jr., a graduate of Howard University in Washington, DC, and of Northwestern University's law school, had been a first lieutenant in a Black regiment in World War I and was now a prominent attorney and politician in Chicago.

25 **"feast . . . educators":** Roundtree and McCabe, *Mighty Justice*, p. 23.

26 **Nabrit and Norris recommendations:** "Confidential Estimate of Applicant for Admission," DJR Alumna File, Spelman, Folder 1934a, pdf pp. 18–21. Nabrit's is undated. Norris's is dated May 25, 1934.

26 **"as much a warrior . . . her time":** Roundtree and McCabe, *Mighty Justice*, p. 24.

27 **"She taught . . . light for me":** Judith Weinraub, "A Long Life of Sweet Justice," *Washington Post*, February 4, 1995, https://www.washingtonpost.com/archive/lifestyle/1995/02/04/a-long-life-of-sweet-justice/eb378931-d7ec-417f-9282-5401262f87b7/?utm_term=.3680dc779a65. Last accessed February 24, 2020.

27 **Harvard anniversary:** Dovey Johnson, "The Harvard Tercentenary," *Campus Mirror*, November 15, 1936, p. 4, https://gahistoric newspapers.galileo.usg.edu/lccn/sn38019897/1936-11-15/ed-1/seq -4.pdf. Last accessed February 24, 2020.

27 **Rockefeller's death:** Dovey Johnson, "Spelman Loses a Friend," *Campus Mirror*, May–June 1937, p. 13, https://gahistoricnews papers.galileo.usg.edu/lccn/sn38019897/1937-05-01/ed-1/seq-15/. Last accessed February 24, 2020.

27 **Japanese woodcuts:** Dovey Johnson, "Exhibits of Japanese Wood-Cuts Open at Atlanta University Library," *Campus Mirror*, October 15, 1937, p. 1, https://gahistoricnewspapers.galileo.usg.edu/lccn/sn 38019897/1937-10-15/ed-1/seq-1/. Last accessed February 24, 2020.

27 **Rufus Jones:** Dovie [sic] Mae Johnson, "The Challenge of the Closed Door," *Campus Mirror*, October 15, 1936, p. 2, https:// gahistoricnewspapers.galileo.usg.edu/lccn/sn38019897/1936-10 -15/ed-1/seq-2/. Last accessed February 24, 2020.

29 **Howard Thurman:** Dovey Johnson, "Mr. Howard Thurman Addresses Spelman Students," *Campus Mirror*, November 15, 1936, p. 5, https:// gahistoricnewspapers.galileo.usg.edu/lccn/sn38019897/1936-11-15/ ed-1/seq-5/. Last accessed February 24, 2020.

29 **Etta Moten:** Dovey Johnson, "Etta Mot[e]n Speaks to Spelman Students," *Campus Mirror*, December 15, 1936, p. 7, https:// gahistoricnewspapers.galileo.usg.edu/lccn/sn38019897/1936-12 -15/ed-1/seq-7/. Last accessed February 24, 2020.

4: Miracle-Maker

30 **"Thief! You're a thief!":** Roundtree and McCabe, *Mighty Justice*, p. 33.

31 **"nearly numb with terror":** Roundtree and McCabe, *Mighty Justice*, p. 33.

31 **"I knew only one white person . . .":** Roundtree and McCabe, *Mighty Justice*, p. 33.

31 **"Throughout my life . . . if you but believe":** Weinraub, "A Long Life of Sweet Justice."

32 **"dedicated work . . .":** "John W. Stanley Funeralized," *Atlanta Voice*, September 18, 1971, p. 3.

32 **"I climbed the steps . . . doing here?":** Roundtree and McCabe, *Mighty Justice*, p. 36.

33 **"If young men and women . . . steadily":** "Graduates Urged to Bar All Fear," *Atlanta Constitution*, June 9, 1938, p. 2.

33 **loan from Neptune:** "Spelman College, Atlanta, Georgia, June 8, 1938," and "Statement of Debts and Payments of Dovey Mae Johnson of 921 East Hill St. Charlotte, N. Carolina to M. Mae Neptune, Spelman College, Atlanta, Georgia," DJR Papers, NABWH, Folder 9, pdf pp. 7–10. Mary Mae Neptune also made small loans to Dovey. For example, in PDF p. 11 we learn that Neptune lent Dovey $10.25 to get home the summer after she graduated from Spelman.

5: No

36 **No. "There are things . . . right here":** Roundtree and McCabe, *Mighty Justice*, p. 45.

37 **Dovey's work and salary at Finley High and Piedmont Junior College:** "Application for Federal Employment," stamped September 12 and 13, 1946, DJR Papers, NABWH, Folder 1, PDF pp. 3–6.

37 **Grandpa Clyde as helper:** "City Directories, 1822–1995," digital image s.v. "Clyde L. Graham," *Ancestry.com.*

37 **Dovey's family in the 1940 Census:** 1940 United States Federal Census, Charlotte, Mecklenburg, North Carolina, digital image s.v. "Clyde Graham," *Ancestry.com.*

38 **Grandpa Clyde's death:** "North Carolina, Death Certificates, 1909–1976," digital image s.v. "Rev. Clyde Graham," *Ancestry.com.*

38 **"Ill as he had been . . . quiet":** Roundtree and McCabe, *Mighty Justice*, p. 42.

38 **Defense industry earnings:** Doris Weatherford, *American Women During World War II: An Encyclopedia* (New York: Routledge, 2010), p. 342.

39 **Hiring discrimination in defense industry:** "Becoming the Arsenal of Democracy," National WWII Museum, https://www.nationalww2museum.org/war/articles/becoming-arsenal-democracy. Last accessed March 12, 2020.

39 **"We burned logs . . .":** Audrey Thomas McCluskey, *A Forgotten*

Sisterhood: Pioneering Black Women Educators and Activists in the Jim Crow South (Lanham, MD: Rowman & Littlefield, 2014), p. 60.

40 "often worked 12-hour days . . .": Abigail Thernstrom and Stephan Thernstrom, "Black Progress: How Far We've Come, and How Far We Have to Go," Brookings Institute, https://www.brookings.edu/articles/black-progress-how-far-weve-come-and-how-far-we-have-to-go/. Last accessed February 24, 2020.

41 "something powerful . . .": Roundtree and McCabe, *Mighty Justice*, p. 13.

41 "something else in mind": Roundtree and McCabe, *Mighty Justice*, p. 45.

41 "Every clip was logged . . . advice": Roundtree and McCabe, *Mighty Justice*, p. 46.

42 "speechless . . . retreated . . . awe": Roundtree and McCabe, *Mighty Justice*, p. 48.

42 "No person . . . getting down to business": Roundtree and McCabe, *Mighty Justice*, p. 48.

6: No Glamour Girls Need Apply

44 "behind-the-lines assignments": "Women Army Bill Passed By House," *Dayton Journal*, March 18, 1942, p. 1.

44 "Who will do the cooking . . .": Kara Dixon Vuic, "American Women in World War II," *The Routledge Handbook of American Military and Diplomatic History, 1865 to the Present*, ed. Antonio S. Thompson and Christos G. Frentzos (New York: Routledge, 2013), p. 152.

44 "Heavy Guard . . .": headline, *Washington Post*, December 8, 1941, p. 3.

45 "silliest piece of legislation . . . duty of men": Yashila Permeswaran, "The Women's Army Auxiliary Corps: A Compromise to Overcome the Conflict of Women Serving in the Army," *History Teacher* 42, no. 1 (November 2008): 97.

45 "to pass a physical examination . . .": Jennifer Nichol Stewart, "Wacky Times: An Analysis of the WAC in World War II and Its Effects on Women," *International Social Science Review* 75, no. 1/2 (2000): p. 29.

46 "No glamour girls need apply": Lee Carson, "WAAC Volunteers Face Hard Tasks," newspaper clipping in DJR Papers, NABWH, Folder 14, pdf p. 14.

46 "grand lobbyists": Kellie Patrick, "WAC Veteran Recalls Pain of Discrimination," *The Sentinel*, August 25, 1992, p. A4.

46 "consumed...terrifying months": Roundtree and McCabe, *Mighty Justice*, p. 48.

46 "Bethune saw in the WAAC...": Putney, *When the Nation Was in Need*, p. 3.

46 "handpicked and approved": Putney, *When the Nation Was in Need*, p. 2.

47 "more open": Roundtree and McCabe, *Mighty Justice*, p. 56.

47 Ally Laury and family: 1940 United States Federal Census, Richmond, Richmond City, Virginia, digital image s.v. "Allie C. Laury," *Ancestry.com*.

47 "interrogated...educational background": Roundtree and McCabe, *Mighty Justice*, p. 56.

47 "Miss Dovey Johnson Passes WAAC Exams": *Baltimore Afro-American*, July 4, 1942, p. 16.

47 "uniforms...military discipline: "Five Virginians Sworn In for WAAC Training," *Staunton News-Leader*, July 14, 1942, p. 3.

47 Dovey's height and weight: "US, World War II Army Enlistment Records, 1938–1946," digital image s.v. "Dovey M. Johnson," *Ancestry.com*.

7: All-In

49 "I was dumped out...White women on the other": Roundtree and McCabe, *Mighty Justice*, pp. 56–57.

49 Racial classifications: Dovey Johnson Roundtree, "Out of the Service Into New Careers," *Opportunity*, January–March 1947, p. 83.

50 "I know that you understand...do that": Roundtree and McCabe, *Mighty Justice*, p. 57.

50 Occupations of some Black WAACs: Charity Adams Earley, *One Woman's Army*, p. 24.

50 "Though a high school...their children's children": "40 Negro

Women Report to Training Center at Fort Des Moines, Iowa, for the WAACs," *New York Age*, August 1, 1942, p. 3.

51 **"so tight on . . .":** Earley, *One Woman's Army*, p. 26.

51 **"You are a member . . . every day of the month":** War Department, FM 35–20, *WAC Field Manual, Physical Training* (Washington, DC: US Government Printing Office, 1943), p. iv.

51 **Recreational outlets:** Putney, *When the Nation Was in Need*, p. 18.

52 **"Swinging along . . . infantry drill":** https://digitalcollections.nypl.org/items/510d47df-fa11-a3d9-e040-e00a18064a99.

54 **thirty-six Black officer candidates:** Dovey M. Johnson, "The Negro and the Women's Army Auxiliary Corps," speech to be given on the "Wings of Jordan" radio program, January 10, 1943, DJR Alumna File, Spelman, Folder 1940sb, pdf p. 6.

54 **"serious, challenging . . . their sex":** Roundtree, "Out of the Service Into New Careers," p. 83.

54 **"You darkies move . . .":** Roundtree and McCabe, *Mighty Justice*, p. 60.

55 **"agitators":** Roundtree and McCabe, *Mighty Justice*, p. 61.

55 **"Colonel Morgan's scare . . . was not it:** Putney, *When the Nation Was in Need*, p. 55.

55 **"We might be agitators . . .":** Roundtree and McCabe, *Mighty Justice*, p. 61.

55 **"I believed in the war effort . . .":** Roundtree and McCabe, *Mighty Justice*, p. 63.

55 **Black lack of interest in the WAAC:** Roundtree and McCabe, *Mighty Justice*, p. 62.

56 **rumor about the WAAC and prostitution:** Putney, *When the Nation Was in Need*, p. 38.

56 **recruiting in Orangeburg, South Carolina:** "WAAC Officers on Recruiting Duty in S.C.," *Pittsburgh Courier*, December 26, 1942, p. 11.

56 **recruiting in Macon, Georgia:** "WAACS to Appear Here Sunday at Steward Chapel Church," *Macon Telegraph*, January 15, 1943, p. 12; "WAAC Offers Many Jobs for Women," *Macon Telegraph*, January 19, 1943, p. 5.

57 **"Lt. Dovey M. Johnson . . . WAACs":** *Orlando Morning Sentinel*, February 9, 1943, p. 10.

57 "NEGRO OFFICERS . . .": *Tampa Sunday Tribune*, February 21, 1943, Part 2, p. 3.

57 "sense of oneness": Roundtree and McCabe, *Mighty Justice*, p. 65.

57 "I am traveling . . . by this bus": Roundtree and McCabe, *Mighty Justice*, p. 66.

8: Of Courage and Conviction

59 "My job . . . any other citizen": "First Negro WAAC Arrives in Texas," *Pampa News*, March 23, 1943, p. 1.

59 Dovey's March letter to Read: March 29, 1943, DJR Alumna File, Spelman, Folder 1940sa, pdf p. 8.

59 Dovey's April letter to Read: undated, DJR Alumna File, Spelman, Folder 1940sb, pdf p. 8.

61 "Sir, you are setting . . .": Roundtree and McCabe, *Mighty Justice*, p. 70.

61 "stated that if . . . ": Putney, *When the Nation Was in Need*, pp. 15–16.

61 "I am interested only . . .": "Wac Capt. Johnson Opens Ohio Drive for Recruits," unidentified newspaper, DJR Papers, NABWH, Folder 14, pdf p. 32.

61 "Brown America . . .": "Capt. Dovey Johnson Lauds Fellow Members of Corps," unidentified newspaper, DJR Papers, NABWH, Folder 14, pdf p. 33.

62 "without doubt . . .": "Toki Types," *Pittsburgh Courier*, May 13, 1944, p. 9.

62 "PEACE! It's Over": *Charlotte Observer*, August 15, 1945, p. 1.

63 "All around me . . . peace": Roundtree and McCabe, *Mighty Justice*, p. 74.

63 Black men in the army: National WWII Museum, "Fighting for the Right to Fight: African American Experiences in WWII," http://righttofightexhibit.org/during-war/army.php. Last accessed March 15, 2020.

63 Tuskegee Airmen: "Tuskegee Airmen," Oxford African American Studies Center, https://oxfordaasc.com/page/guest-editorial-tuskegee-airmen/tuskegee-airmen. Last accessed March 16, 2020.

64 **Black men in the Navy:** Rich Koone, "African Americans in World War II, the Asiatic-Pacific Theater," Texas Historical Commission, https://www.thc.texas.gov/blog/african-americans-world-war-ii-asiatic-pacific-theater. Last accessed March 15, 2020.

64 **Black Marines:** Anna Hiatt, "Who Were the Montford Point Marines," *JSTOR Daily*, June 26, 2019, https://daily.jstor.org/who-were-the-montford-point-marines/. Last accessed March 16, 2020.

64 **Black men in the Coast Guard:** William H. Thiesen, "The Long Blue Line: A History of African-Americans in Coast Guard Combat," https://coastguard.dodlive.mil/2018/02/tlbl-african-americans-in-uscg-combat/. Last accessed March 15, 2020.

64 **Army Nurse Corps:** Gordon R. Sullivan, *The Army Nurse Corps*, https://history.army.mil/books/wwii/72-14/72-14.HTM. Last accessed March 16, 2020.

64 **Navy Nurse Corps:** United States Navy Nurse Corps, https://en.wikipedia.org/wiki/United_States_Navy_Nurse_Corps. Last accessed March 16, 2020.

64 **WACs:** "'Efficiency, Skill, Spirit, and Determination': American Women in World War II," Friends of the National WWII Memorial, https://www.wwiimemorialfriends.org/blog/american-women-wwii/. Last accessed March 16, 2020.

64 **WAVES:** Christine Heidenrich, "Women Accepted for Volunteer Emergency Service: The WAVES Program in World War II," Smithsonian National Air and Space Museum, September 14, 2020, https://airandspace.si.edu/stories/editorial/waves-program-color-world-war-2ri. Last accessed October 15, 2020.

64 **SPARS:** "'Efficiency, Skill, Spirit, and Determination': American Women in World War II," Friends of the National WWII Memorial, https://www.wwiimemorialfriends.org/blog/american-women-wwii/. Last accessed March 16, 2020.

65 **WASPS:** National WWII Museum, "The Legacy of WASP Dorothy Britt," March 11, 2020, https://www.nationalww2museum.org/war/articles/legacy-wasp-dorothy-britt. Last accessed March 16, 2020.

9: Her Legacy to Me

67 **Statistics of FEPC and Black employment:** Waleed Shahid, "This New Deal Agency Promoted Civil Rights. Trump Wants to Kill It," *The Nation*, June 28, 2017, https://www.thenation.com/article/archive/this-new-deal-agency-promoted-civil-rights-trump-wants-to-kill-it/?print=1. Last accessed March 16, 2020.

67 **Randolph's letter to Du Bois:** "Letter from National Council for a Permanent F.E.P.C. to W. E. B. Du Bois, January 3, 1944," W. E. B. Du Bois Papers (MS 312). Special Collections and University Archives, University of Massachusetts Amherst Libraries, https://credo.library.umass.edu/view/full/mums312-b103-i450. Last accessed March 11, 2020.

68 **Randolph's Senate speech:** "Randolph Lays R.R. Manpower Shortage to Race Bias," *Plaindealer* (Kansas City, Kansas), March 23, 1945, pp. 1, 2.

69 **"been fired from a cannon":** Roundtree and McCabe, *Mighty Justice*, p. 77.

70 **"Mama's face fell . . .":** Roundtree and McCabe, *Mighty Justice*, p. 78.

70 **"Always, she'd lived modestly . . . and worn rugs":** Roundtree and McCabe, *Mighty Justice*, p. 79.

70 **Dovey's army pay:** "WAC ranks (September, 1943–1945)," https://en.wikipedia.org/wiki/Women%27s_Army_Corps. Last accessed March 15, 2020.

70 **"What on earth is this . . .":** Roundtree and McCabe, *Mighty Justice*, p. 80.

71 **"groping for some way. . .":** Roundtree and McCabe, *Mighty Justice*, p. 80.

71 **"stimulating . . . to be busy":** March 22, 1946, DJR Alumna File, Spelman, Folder 1940sa, pdf p. 5.

71 **"California has a peculiar . . . marked 'for white only'":** *Vallejo Observer*, December 24, 1945, p. 2, DJR Papers, NABWH, Folder 14, pdf p. 12–13.

72 **"soul on fire":** Roundtree and McCabe, *Mighty Justice*, p. 84.

10: Shatter the Monster

73 "The answer for black people . . .": Roundtree and McCabe, *Mighty Justice*, p. 84.

75 "As I studied her . . . swallowed me up": Roundtree and McCabe, *Mighty Justice*, p. 84.

75 "The more I processed . . . ": Roundtree and McCabe, *Mighty Justice*, p. 86.

75 Statistics on lawyers: J. Clay Smith Jr., *Emancipation: The Making of the Black Lawyer, 1844–1944*, Appendix 2, "1940 Table 13" (Philadelphia: University of Pennsylvania Press, 1993), pp. 634–637.

76 "so tall and so handsome": Roundtree and McCabe, *Mighty Justice*, p. 27.

76 Bill Roundtree's color and work history: "US WWII Draft Cards Young Men, 1940–1947," 1930 United States Federal Census, Atlanta, Fulton, Georgia; "US, World War II Army Enlistment Records, 1938–1946," Atlanta, Fulton, Georgia, digital images s.v. "William Andre Roundtree," "William Roundtree," and "William A. Roundtree," *Ancestry.com*.

76 Dovey's wedding: "Xmas Eve Newlyweds," *Portland Inquirer*, January 18, 1946, newspaper clipping without page number, DJR Papers, NABWH, Folder 1, pdf p. 1.

77 "the madness . . .": Roundtree and McCabe, *Mighty Justice*, p. 88.

77 "The more I talked . . . overseas again": Roundtree and McCabe, *Mighty Justice*, pp. 89–90.

77 Dovey at Wake Hall: "Application for Federal Employment," stamped September 12 and 13, 1946, DJR Papers, NABWH, Folder 1, pdf p. 3.

11: Of Sacredness

79 "Are you registering . . . the male veterans": Roundtree and McCabe, *Mighty Justice*, p. 92.

80 "either a social engineer . . . parasite on society": Quoted in "Separate Is Not Equal: Brown v. Board of Education," Smithsonian

National Museum of American History, Behring Center. http://americanhistory.si.edu/brown/history/3-organized /charles-houston.html. Last accessed March 10, 2020.

81 **"and his band . . . of the cases":** Roundtree and McCabe, *Mighty Justice*, p. 96.

81 **"No one forgets the . . . Texas drawl":** "Class of '50 in Retrospect,"
· *The Bison: 1950*, Howard University Yearbook, p. 134.

82 **"the venerable master . . . made me a lawyer":** Roundtree and McCabe, *Mighty Justice*, p. 98.

82 **"earliest understanding . . . thing of sacredness":** Roundtree and McCabe, *Mighty Justice*, pp. 97, 96.

82 **"drowning":** Roundtree and McCabe, *Mighty Justice*, p. 97.

82 **"mother hen. . . . You can do it":** Roundtree and McCabe, *Mighty Justice*, pp. 94, 95.

82 **Women at Howard Law:** "Law School," *The Bison: 1950*, Howard University Yearbook, pp. 128–130. The other two women (also Black) in Dovey's class were Ida I. Stephens, who later joined the WAVES, and Romae L. Turner, who later practiced law in Atlanta.

82 **Dovey's activities at Howard:** "Law School," p. 129. Her involvement in the Portia Club is found in the 1949 *Bison*, p. 123.

84 **"Grandma was limping . . .":** Roundtree and McCabe, *Mighty Justice*, p. 112.

84 **Train's route from Charlotte to DC:** Streamliner Schedules, http:// www.streamlinerschedules.com/concourse/track1/crescent195008 .html. Last accessed March 12, 2020.

85 **"collapsed on the closed . . .":** Roundtree and McCabe, *Mighty Justice*, p. 113.

85 **"They were bruised and bleeding":** Roundtree and McCabe, *Mighty Justice*, p. 113.

86 **"All through the whirlwind . . .":** Roundtree and McCabe, *Mighty Justice*, p. 114.

86 **Spelman-Morehouse concert:** Telegram, December 17, 1950, DJR Alumna File, Spelman, Folder 1950s, pdf p. 8.

86 **"14 Women . . .":** *Evening Star*, February 24, 1951, p. A2.

86 "busy at it . . . eight months": Letter, May 15, 1951, DJR Alumna File, Spelman, Folder 1950s, pdf p. 7.

12: A Calling

87 "It was, in my mind . . .": Roundtree and McCabe, *Mighty Justice*, p. 123.

88 "We took every case . . . operation": Roundtree and McCabe, *Mighty Justice*, p. 121.

88 "a calling": Roundtree and McCabe, *Mighty Justice*, p. 120.

91 "The US Supreme Court opinion . . .": "Beginning of the End," *Crisis*, July 1946, p. 201.

92 "That September afternoon . . . to map out the basis of": Roundtree and McCabe, *Mighty Justice*, p. 127.

93 "undue and unreasonable prejudice . . . District of Columbia": Roundtree and McCabe, *Mighty Justice*, p. 131.

94 "Today, education is . . . inherently unequal": Chief Justice Earl Warren, Opinion, May 17, 1954, Digital History, http://www .digitalhistory.uh.edu/disp_textbook.cfm?smtID=3&psid=1120. Last accessed March 12, 2020.

95 "If segregation is unconstitutional . . .": Angie Maxwell, *The Indicted South: Public Criticism, Southern Inferiority, and the Politics of Whiteness* (Chapel Hill: University of North Carolina Press, 2014), p. 194.

95 "The disadvantages . . . unreasonable": "ICC Bans Segregation on Interstate Carriers," *Dallas Morning News*, November 26, 1955, Part 1, p. 1.

95 "This is just the greatest . . . American people as well": "ICC Ruling 'Frees' Brooklyn Girl," *New York Age*, December 3, 1955, p. 1.

95 "spent a great deal of their time . . .": "Winner Acclaims Decision by I.C.C.," *New York Times*, November 27, 1955, p. 84.

96 "nobody will shout . . . human power": Martin Luther King Jr., "Where Do We Go From Here?" August 16, 1967(?), King Papers, https://kinginstitute.stanford.edu/king-papers/documents/ where-do-we-go-here-address-delivered-eleventh-annual-sclc -convention. Last accessed March 12, 2020.

98 "a different person . . .": Roundtree and McCabe, *Mighty Justice*, p. 156.

13: Hurting in Every Way

99 **"To our doorstep came . . ."**: Roundtree and McCabe, *Mighty Justice*, p. 157.

99 **Vanison case**: "Woman Awarded $25,000 Damages," *News-Press* (Fort Myers, FL), January 24, 1957, p. 3.

100 **"as hopeless"**: "Julius W. Robertson, Washington Attorney," *Evening Star*, November 4, 1961, p. A14.

100 **"on a motion . . ."**: "Girl Committed in Death of Baby," *Evening Star*, September 21, 1957, p. A26.

101 **"Attorney Dovey Roundtree . . . by police"**: "Arson Trial Set for 3 Boys," *Evening Star*, April 9, 1958, p. B14.

101 **break-ins**: Andrew W. Bingham, "Court Cautions Police on Juvenile Rights," *Evening Star*, July 30, 1958, p. B13.

101 **"ninety-one children jammed . . . "**: Frank Sartwell Jr., "Deplorable Conditions Found on Visit to Receiving Home," *Evening Star*, March 16, 1955, p. A3.

102 **"the order of the day . . ."**: Martin Luther King Jr., "A Look to 1964," *Amsterdam News*, January 4, 1964, p. 6.

102 **"an end to poverty and racial injustice"**: Lyndon B. Johnson, "Commencement Speech at the University of Michigan," May 22, 1964, https://teachingamericanhistory.org/library/document/great-society-speech/. Last accessed March 12, 2020.

14: Incapable

105 **"If anyone bothers you . . ."**: Roundtree and McCabe, *Mighty Justice*, p. 193.

105 **"disgust the white prison guards . . ."**: Roundtree and McCabe, *Mighty Justice*, p. 193.

105 **"I don't know nothin' . . . nobody"**: Roundtree and McCabe, *Mighty Justice*, p. 193.

106 **"Incapable . . . his predicament"**: Roundtree and McCabe, *Mighty Justice*, p. 191.

106 **"The crime just . . ."**: Janney, *Mary's Mosaic*, p. 95.

106 **"purposely and with deliberate . . ."**: *Crump*, Folder 1, pdf p. 76.

106 "found coatless...": "Crump Indicted in Canal Death of Mrs. Meyer," *Washington Post*, October 20, 1964, A3.

108 "is not bound ... 44th birthday": George Eagle, "Grand Jury to Hear Evidence Today in Mary P. Meyer Death," *Washington Post*, October 15, 1964, C18.

108 Plea: "Plea of Defendant," *Crump*, Folder 1, pdf p. 41.

108 "an old stone building...": Burleigh, *A Very Private Woman*, pp. 255–256.

109 "Judge Matthews ... danger to the community": Janney, *Mary's Mosaic*, p. 100.

109 "In June 1963 ... of the capital city": Burleigh, *A Very Private Woman*, p. 240.

109 "explosion": Dorothy Gilliam, "Mrs. Meyer Urges United Attack to Avert Race Disaster in Capital," *Washington Post*, April 16, 1963, p. A17.

110 "I held that without...": Roundtree and McCabe, *Mighty Justice*, p. 194.

110 "Release Bid Is Refused in Slaying": *Washington Post*, November 10, 1964, p. A47.

110 "shrewd move ... intervening months": Janney, *Mary's Mosaic*, pp. 101.

111 Psychiatric evaluation: "Motion for Mental Examination," November 12, 1964, and "Order" by Judge Matthew McGuire, November 13, 1964, *Crump*, Folder 1, pdf pp. 10–11 and pdf pp. 35–36.

111 Ray's transfer to St. Elizabeths: "US Marshall's Return of Service," *Crump*, Folder 2, pdf p. 76.

15: Minister in the Family

112 "I was the minister...": Roundtree and McCabe, *Mighty Justice*, p. 185.

112 "not enough...something else": Roundtree and McCabe, *Mighty Justice*, p. 163.

113 "live out his legacy...": Roundtree and McCabe, *Mighty Justice*, p. 17.

114 "The whole neighborhood...": Roundtree and McCabe, *Mighty Justice*, p. 185.

114 "a long illness": "Miss Mary Neptune," *Times Recorder* (Zanesville, Ohio), January 14, 1964, p. A2.

114 "a million eyes": Janney, *Mary's Mosaic*, p. 106.

16: No Words. Only Breathing.

115 "suffering from a mental...": Dale C. Cameron, January 13, 1965, *Crump*, Folder 1, pdf p. 8.

115 "deteriorated daily...": Roundtree and McCabe, *Mighty Justice*, p. 198.

115 "guards' hatred...": Roundtree and McCabe, Mighty Justice, p. 199.

115 "Four months after... other people": Janney, *Mary's Mosaic*, p. 106.

116 Dovey's request for information and prosecution's response: "Motion for Bill of Particulars," February 18, 1965, "Bill of Particulars," March 5, 1965, and "Supplemental Bill of Particulars," March 12, 1965, *Crump*, Folder 2, pdf pp. 52–53, pdf pp. 41–44, and pdf p. 34.

117 "Oh, brother!...": Janney, *Mary's Mosaic*, p. 107.

117 "Tall, prepossessing... bully": Janney, *Mary's Mosaic*, p. 108.

118 "most Saturday afternoons...": Janney, *Mary's Mosaic*, p. 102.

118 "My very presence, I knew...": Roundtree and McCabe, *Mighty Justice*, p. 202.

119 US Court of Appeals ruling: *Raymond Crump, Jr., Appellant, v. Sam Anderson, Superintendent, District of Columbia Jail, Appellee*, 352 F.2d 649 (D.C. Cir. 1965).

17: Voir Dire

120 "foolishness in his courtroom...": Roundtree and McCabe, *Mighty Justice*, pp. 203–204.

121 Jurors eliminated and scribbles: "July 1965 Jurors," "Jurors," and Judge Corcoran's certification of the 12 main jurors and 4 alternates, July 19, 1965, *Crump*, Folder 1, pdf pp. 12–20, 65–68, and 84.

121 Composition of the jury: Janney, *Mary's Mosaic*, p. 110.

123 **"influenced their judgment":** "Jury Ready for Trial of Crump," *Washington Post*, July 20, 1965, p. A3.

18: Scared to Death

124 **Hantman's opening statement:** "Opening Statement on Behalf of the Government," *Crump*, Folder 3, trial transcript pp. 2–17.

126 **Hantman's exhibits:** *Crump*, Folder 1, pdf pp. 21–23.

126 **Hantman's witnesses:** *Crump*, Folder 1, pdf pp. 49–53.

126 **"I was scared . . . going to present":** Janney, *Mary's Mosaic*, p. 113.

127 **Dovey and Hantman before the bench:** *Crump*, Folder 6, trial transcript pp. 20–30.

127 **Corcoran's talk to jurors:** *Crump*, Folder 6, trial transcript pp. 30–33.

128 **"inflammatory . . . your record:** *Crump*, Folder 6, trial transcript p. 36.

128 **"The courtroom was quiet . . .":** Roundtree and McCabe, *Mighty Justice*, p. 205.

128 **"If it please the Court . . .":** *Crump*, Folder 6, trial transcript p. 37.

128 **"There are times . . . opening":** Roundtree and McCabe, *Mighty Justice*, p. 205.

129 **"No, I don't think . . .":** *Crump*, Folder 6, trial transcript p. 38.

19: Thank You, Sir

130 **Bradlee's upcoming move to the *Washington Post*:** "Top of the Week," *Newsweek*, July 19, 1965, p. 7.

130 **"scheduled Bradlee . . .":** Zalin Grant, "Mary Meyer: A Highly Suspicious Death," http://pythiapress.com/wartales/Meyer.html. Last accessed March 12, 2020.

131 **Bradlee on the stand:** *Crump*, Folder 6, trial transcript pp. 41–47.

132 **"the world's greatest cross-examiner":** Janney, *Mary's Mosaic*, p. 106.

132 **Brown Construction Company:** *Crump*, Folder 1, "Affidavit in Support of Application to Proceed Without Prepayment of Costs," October 20, 1964, pdf p. 44.

132 Ray's work as a paving contractor: "Nab Laborer in Killing of Prominent Artist," *Chicago Defender*, October 14, 1964, p. 3.

132 "fooled around a little": Roundtree and McCabe, *Mighty Justice*, p. 195.

133 "city of Washington inside out": Roundtree and McCabe, *Mighty Justice*, p. 195.

133 "hard, and tough, and angry": Roundtree and McCabe, *Mighty Justice*, p. 195.

133 "barrage . . . collapse, probably into tears": Roundtree and McCabe, *Mighty Justice*, p. 201.

133 "shaking and reaching out . . . behind us": Roundtree and McCabe, *Mighty Justice*, p. 202.

133 "like a veritable sea . . . white women": Roundtree and McCabe, *Mighty Justice*, p. 202.

134 "unnerved by the racial tension . . .": Burleigh, *A Very Private Woman*, p. 260.

134 "I sat next to the jury box . . . the jury noticed": Robert S. Bennett, *In the Ring: The Trials of a Washington Lawyer* (New York: Crown, 2008), pp. 36, 35, 38.

134 Dalinsky on the stand: *Crump*, Folder 6, trial transcript pp. 48–52.

135 Worrell on the stand: *Crump*, Folder 6, trial transcript pp. 52–64.

139 Rayford on the stand: *Crump*, Folder 6, trial transcript pp. 64–97.

140 "With military precision . . .": Bennett, *In the Ring*, p. 37.

140 "I'd walked each...": Roundtree and McCabe, *Mighty Justice*, p. 207.

140 Ronsisvalle on the stand: *Crump*, Folder 6, trial transcript pp. 100–127.

140 "Wiggins—a black man . . .": Janney, *Mary's Mosaic*, p. 51.

20: To Simplicity

142 Wiggins on the stand: *Crump*, Folder 6, trial transcript pp. 127–145.

143 "Enshrouded in trees . . . to simplicity": Roundtree and McCabe, *Mighty Justice*, p. 211.

143 Wiggins back on the stand: *Crump*, Folder 8a, trial transcript pp. 204–281.

146 "Witness Identifies Crump...": William Chapman, *Washington Post*, July 22, 1965, p. A3.

146 "Witness Says Defendant...weighing 185 pounds": William Basham, *Evening Star*, July 21, 1965, p. A15.

147 Ray's height and weight on driver's license and in DC Jail: Janney, *Mary's Mosaic*, p. 115.

21: Hair Is Not Like Fingerprints

148 Branch on the stand: *Crump*, Folder 8a, trial transcript pp. 291–318.

148 Cops on the stand: They were Robert E. Decker and Harry L. Beagle, both with the Metropolitan Police. *Crump*, Folder 8a, trial transcript pp. 282–290b and pp. 318–329.

148 Sylvis on the stand: *Crump*, Folder 8b, trial transcript pp. 340–355.

149 Warner on the stand: *Crump*, Folder 8b, pp. 355–388.

149 Weber on the stand: *Crump*, Folder 3, trial transcript pp. 422–458.

150 Perkins on the stand: *Crump*, Folder 3, trial transcript pp. 467–477 and 484–507.

151 "I am a one-woman office": *Crump*, Folder 3, trial transcript p. 392.

151 "There will be all...weekend": *Crump*, Folder 3, trial transcript pp. 542–543.

151 "some 40 policemen...shorter and slender": William Basham, "Meyer Witness Links Cap to Crump," *Evening Star*, July 23, 1965, p. A14.

152 Mitchell on the stand: *Crump*, Folder 4, trial transcript pp. 653–667.

153 Semmes on the stand: *Crump*, Folder 5, trial transcript pp. 781–792.

153 Stombaugh on the stand: *Crump*, Folder 5, trial transcript, pp. 798–809, and pp. 831–865.

154 "Your Honor please...": *Crump*, Folder 5 trial transcript, p. 866.

22: Exhibit A

155 Dovey's opening statement: "Opening Statement on Behalf of the Defendant," *Crump*, Folder 7, trial transcript pp. 881–883.

156 Dovey's witnesses on the stand: *Crump*, Folder 7, trial transcript pp. 883–892.

156 "At this time, if it please the Court...": *Crump*, Folder 7, trial transcript p. 892.

156 "There wasn't a sound...": Roundtree and McCabe, *Mighty Justice*, p. 214.

156 Sidebar: *Crump*, Folder 7, trial transcript pp. 893–899a.

157 "I hate to keep this jury...": *Crump*, Folder 7, trial transcript p. 896.

157 Corcoran to the jury: *Crump*, Folder 7, trial transcript p. 899a.

23: Adler Heels

158 Hantman's closing: "Argument to the Jury on Behalf of the Government," *Crump*, Folder 7, trial transcript pp. 903–926.

159 Dovey's closing: "Argument on Behalf of the Defendant," *Crump*, Folder 7, trial transcript pp. 927–944.

162 Hantman's rebuttal: "Rebuttal Argument on Behalf of the Government," *Crump*, Folder 7, trial transcript pp. 944–958.

24: If Justice Is to Be Done

164 Corcoran's thanks and charge to the jury: "Charge to the Jury," *Crump*, Folder 7, trial transcript pp. 963–986.

165 Jury's first note to Corcoran and his response: *Crump*, Folder 7, trial transcript pp. 991–992.

166 Jury's second note to Corcoran and his response: *Crump*, Folder 7, trial transcript p. 993.

166 Martha Crump: William Chapman, "District Court Jury Ponders Meyer Slaying," *Washington Post*, July 30, 1965, p. A3.

25: Wept

168 Verdict and "Raymond Crump...": "Verdict of the Jury," *Crump*, Folder 7, trial transcript p. 995.

168 "cried out...from church": Roundtree and McCabe, *Mighty Justice*, p. 216.

168 "Is there anywhere...home": Roundtree and McCabe, *Mighty Justice*, p. 216.

168 "swayed forward . . .": William Chapman, "Crump Free in Murder on Towpath," *Washington Post*, July 31, 1965, p. A1.

168 "wept": "Laborer Acquitted of Murder," *The (Columbia, South Carolina) State*, July 31, 1965, p. 3A.

Coda

169 "There were so many . . . ": Chapman, "Crump Free in Murder on Towpath," p. A1.

169 Ray's letter to Dovey: DJR Papers, NABWH, Folder 3, pdf pp. 34–36.

170 Ray's post-acquittal crimes: Burleigh, *A Very Private Woman*, pp. 278–280.

170 Ray Crump's death: Crump Raymond, Jr., *Washington Post*, June 13, 2005. https://www.legacy.com/obituaries/washingtonpost/obituary.aspx?n=raymond-crump&pid=14253303.

170 "heartsick . . . afterward": Roundtree and McCabe, *Mighty Justice*, p. 218.

170 *National Enquirer* story: Don Oberdorfer, "JFK Had Affair With D.C. Artist, Smoked 'Grass,' Paper Alleges," *Washington Post*, February 23, 1976, pp. A1, A9.

171 "author and lecturer": Roundtree and McCabe, *Mighty Justice*, p. 189.

171 On Cord Meyer: Ben A. Franklin, "Woman Painter Shot and Killed on Canal Towpath in Capital," *New York Times*, October 14, 1964, p. 40.

171 "took a vacuum cleaner . . .": Bennett, *In the Ring*, p. 36.

171 "impossible for the matter . . . gratified": Roundtree and McCabe, *Mighty Justice*, p. 217.

172 "the kind of success . . .": Roundtree and McCabe, *Mighty Justice*, p. 217.

172 "for other men . . .": Roundtree and McCabe, *Mighty Justice*, p. 217.

172 BADC endorsement: Jacob A. Stein to John N. Mitchell, March 12, 1969, DJR Papers, NABWH, Folder 15, pdf pp. 1–2.

172 Letters of recommendation: DJR Papers, NABWH, Folder 15.

173 **"for seminars ... July 1965"**: Roundtree and McCabe, *Mighty Justice*, p. 217.

173 **"More and more ... one from another"**: Roundtree and McCabe, *Mighty Justice*, p. 220.

173 **Address to cosmetologists:** Lillian Wiggins, "Attorney Says Beauty Is Within," *Washington Afro-American*, June 29, 1974, pp. 1, 9, DJR Papers, NABWH, Folder 8, pdf pp. 12–13.

173 **Address to Tots and Teens:** "Attorney Roundtree Speaks at Founders Day Celebration," *Washington Afro-American*, June 21, 1975, p. 8, DJR Papers, NABWH, Folder 8, pdf p. 14.

173 **Address at US Army Military History Institute:** Kellie Patrick, "WAC Veteran Recalls Pain of Discrimination," *The Sentinel*, August 25, 1992, p. A4.

SELECTED SOURCES

Burleigh, Nina. *A Very Private Woman: The Life and Unsolved Murder of Presidential Mistress Mary Meyer*. New York: Bantam, 1999.

Earley, Charity Adams. *One Woman's Army: A Black Officer Remembers the WAC*. College Station: Texas A&M University, 1996.

Flono, Fannie. *Thriving in the Shadows: The Black Experience in Charlotte and Mecklenburg County*. Charlotte, NC: Novello Festival Press, 2006.

Janney, Peter. *Mary's Mosaic: The CIA Conspiracy to Murder John F. Kennedy, Mary Pinchot Meyer, and Their Vision for World Peace*. 3rd edition. New York: Skyhorse Publishing, 2016.

Jones, Dr. Ida E. *Mary McLeod Bethune in Washington, DC: Activism and Education in Logan Circle*. Charleston, SC: The History Press, 2013.

Lunsford, Brandon. *Charlotte Then and Now*. London: Pavilion Books, 2013.

Putney, Martha S. *When the Nation Was in Need: Blacks in the Women's Army Corps During World War II*. Lanham, MD: Scarecrow Press, 2001.

Roundtree, Dovey Johnson. Dovey Johnson Roundtree Papers, NABWH_005. National Archives of Black Women's History, Mary McLeod Bethune Council House, Washington, DC.

———. Dovey J. Roundtree Spelman Alumna File. Spelman College Archives, Atlanta, Georgia.

———, and Katie McCabe. *Mighty Justice: My Life in Civil Rights*. Chapel Hill: Algonquin, 2019.

United States v. Raymond Crump Jr., Criminal No. 930–64, US District Court for the District of Columbia, 1965.

PICTURE CREDITS

INDEX

Note: Page numbers in *italics* refer to illustrations.

Tigers, Not Daughters

ALSO BY SAMANTHA MABRY

A Fierce and Subtle Poison

All the Wind in the World

Tigers, Not Daughters

SAMANTHA MABRY

ALGONQUIN 2020

Published by
Algonquin Young Readers
an imprint of Algonquin Books of Chapel Hill
Post Office Box 2225
Chapel Hill, North Carolina 27515-2225

a division of
Workman Publishing
225 Varick Street
New York, New York 10014

LIBRARY OF CONGRESS CATALOGING-IN-PUBLICATION DATA

Names: Mabry, Samantha, author.
Title: Tigers, not daughters / Samantha Mabry.
Description: Chapel Hill, North Carolina : Algonquin Books of Chapel Hill, 2020. |
    Audience: Ages 14 and up. | Audience: Grades 10–12. | Summary: "Three sisters
    in San Antonio are shadowed by guilt and grief over the loss of their oldest sister,
    who still haunts their house"—Provided by publisher.
Identifiers: LCCN 2019037812 | ISBN 9781616208967 (hardcover) | ISBN
    9781643750545 (ebook)
Subjects: CYAC: Sisters—Fiction. | Family problems—Fiction. | Grief—Fiction. |
    Ghosts—Fiction. | Hispanic Americans—Fiction.
Classification: LCC PZ7.1.M244 Tig 2020 | DDC [Fic]—dc23
LC record available at https://lccn.loc.gov/2019037812

10 9 8 7 6 5 4 3 2 1
First Edition

For my students

Tigers, Not Daughters

The Night the Torres Sisters Tried to Run Away from Southtown

THE WINDOW TO Ana Torres's second-story bedroom faced Hector's house, and every night she'd undress with the curtains wide open, in full view of the street. We'd witnessed this scene dozens—*hundreds*—of times, but still, each night Ana had us perched there, pained and floating on the edge of something tremendous.

With her back to us, Ana would strip off her shirt and her bra—that bra made of white cotton, the fabric so thin we could see the shimmer of her sandstone skin through it—and toss them onto the floor at the foot of her never-made bed. She'd lift up her arms, stretch her spine like a cat, and roll her head side to side to ease out the kinks in her neck. She'd run her fingers through her long, ink-black hair before gracefully winding it up into a knot. Then she'd turn—so slowly it made our eyes gloss with tears. She'd sigh and gaze through her window—never straight at our faces, which were always twisted tightly with hope—but always past us, over the top of the crooked oak tree in her front yard, over the top of Hector's two-story house, over the tops of tilted palms several streets away, to some faraway place. She'd have this wistful expression on her face, like she was waiting for something, or some*one,* to come down from the night sky and take her away.

We were barely fifteen, and Ana was nearly eighteen, but we were convinced that we could be her heroes. We could be the ones to rescue her and take her wherever she wanted to go. Up and over into New Mexico? No problem. Down into Matamoros? Just say when. Peter knew the basics when it came to driving a car, and Luis had close to fifty bucks stashed away in a drawer. We would do whatever it took and would suffer any number of indignities to be with her, this girl of our young, fresh dreams, to save her from our old neighborhood, with its old San Antonio families and its traditions so strong and deep we could practically feel them tugging at our heels when we walked across our yards. We wouldn't have cared if Ana made fun of our gangly bodies, our terrible, squeaky voices, the way no deodorant could come close to covering up our puberty-stink, or the very, very dumb things we inevitably would say.

Just tell us where you want to go, Ana. And we'll take you there.

We never got the chance.

Just over a year ago, on an unusually warm spring night during Fiesta, Ana Torres opened her second-story window and stuck out her head. She was checking to make sure the street was clear before she latched on to the sturdy branches of the old oak tree. She shimmied down the wide trunk, and once the soles of her flip-flops landed on the patchy grass, she dusted off the bits of bark from her palms and turned her gaze up.

There, at Ana's window, was her sixteen-year-old sister, Jessica. Jessica tossed down a pink backpack, then a blue one, then two matching tweed suitcases like the kind traveling salesmen used to carry back when there were such people as traveling salesmen. Ana caught each of them, one after the other, her knees buckling only slightly under the weight. She set them in a row near the base of the tree and looked up again, to watch Jessica hitch her left leg awkwardly through the window and then reach for the nearest branch with unsure hands.

Even from across the street at Hector's house, we could see Jessica's lips pulled back and her teeth clamped together in cold determination. She was gripping too hard—first to the window frame, then to the branches. It was obvious

3

she'd never done anything like this before. Her fingers were popping the leaves loose, and the soles of her high-tops were chipping off bits of bark. Both the leaves and the bark were fluttering to the ground, right to where Ana was bouncing on the balls of her feet. We could tell Ana wanted to call out to her sister. She couldn't say anything, though—couldn't risk it—because the base of the tree, right by the row of luggage, was directly in front of their dad's bedroom window.

By now, fifteen-year-old Iridian—the girls, we realized, were making their escape in birth order—was leaning half-way out the window, scowling at Jessica's slow and clumsy progress. She kept glancing nervously over her shoulder, then down to the top of her sister's head. Her fingers drummed against the window frame. Finally, she couldn't wait anymore. She pulled her hair back into a quick bun and climbed out. Her movements—like Ana's—were solid and sure. She knew exactly where to grip, how to shift her balance, when to inhale, when to exhale. Soon though, Iridian was forced to pause and dangle, waiting for Jessica. She glanced to the window above, where the youngest of the Torres sisters, Rosa, who was twelve, was starting to emerge.

Finally, Jessica hit the ground—hard and flat-footed. Her arms pinwheeled like a cartoon character's until she caught her balance. Seconds later, Iridian swung off a high branch and landed in a crouch in the grass. She pulled her hair out from her bun, and the strands spilled across her shoulders.

Now that the three of them—Ana, Jessica, and Iridian—were all on solid ground, they looked up in unison. Rosa was wearing a calf-length dress because Rosa always wore a calf-length dress. Tonight, though, in honor of Fiesta, the front of that dress was covered in medals—like awards, like pins in the style of a Purple Heart, except most of hers were made of plastic with bright, multicolored ribbons attached to them. As Rosa was suspended with just the tip of one bulky shoe braced against the window frame, the fabric of her dress caught in a breeze, and we wouldn't have been surprised if, instead of climbing down to join her sisters, Rosa climbed *up* into the tallest, most tender branches of the tree to search for birds' nests or pluck off the prettiest leaf or just be closer to the stars in the night sky. We'd always thought that if Rosa were an element, she'd be air, the lazy kind that gets tossed around a room when a ceiling fan is on its lowest setting.

Rosa did decide to climb down instead of up, but just as she was about to take the final, short leap to the ground, her dress got caught on something—maybe the sharp nub of a snapped-off limb—and her skirt was hoisted up to her ribs, exposing not just her pale underwear but the bottom edge of her bra. Our breaths caught—all at the same time. We saw Ana reach over and grip Jessica's wrist. Iridian took a step forward, then stopped, then put her hand over her mouth. Rosa shifted her weight, released one hand from the tree branch and pulled—once, twice—before the fabric gave way. Then, finally, she leapt.

From there, the girls didn't hesitate. They each grabbed a piece of luggage and were gone, down Devine Street and then north and away from Southtown.

For a moment, we just stood there, shoulder to shoulder at Hector's bedroom window, our skin buzzing with the kind of feeling a person gets before jumping off a high cliff into water: bravery mixed with low-level terror. Eventually, we looked at one another. We knew that *this* was our moment. We crept out of Hector's room and tiptoed down the stairs. One by one, we pushed through the Garcias' squeaky storm door and stepped out into the night.

If the Torres sisters were headed north and carrying luggage, we figured their destination was the Greyhound station on St. Mary's and Martin, even though it was over a mile away and on the other side of downtown. Sure enough, when we got to the end of Devine, we saw the sisters hustling in that direction. We didn't know for sure where they'd catch a bus to, but if we had to guess, we would've said the girls were heading south, to the Rio Grande Valley, where their aunt Francine lived in a big house in the middle of the orange groves.

Ana led the way. Behind her was Iridian. Then Rosa. Bringing up the rear was Jessica. Her suitcase was so heavy it banged against the side of her leg with every step, and she had to keep switching it from her right hand to her left and back.

All warm, star-flecked spring nights in downtown San Antonio bring out the tourists, but this night was different from the other warm, star-flecked nights. The girls were making their getaway on one of the busiest nights of the year, during Fiesta, when the streets were packed, even in the middle of the night—and not just packed with tourists, but with locals draped in medal-covered sashes and wearing crowns made from paper flowers. They were out in droves to celebrate the Texians who fought long ago in the battles of the Alamo and San Jacinto. And even when we were still a couple of blocks away from downtown proper, we could hear the music—the blare of horns, the percussive thumps of guitars. Little bits of colored crepe paper floated through air and covered the sidewalks and the streets.

The girls chose to run away during Fiesta probably because they thought they could disappear in the huge, ambling crowd and no one would notice them, and maybe that was a good plan. We, however, could do nothing *but* notice them. None of the Torres sisters was particularly tall—Iridian was the tall*est*, but still not tall. Their heads didn't bob above the crowd, but we could still see it shift and part as the girls pushed through. We followed, shouldering and ducking our way through people who

7

smelled like beer and cinnamon and drugstore cologne. We thought we could stay hidden and that *we* could go unnoticed, but once the sisters had finally plowed through the crowd's northernmost edge and were picking up their pace, Jessica, who was still bringing up the rear, glanced over her shoulder and saw us.

She stopped. Her eyes narrowed. We froze. She advanced.

"Shit," Jimmy squeaked.

Even with a little square of pink crepe paper stuck just above her right eyebrow, Jessica Torres was still scary as hell. It seemed like she was always, *always* angry. In kindergarten, she bit a teacher on the wrist because snack time was over and he tried to take away her peanut butter crackers. In junior high, she keyed Jenny Sanchez's mom's car because she didn't like the color of it, and just this last December, she got detention for three days after she'd jammed the tip of a lead pencil into Muriel Contreras's pinky finger. The lead is still in there. Muriel tries to say it's a freckle, but everyone knows the truth.

For a moment, there on the far edge of the Fiesta celebration, none of us spoke. Jessica stared us down. Her teeth were clamped together, bared slightly, just like they were when she was climbing down that tree. The other Torres sisters—realizing Jessica was no longer with them—halted and spun around.

It was Hector who finally mustered up some courage. He cleared his throat and asked, "Where are you going?"

"We can help," Calvin quickly chimed in.

Ana took a step forward. She shrugged off her heavy backpack and slid herself in front of Jessica. She looked us over, met each of us in the eye for the briefest moment, but said nothing. A breeze caught her hair, lifting the strands, blowing them in our direction.

We'd never been this close to Ana Torres before, and it was disorienting. She was so, so beautiful. We'd imagined before—*many* times—what she might've smelled like. Maybe it was roses, vanilla, lemons, or maybe the first, fresh slice of white bread pulled from the plastic sleeve. But until then, we never truly knew.

It was laundry. She smelled like laundry, like dryer sheets mixed with a little stubborn sweat.

"We can help," Calvin repeated.

"Boys." Ana's tone was full of scorn, and it burned our soft hearts. "Go home. We don't need your help."

Ana was suddenly lit up from the side. All four of the girls turned, and in that moment we knew from the loud rattle of the overstressed engine coming our way that Rafe Torres had discovered his daughters' escape and had tracked them down in his truck.

Hector cried out, "Run!"

But the girls didn't run.

They just waited and watched as their dad honked his horn twice and brought his old green Ford pickup to a stop in the middle of the street. Jessica's heavy suitcase fell to the ground with a thud. Rafe, dressed in a white V-neck undershirt and jeans, jumped from the truck while the engine was still running and went straight for Ana. He gripped her arm, digging his thumb right into her shoulder joint.

"What were you thinking?" he barked. "Huh?"

Ana said nothing. She didn't even wince. She just slowly turned her head to the side, and her gaze slid northward, in the direction of the bus station.

The passenger door of Rafe's truck opened, and out came Hector's mom, wearing fuzzy slippers and a red flannel robe over a long nightgown. She was watching Rafe and Ana with a strange expression on her face. It was a mix of things: like she was relieved, like she was furious, like she was guilty, like she felt sorry for the Torres girls, like she knew, deep down, that it may have been better for them to have caught a bus to the Valley or wherever else they'd hoped to go than to stay with their sad dad in Southtown.

Hector's mom then turned toward us. She ticked up her chin and pointed down the street.

"Walk," she commanded.

We walked. The last thing we saw before we were again swallowed by the noisy, sweaty Fiesta crowd was

Jessica arguing with her father, refusing to get in the truck. If anyone else had noticed what was happening between the Torres girls and Rafe, they didn't let on; everyone knew families were complicated and that dads were always dealing with unruly teenage daughters. Rafe gripped Jessica's arm, then her waist, and then pushed her into the extended cab. She managed to pin us with one more stare, full of hot fury. We deserved it.

We learned on the walk back what had happened. Hector's mom had heard us leave. It took her a minute to figure out what was happening and then to get up and wrestle on her robe. Once she got out into the front yard, she saw Ana's wide-open second-story window. She went across to the Torres house and rang the doorbell until Rafe answered, still half asleep. Together, in Rafe's truck, they drove around the neighborhood, searching for their runaways. At the time, Rafe didn't seem all that mad, Hector's mom told us. Instead, he seemed scared. His fingers were trembling against the steering wheel. He kept repeating, "My girls. My girls." He kept asking Hector's mom, "What will I do if they leave me?"

This is how we learned that we were the ones who had destroyed the Torres girls' chance at escape. If it weren't for us, things would've turned out differently. If it weren't for us, Ana wouldn't have died two months later and her sisters wouldn't have been forced to suffer at the hands of her angry ghost.

Iridian
(Sunday, June 9th)

THE ROUTINE ON Sunday was simple. Rosa got up first. She'd shower, dress for church, and then go out into the backyard for an hour or so and try to talk to the animals. Jessica got up next. The first thing she'd do, even before using the bathroom, was check on Dad. Knowing him, he'd probably have gotten home just as the sun was coming up and would sleep well into the afternoon. After going downstairs to peek into his room, Jessica would head back upstairs and get ready to go to work, which usually took a while, given that she never left the house without looking flawless. Jessica's Sunday shift at the pharmacy didn't start until 11 a.m., but before that she'd pick up her boyfriend John from his house a couple of blocks away so they could go get breakfast somewhere.

Iridian had nowhere to be, so she got up last.

On this particular Sunday, which she hoped would be the same as every other Sunday, Iridian got dressed and went downstairs to the kitchen. After pouring some cereal—chocolate puffs, her favorite—she hopped up on the counter so she could have a better view of Rosa, who was sitting on a wooden chair in the middle of the backyard, facing away from the house. When Rosa wasn't outside, her long hair was the blandest shade of tree-bark brown, but in the sun, especially the morning sun, it was an array of earth tones: pecan, rust, russet.

Rosa's hands were resting on her lap. Her palms were facing up. The light morning breezes tugged at the folds of her faded red dress and the gleaming strands of her hair.

Next door, Mrs. Moreno was out watering the cherry tree she'd just planted. She was frowning at Rosa but also at the Torreses' backyard. It had always been more dirt than grass, and in a corner close to the alley was a pile of mangled metal—the bent carcass of a swing set, the remains of a trampoline, and the rusted frame of a trundle bed. Eventually, Mrs. Moreno realized that Iridian was spying on her spying. Their gazes caught, and Iridian raised her hand to give the older woman a wave. Mrs. Moreno's upper lip stuck on dry teeth in her attempt to smile. As she turned away, the arc of water from her hose swung from the cherry tree to a sorry-looking rosebush that was losing its battle against summer.

Iridian watched as Rosa's shoulders lifted, then lowered. It was a tiny, almost imperceptible movement: a sigh. Iridian saw that little sigh every Sunday morning, and every Sunday morning, it killed her. The day had just started, but already Rosa was disappointed. She woke up full of hope only to have that hope punctured.

Iridian was shoveling in another spoonful of cereal when Rosa stood, dragged her chair back to the porch, and came inside.

"Any luck?" Iridian asked, as the screen door bounced in its frame.

Rosa shook her head and ran her hands over her dress to try to smooth out the creases. She may have been the youngest Torres sister, but Rosa dressed as if she were older—older, like from another century. She wore the same thing every day: a thrift-store dress and bulky brown oxfords. The dresses were short-sleeved, with hems that went at least to her calves, and were buttoned all the way down the front. They reminded Iridian of the kind of clothes that women in Depression-era photographs wore, more fit for standing in a bread line than going to church.

"There was nothing," Rosa replied. "For a second I thought there might be something, but . . ."

Out in front of the house, a car honked its horn.

"Tell Walter and Mrs. Mata hello," Iridian said.

The Matas had been Rosa's ride to church every Sunday for a year. Walter was a year and a half older than Rosa, and they'd gone all through elementary school and junior high together. The Torres sisters' neighbors and parents of classmates had all taken on various roles—there were bringers of casseroles and mowers of lawns. Mrs. Mata had become transporter to church. The rest of the Torres family stopped going to regular mass soon after Ana died, but Rosa's faith remained big enough for all of them. At Ana's vigil, their old priest Father Canty told Rosa she was special—"full of God" or "touched by God," something like that. He'd insisted Rosa had a purer heart than most people. It was a gift that needed to be nurtured, honed, and then put to use. According to the old priest, if Rosa tried very hard and was very patient, she could see into the hearts of God's creatures, especially those that were small and in need of care. He said her purpose in this life was to soothe the suffering of others.

Father Canty died in his sleep exactly two weeks after Ana's funeral, so he was never able to guide Rosa any further down her spiritual path than that. His replacement was a much younger man, Father Mendoza, who, shortly after arriving to town, got in a fistfight with the still grief-stricken Rafe Torres in the produce section of the grocery store and swore he'd never come near the family again. Iridian was fine with that—she'd fallen asleep during mass for as long as she could remember; the droning words of the sermon softly bounced off her head, never finding their way in—and Jessica had never liked priests because she'd always hated old men telling her what to do. Jessica thought Father Canty's message to Rosa meant that she should volunteer at the children's hospital or the food pantry. Rosa, though, interpreted creatures "small and in need of care" as the animals around the neighborhood, and her sisters eventually just went with it.

"Dad's not in his room," Jessica declared, entering the kitchen and pinning her name tag to her shirt. "Mrs. Mata's outside, Rosa."

The horn sounded again, and Rosa blinked, like she'd briefly forgotten where she was.

"I can't find my keys," Rosa said. "But you'll be here all day, right, Iridian?"

"That's the plan."

Rosa fluttered away, out of the kitchen and through the living room. Once the front screen door clicked shut, Iridian turned to her older sister. Jessica's work uniform consisted of a blue collared shirt and khakis, and it was obvious she'd gone the extra mile that morning to try to offset the unflattering clothes she was forced to wear. Long, loose curls fell down past her shoulders. She smelled like burned hair and aerosol. Her eyes were rimmed with black pencil, and her lips were painted a deep plum color.

"There's cereal if you want some," Iridian said.

"Did you hear me? Dad's not in his room. He won't answer his phone, either." Jessica paused. "I'm worried about him—because of today."

Because of today.

Iridian knew, despite how hard she might hope, that this Sunday wouldn't be like all the other Sundays. That was because this Sunday was June ninth, a year to the day her sister Ana had fallen to her death from her window. Iridian had woken up sick in her sadness—even if *sadness* didn't come close to describing the deep, persistent gnawing that she felt. Emotions were hard for Iridian. She liked to read about them in books, but hated when they crept and settled in her own bones. They made her edgy. They made her sweat. Over the course of the last year, she'd convinced herself she'd gotten really good at ignoring them, brushing them aside, dodging them like a car swerving around a dead animal in the road.

"Dad stayed out." Iridian swallowed a mouthful of now-soggy chocolate globes. "He probably met some fine lady last night and—"

"Stop." Jessica put up her hand and then snatched her car keys off the kitchen table. "I get it. Just let me know when you hear from him, alright?"

Once Jessica was gone, Iridian finished the last of her breakfast, drank the milky dregs, and put the bowl in the sink. Upstairs in her room, she climbed under the covers, then reached under her pillow for her favorite book, *The*

Witching Hour by Anne Rice, which she was just starting again even though she'd already read it over a dozen times. The paper cover had fallen off and was now rubber-banded to the rest of the pages. Iridian could practically recite entire paragraphs by memory, especially the sexy parts between Rowan and Lasher, the ghost that, for centuries, had plagued the women of the Mayfair family, women who also just so happened to be witches.

It was the greatest book ever written.

Bleary-eyed, Iridian looked up to her doorway. She could've sworn she heard someone coming up the stairs and calling her name, but no one was there. She blinked and then glanced at the clock on her nightstand. It was 2:05 in the afternoon. She'd been reading for over four hours. Her right arm was asleep from the elbow down because she'd been lying on it weird.

The front door opened with a high, quick whine.

"Iridian! *Iridian!*"

It was Rosa. She was shouting. Something was wrong. Rosa *never* shouted. Iridian bolted down the stairs and saw her sister standing at the front door.

"It's Dad," Rosa said breathlessly. "In the street."

Iridian pushed past her sister. She was out of the house and running—across the front yard; across Mrs. Moreno's yard, where the water from the sprinkler was creating little suspended prisms in the sunlit air; down the sidewalk; under the shady canopies of the oak trees; and then out into the middle of the street. Down at the intersection, there was a jumble of cars facing every which way.

Iridian's heart lurched, then sank. She was thinking, *There's been a wreck.* Her dad must've been out drinking. Less than a block away from the house, he must've run his truck through a stop sign and into another car, or a couple of cars, or worst of all, a kid out on her bike.

Jessica's old white Civic was there, too, in the middle of the road, with the driver's-side door flung open. She must've been coming home from work on a break. For a panicked moment Iridian was convinced that *she* was the one Rafe had hit.

All around Jessica's car were other cars. The people in them were honking their horns, shouting, waving their arms out the window; but what they *weren't* doing was moaning in pain or calling for help.

Iridian wove through the cars and saw Jessica—her dark hair and the blue of her work shirt. She was crouched down in the intersection next to their dad. He was sitting in the middle of the road in his work coveralls. Sitting and sobbing.

"My girl!" he wailed. "My beautiful girl!"

Jessica had her arms around her dad's shoulders and was talking to him, trying to calm him down, but he didn't seem to realize she was there. Behind them, the green Ford

19

pickup was parked at a diagonal, taking up most of the intersection. Its driver's-side door was open. The engine was still running, so Iridian went over and yanked the keys from the ignition.

"My baby." Rafe collapsed to the side, his face landing hard against the hot asphalt. He closed his eyes. Iridian thought that maybe he'd passed out, but then he curled himself into a ball and started muttering to himself.

"Christ," Jessica said. "Shit, shit, *shit*."

A long stripe of blood was on the road close to the Ford's front bumper, but from what Iridian could see of her dad's hands, legs, arms, and face, he wasn't hurt.

"Iridian!" someone yelled. "Get your father and his truck out of the damn road!"

Iridian turned, grateful for the distraction. Old Mr. Garza was in his idling pickup on the other side of the intersection. His wife was in the passenger seat. They were both dressed for afternoon mass. Mrs. Garza's arms were folded across her chest, and she was giving Iridian her very best, most judgmental glare.

Just beyond the Garzas' truck, a flash of red caught Iridian's eye. It was Rosa. She'd run into the yard of a nearby house. Iridian watched her sister land on her knees in front of a large wheat-colored dog. The dog was on its side, breathing fast. Rosa put her hand gently on its body, against its rib cage, and when she pulled it away, there was blood—blood from the dog, blood on the street.

Rosa looked up—to Iridian, and then past her sister and around. Iridian followed the direction of Rosa's gaze and saw that the entire neighborhood had come out to witness the hideous spectacle of the Torres girls and their father. There were the Matas. Mrs. Moreno. The Johnsons. The Avilas. Hector Garcia from across the street and the boys who hung out at his house all hours of the day and night. Teddy Arenas was in his driveway, leaning against his perpetually broken-down Dodge Charger and drinking a beer. Even Kitty Bolander, the little girl Ana used to babysit, had come up on her bike.

Iridian closed her eyes and gulped, trying to calm down and also magically will the day to start over. When she opened her eyes, there was Rosa again. Her hands were back on the dog. She'd tossed her hair over one shoulder and was lowering her ear against the animal's side. It was only a matter of seconds before Iridian saw the dog shudder, all the way from its nose to the tip of its tail, as if a current had passed through it.

In that same moment, Rafe mumbled, "Ana, my heart."

Sirens bleated in the near distance, which meant that someone had called 9-1-1. Even more people had come out of their houses or stopped their cars along the side streets, attracted to this awful scene like flies on a fresh kill. They were all murmuring, buzzing. Iridian tried to take a big breath in, but the air was thick with exhaust. She erupted into a coughing fit.

"Dad, come on!" Jessica pled. "You *have* to move. Iridian, help!"

Jessica stood and started tugging on Rafe's limp arm. She was crying. The once-perfect black rims around her eyes were blurred. The waves in her hair had flattened. She was yelling at the people in their cars to stop honking their horns and *shut up*.

"Dad, please!" she gasped. "Iridian, do something. *Help me!*"

Iridian didn't help. She didn't move. Instead, she looked back at Rosa, who had left the dog in the yard and was now taking slow steps into the road.

Kitty Bolander's mom was calling out her daughter's name. When she finally reached her, she started to steer Kitty in the direction of home, but then stopped and put her hand on Iridian's shoulder.

"I'm so sorry," she said. "I know this day must be so hard for your family, especially your poor father."

Mrs. Bolander was probably being sincere. Most everyone there probably felt genuinely sorry for Iridian and her family, but that didn't make things any better. If anything, it made Iridian feel like the air was thinning out even more, like all these supposedly well-intentioned people were stealing it from her.

"Iridian!" Again, Mr. Garza honked his horn. "Rafe! Vámanos, man!"

Rafe couldn't hear Mr. Garza. Rafe was lost. He was

still crying, moaning about the pain in his heart and his lost, beautiful daughter. At last, he lifted his bleary gaze to Iridian, and for a moment, they stared at each other. He looked terrible, ill. There were bags around his eyes, large and swollen. His hair, usually pomaded and carefully slicked back, was stuck into spikes as if he'd been trying to yank it from his scalp.

His lips slid against each other. They puckered. He was trying to tell Iridian something, but he couldn't get any words out. That was fine, because Iridian didn't want to hear whatever it was he had to say. All she wanted was to get out of there.

"Rosa," she croaked.

Rosa, the sister whose heart was crafted to ease the suffering of others, came forward, linked her arm with Iridian's, and steered her away. When they were knitted together like this, Iridian felt safer. She didn't even care about the dog's bright blood transferring from Rosa's skin onto hers.

"I think I might've felt it," Rosa whispered excitedly, as the two of them turned back to the house. "Its spirit."

"Where are you two *going*?" Jessica cried out, her voice going shrill. "Iridian, what the fuck? You can't just leave me here with him!"

But that's exactly what Iridian was doing. She didn't even spare a glance over her shoulder.

"Iridian!" Jessica shouted. "Rosa! *Get back here!*"

"I hate him," Iridian said to Rosa, quietly, so only her sister could hear.

"I know."

"We loved her, too. It's like he's forgotten that."

Rosa didn't reply. The sisters kept walking, just the two of them, at a slow and steady pace back to their house.

"I hate him," Iridian repeated. "He doesn't deserve our help."

"I know," Rosa said.

"Iridian!" Behind them, Jessica was nearly hysterical. *"You fucking coward!"*

"Don't pay attention to her." Rosa leaned in. "Maybe just try to walk a little faster?"

Jessica
(Monday, June 10th)

JESSICA REALLY HAD to hand it to her dad. He always tried so hard to make his apologies appear convincing. There was the way he'd start off by looking each of his daughters in the eye, but then duck his head down real quick as if he were just so overcome with emotion. Or there was the way the sides of his mouth would dip into a big-ass frown, the exaggerated kind that a clown would paint on his face. Or there was his voice, how it would get all wobbly, like a kid who tripped on a curb but wanted you to think he was pushed off a building or some shit.

"Girls, listen," Rafe said, staring down at the surface of the kitchen table. He'd even gone the extra mile and shaved that morning. A white strip of dried foam clung to his earlobe.

"I'm so sorry. I didn't know how I'd be when yesterday came around, and I wasn't myself. As you saw." He paused, took a breath, shook his head slowly, and started running his pointer finger down a long gouge in the wood. "You girls are my everything. You know that."

Jessica couldn't help it. Her lower lip started to quiver.

Iridian sat across the table with her arms folded, scowling at Jessica and scowling at Rafe. Rosa was also there, but she was distracted by something out in the backyard.

"Do you see?" Rosa said softly. "It's—"

"I try to be a good father." Rafe's voice broke as he interrupted Rosa. "I *am* a good father, verdad?"

"Yes," Jessica replied, automatically.

Rafe reached across the table for Jessica's hand, and she let him take it. Iridian made a sound, a little cluck of disgust that their dad didn't register.

"This year—" He squinted at Jessica with bloodshot eyes. "This year will be different. I'll change. I promise. I have a plan."

Jessica nodded, but the thing was, he'd said this exact same thing before, almost exactly one year ago.

After Ana died, and after a brief but catastrophic mourning period, Rafe had emerged from his bedroom one day in the middle of July and had made a plan. To his credit, he'd short-term stuck to that plan. He'd gotten up early on Saturday mornings and helped the neighbors fix their cars and their fences and let them use his truck to haul away bulk trash. He didn't go to the bar so much. He paid back a guy that he worked with who had lent him some money. He'd taken Rosa to church, and then to lunch, and then to the art museum. He'd bought Iridian a book. He'd told Jessica to invite a couple of her friends over for a cookout. He'd grilled up hot dogs and cobs of corn. They'd had an okay time.

It didn't last, though. By the end of summer, he was back to his old ways, breaking all kinds of promises. He said he was going to take his girls out for pizza, and then he forgot. He said he was going to be right over to give Jessica's car a jump and then never showed up. Strange dudes started calling at all hours, asking to speak to Rafe, and then made Jessica and her sisters take down messages about "debts" and "payment for services rendered." Those dudes had all said something like, "He knows what we're talking about." A couple of them, before they'd hung up, had asked the girls how old they were.

Back at the breakfast table, Rafe coughed without covering his mouth.

"Are you sick?" Jessica asked. "Do you want me to bring you something from work?"

He shook his head and gave her hand a squeeze. His palm, was it too warm?

"I'm alright."

27

"Are you sure? It's not a prob—"

"You should go, Dad," Iridian said, interrupting. "It's already after eight. You don't want to be late again. Remember what you told us? About your boss? No more warnings."

"Uh, right." Rafe cleared his throat, removed his hand from Jessica's, and checked his watch. "Right. Jessie, just give me a minute."

He pushed his chair back from the table and went to his bedroom. The police had shown up the previous day, but since a sobriety test had proven Rafe wasn't drunk and no one had actually seen him hit the dog, no charges had been filed. Still, Jessica was worried about her dad behind the wheel—for everyone's sake—so that morning she'd hidden his keys and offered him a ride.

"We all know how you feel about him, Iridian," Jessica said, once their dad was out of earshot. "You could make it a little less obvious."

"He's awful," Iridian snapped. "He's awful, and he doesn't deserve our comfort or your hand-holding."

Jessica wiped away the tear that was threatening to spill from the corner of her eye, and her finger came away smudged black from her eyeliner.

Iridian snickered. "I can't believe you shed tears for that man."

"Like you're so fucking perfect," Jessica replied.

Iridian shoved away from the table, the legs of her chair

squealing against the linoleum floor. She stalked into the living room, turned on the television, and started to flip through the channels.

Rosa moved her chair so that she could sit facing Jessica. She then lifted her fingers up to her sister's face to smooth out the eyeliner. The rising sun coming in from the windows lit Rosa up from behind. In that light, she was weirdly pale. Her eyelids, nostrils, and the upper crest of her ears were practically translucent. Jessica closed her eyes and took a deep breath. Rosa's skin was cool, and the light pressure of her fingers was soothing.

Out in the living room, Iridian landed on what sounded like the local news. With her eyes still closed, Jessica listened for updates about the weather. Overnight there'd been another thunderstorm. Hurricane season had come early that year. Even this far inland, they'd been hit with bad storm after bad storm.

Jessica heard updates, but they weren't about the weather.

> *. . . already at least a couple of sightings near Concepcion Park. If you see the animal, please don't approach it. Do not attempt to feed or capture it. Instead, call police immediately . . .*

"Iridian!" Rosa called out. "What is it?"
"What is *what*?"

"The animal that escaped. What is it?"

Iridian took a couple of seconds before replying. "A spotted hyena. It escaped from the zoo yesterday morning. Those things are gross. They eat babies."

"They do *not* eat babies," Jessica said.

"They do," Iridian insisted. "They come into people's houses at night, steal the little babies, and eat them. I read about it."

"Did the storm wake you last night?" Rosa asked Jessica, giving the corner of her sister's eye one last dab with her finger.

"Yeah," Jessica replied, "I thought the thunder might break my window."

"Ready, Jessie?"

Jessica opened her eyes. Rafe was standing in the entrance to the kitchen. That little crust of foam was still there on his ear, and Jessica's traitor heart clenched at the sight.

"Ready," she said.

The air-conditioning in Jessica's car had been broken for months, so she always kept the windows rolled down while she drove. It was hard to have a conversation or listen to the radio because the wind and the street noise drowned everything out. This meant Jessica couldn't really talk to her dad as she drove him across town to the factory, where he had a job building cars on an assembly line. The silence was fine with her.

Jessica pulled into the lot and let the car idle as her dad climbed out of the passenger seat. After shutting the door, he leaned in through the open window and clasped his calloused hands together. He really did look bad. The sunlight made it worse.

"Jessie. Keep the faith for your old man, huh?"

Jessica smiled. She imagined it looked unconvincing.

"And don't worry about coming to get me later." Rafe gazed up, squinting into the sun. The fingers on his right hand twitched. Jessica worried that he was going to try to reach for her hand like he did earlier at the kitchen table, but he didn't. "I'll figure out a way back. Catch the bus, find a ride or something."

Jessica's phone buzzed in her cup holder. She glanced down to see several missed messages—calls and texts—from John. She'd never heard any of them come in.

Her smile—convincing or otherwise—disappeared completely.

Iridian

(Monday, June 10th)

IN THE WEEKS following their sister's death, the Torres girls would play a game called Who Loved Ana Most. Iridian would always win because she was the best at remembering small details. For example: Ana's left eye sat a little lower on her face than her right. There was a freckle on the inside of her right wrist, at the pulse point. There was a spot on the crown of her head where gray hairs would always sprout. Iridian knew about that last thing because sometimes Ana would ask her to sit up on the bathroom counter and pull those hairs out with tweezers. Ana's favorite movie was *The Princess Bride*, but she'd tell people it was *The Craft*. When she was thirteen, Ana decided she wanted to be a majorette, not because she had school spirit—she didn't—but because the girls' mother was once a majorette, and, most of all, because Ana liked the idea of going out on a great big football field and being the only one of her kind.

The grand prize for Who Loved Ana Most was her room, her clothes and shoes, her makeup, her hairbrushes, and the ancient pack of cigarettes she kept hidden behind the stack of towels in her bathroom cabinet. Jessica, though, kept crying about losing (shocking!), so Iridian caved and gave most of her winnings—Ana's room, Ana's clothes—to her older sister. One night, Iridian spied on Jessica sitting on the edge of the bathroom sink. She had on one of Ana's long, ratty T-shirts and a pair of her old underwear and was wearing her bright pink lipstick. She was leaning against the frame of the open window, trying to mimic Ana's far-off, dreamy look. Iridian hid behind the door and watched Jessica smoke four stale cigarettes, one right after the other. She was puckering her lips so that a perfect hot-pink O would form on the filter. Later, after Iridian had gone back to her room, she could hear her sister throwing up from all the way down the hall. Sometimes Jessica tried too hard.

When Iridian decided to let Jessica have most of Ana's old room, she had one condition: She would get to keep Ana's collection of romance novels, all of which Ana had arranged in three three-foot stacks at the back of her mess of a closet, with the spines facing the wall so that the titles were hidden. It was obvious that most of them had been stolen from the library because they still had the yellowing call slips in them, and because their covers were soft and curled from being read hundreds of times by hundreds of different ladies. The responsible thing would've been to return Ana's books to the library, but Iridian didn't do that. Instead, she carried them all to her room and arranged them the same way Ana had arranged them—in three stacks at the back of her closet, spines facing the wall.

It took a few months to read Ana's old novels, and when Iridian was done, she had a clear sense of her purpose in life: She decided that she wanted to write her own book—a slightly disturbing kind of romance with a slightly disturbing kind of ghost or witch or were-person as the love interest. She had several notebooks full of ideas. She'd brainstormed possible character names: Leticia or LaTisha or Letisha, Gabriel, Viridiana, Sam. She had character descriptions: long chestnut hair, curly auburn hair, crow-black hair, eyes like clear pools, earth-toned skin, freckly skin, freckles that danced across skin, membranous wings, glistening fangs, delicate fingers, scents like clove, lemon, cinnamon, and other things found in a hot tea bag. She'd come up with hundreds of lines of witty banter, and had drawn out intricate family trees featuring the offspring of humans and nonhumans. She'd written out page after page of what it felt like to have body parts come in contact with other body parts, and how that contact would result in gasps, moans, twitches, and full-body shudders. The main characters in most of Ana's novels were fair-skinned and had corn-silk hair that gleamed in the sun, but in Iridian's, the heroines all had hair and skin in various shades of brown.

There was only one book of Ana's that Iridian didn't keep: a school copy of Shakespeare's *King Lear*. It not only had Ana's writing in it—Iridian could tell it was Ana's because of the way she wrote her *a*'s, typed-style with the curl on top—but layers and layers of other students' notes and highlights. Most of the pages were dog-eared and smelled like other people's houses, like cat litter and corn. Iridian wasn't interested in reading a story about daughters and their father—it was a story she lived every day. She took the book back to the school, handed it to Ana's former teacher, and that was that.

After spending the day finishing her reread of *The Witching Hour* in a mostly empty house, Iridian opened her notebook and clicked her pen. Just as she was about to start a conversation between a witch and vampire who were falling in love despite a multigenerational curse, she heard someone coming up the stairs. She knew who it was because the steps were too slow to be Jessica's and too heavy to be Rosa's. Iridian slammed her notebook shut and crammed it into the space between her bed and the wall. She then barreled across her room and braced herself against the doorframe.

"You're not supposed to be here," she said, barring her dad's entrance. "Did you get fired?"

"No, I did not *get fired*, Iridian," Rafe sneered. "My boss let me come home a couple of hours early."

Rafe worked twelve-hour shifts on the line, which meant he shouldn't have been home until after 9 p.m. Iridian glanced at her clock. It was only 5:30.

"More than a couple," she said. "You're not allowed up here."

Rafe towered over his daughter. It was obvious he'd been crying again. It was too dim to see if his eyes were red, but his eyelids were puffed. His gaze swept the darkened room that Iridian and Rosa shared, taking in the two unmade beds, the carpet that hadn't been vacuumed in months, the clothes thrown all over the place.

"Where's your sister?" he asked.

"I don't know." Iridian paused. "Which one?"

"Your *little* sister."

Rosa hadn't been home since the morning, but Iridian wasn't worried. Rosa was a wanderer, had been since she'd been able to walk.

"You're not allowed up here," Iridian repeated.

"This is my house," Rafe replied. "I can go anywhere."

"What do you want?" Iridian felt her fingers dig into the doorframe. She never would've considered herself brave, but she was ready to use her long, weak limbs to defend the contents of her room.

Again, Rafe peered over Iridian's shoulder.

"I'm wondering if you have anything of Ana's," he said. "Anything that I could have."

"Why? What for?"

Rafe waited a moment. "Do I need a reason?"

"Yes," Iridian said, even though she didn't need or want to hear that reason. It wouldn't matter. It probably had to do with missing Ana and wanting a keepsake, a scrap of something that used to belong to her.

He didn't even need to be there, upstairs and lurking. The whole house was still full of Ana's things. Just last week, Iridian had found one of Ana's hairs bundled up in a pair of socks. She knew it was hers because it was long and dark, with about an inch of gray at the root. She'd squeaked with glee when she'd found it, and then wedged it between a couple of pages of *The Witching Hour* like a macabre little bookmark.

"Are you hiding something?" Rafe asked.

"Probably," Iridian shot back. "Get out of my door."

Rafe leaned forward. Lamplight hit his face, and Iridian could see the pink lines from where recent tears had tracked down his cheeks. They looked like burn marks. They did not make her feel sorry for him.

"You girls don't understand," Rafe said.

Iridian said nothing.

"You girls don't *understand*," Rafe repeated. He braced his weight against the doorframe and then dropped his head, shook it.

Iridian couldn't stand this, how her dad always turned his grief into a performance piece.

"You have *no* idea what it's like," Rafe said. "Ana was my heart."

Oh, Iridian had *some* idea what it was like. For her, Ana was hardly even gone. She was everywhere all the time. She was in the walls. She was in the wood of the walls, the wood of the cabinets, the cheap porcelain of the family's mugs, the loops of the terry-cloth hand towels they used to dry their faces, the threads of the worn sheets they slept beneath at night, the pages of the books all stashed in Iridian's closet. She was in the tiniest details of the ways in which the Torres sisters lived their lives, the choices they made, the directions in which they steered themselves, the shades of lipstick Jessica wore. Ana was the one who told Rosa, long before Father Canty ever did, that she was full of magic, that she was different and had a heart that was better-crafted than most people's.

Sometimes, Iridian felt like Ana was the itch in her skin, like she breathed in pieces of her, and then breathed out pieces of her. She cycled through and through. It was overwhelming. Sometimes, like in that very moment, it was too overwhelming. And when things got too overwhelming, Iridian wished she could just shut herself down.

"Your sister died," Rafe said slowly, "because she was keeping secrets."

God, she hated him. Her hate was a sour film coating the back of her throat.

"My sister *died*," Iridian countered, just as slowly, "because she was trying to get away from *you*."

She stepped back into her room and tried to slam the door, but Rafe was too quick and caught it. His other hand whipped out and wrapped around Iridian's upper arm.

"Apologize," Rafe demanded.

"No!"

"You're a miserable girl. Because you're a miserable girl you try to make everyone else miserable."

Maybe that was true—but was it possible that Rafe thought Iridian was the *only* miserable girl in his house?

"You spread your misery," Rafe hissed, squeezing harder. "You're like a disease."

Iridian wrenched her arm free, slammed her door, and bolted it from the inside. She then braced herself there, with both palms and her forehead pressed against the wood, ready for her father to kick the door down or otherwise try to force his way in. She breathed in and out, inhaling the particles of the paint on the door, the particles of Ana. Eventually, Iridian heard Rafe's footsteps receding down the hall. There was a pause and then a slight rattle as he tried the knob on Jessica's locked door. Then there were more steps, hard and heavy, as Rafe went down the stairs.

Iridian counted to one hundred, and then to one hundred again. The weak limbs she would've used to fight her father started to feel even weaker, like foam. Just blow on her and she'd scatter. Once she was fairly certain that her dad wasn't going to come back, Iridian raced to her bed, reached for her notebook, and smacked it to her chest. She was used to her dad throwing out all kinds of insults: little ones that barely pricked and big ones that were meant to crack bone. The best ones were the ones Iridian could snatch out of the air and then save for later, when she'd make them her own. If she could take Rafe's words—no matter how hard or hurtful they were—and write them in her own hand, it transferred their power and made her feel less insignificant. Iridian needed that, to feel less insignificant.

She reached for her pen and opened to a fresh page.

You're like a disease, she wrote.

Jessica

(Monday, June 10th –
early Tuesday, June 11th)

"IT ATTACKED A little boy in his own front yard, then ran off with one of those pequeño dogs," the older woman said. "What kind is that?"

"A Chihuahua?" Jessica offered.

"No, no. More fur."

"Uh . . . a Yorkie?"

"Sí, a Yorkie."

"Oh. Well," Jessica said. "Your total is $14.23."

The woman on the other side of the register took out her wallet, handed Jessica a bank-fresh hundred-dollar bill, and then dumped out all her coins on the counter to hunt for exact change. Of course this was happening while Jessica was the only person working checkout, and while

41

there were five other people in line who were starting to get visibly impatient. One of them was rocking side to side, right foot to left foot to right foot, like he had to go to the bathroom. A man holding a baby in a car seat with one hand and a jug of laundry detergent with the other let out a loud sigh. The old lady ignored him, or she didn't hear him. She bent over the counter and squinted, trying to tell the difference between a penny and a moldy dime.

Jessica picked up the intercom. "Backup to the registers."

"I stopped letting out my cat," the lady said, still hunched. "All night he scratches at the back door, but I don't want Hudspeth snatched up by a hyena. Can you imagine?"

A high school–aged girl joined the line. She was trying to hide a pregnancy test in the sleeve of her hoodie and was biting her lip like she was about to burst into tears. An older man walked over to the photo-maker, holding a flash drive and looking confused.

"I'm confused," he called out.

Again, Jessica reached for the intercom, but stopped when she saw Peter Rojas jogging up from the back of the store.

"I can help the next person," Peter cheerfully announced, sliding behind the counter while clipping on his name tag.

"Thanks," Jessica muttered.

"No problem."

During the summer, Jessica rarely saw Peter. He usually worked the overnight shift and was clocking in around when Jessica was clocking out. The old ladies who shopped at the pharmacy *loved* him. They always asked Jessica if he was working even though they knew his schedule by heart. They went out of their way to steer their carts into the aisle where Peter was stocking or to ask specifically for him to reach for items on the highest shelves. He asked them about their surgeries, and they showed him their granddaughters' senior portraits and photos from their quinceñeras. He seemed genuinely sad when they would tell him that another one of their old lady friends had died.

They'd gone to the same school, but since Peter was Iridian's age and had just finished his junior year, Jessica didn't know him well—they'd been in choir together; that was it—but he was one of Hector Garcia's friends, which meant that, when he wasn't at work, he was usually camped out at the house across the street from Jessica's. He'd been there yesterday afternoon, in fact, standing out in the street with the rest of his friends, gawking as Jessica was trying to yank her distraught father off the ground. He'd seen her at her unraveled worst, begging her sisters for help and yelling at the neighbors to leave them all alone.

Standing there behind the registers under the industrial blast of air-conditioning, Jessica could feel her face get hot and the sweat start to gather behind her ears as if she were still outside with her father, crouched and crying on the asphalt.

"Here, let me," Jessica said to the woman. She plucked twenty-three cents from the pile of coins and started sorting them into the register. "You know, it's probably just scared."

"What, dear?" The woman looked up. "Oh, hello, Peter."

"Hi, Mrs. Rivas," Peter replied.

"The hyena." Jessica handed the woman her change with a long ribbon of coupons. "It's probably just scared. Imagine if you were lost and alone in a strange place. I bet that would be pretty scary. You might start to do some weird stuff."

Mrs. Rivas looked from Jessica to Peter, then back to Jessica.

"But you know," Jessica couldn't help adding, "that thing about the Yorkie? It's probably just a rumor. People around here *love* to come up with all kinds of stories."

Mrs. Rivas, once so chatty, was apparently at a loss for words.

"Have a nice day," Jessica said with a grin. "I can help who's next in line."

Jessica ended up pulling a double because a coworker had to leave to take her kid to the emergency room after he accidentally smashed his hand in a car door. Even though she was exhausted, she was grateful for the excuse not to go home. She spent her time stocking toilet paper, thermometers, greeting cards, condoms, diapers, and cotton rounds. She worked the register some more and tried not to judge customers by their purchases. She spent ten minutes helping an older man look up a coupon on his phone, only to tell him that it had expired three months ago. She ate a granola bar and a fruit cup, and drank a cherry Diet Coke alone in the break room. She caught herself humming along to a Celine Dion ballad that was coming through the speakers. She'd worked four shifts a week at the pharmacy for nearly five months now, since the beginning of the spring semester of her senior year, and had probably heard that same song three hundred times.

Sometimes, she really loved how boring her job was.

Late in the night and toward the end of her second shift, Jessica was with Peter again, this time in the vitamin aisle, where they were scanning hundreds of little bottles that were about to go on sale. The two of them worked in silence, which Jessica thought was great, until Peter asked what he must've assumed was a simple enough question.

"So," he said. "How are you doing?"

Jessica paused, her finger hovering over the trigger of her hand scanner.

"Fine. Why?"

"I don't know." Peter shrugged. "After yesterday. Because of yesterday."

What, Jessica wondered, did Peter think the answer to his question could be? Did he want to know how Jessica went to sleep last night clutching one of Ana's old shoes—one of her *shoes*—because the stink from the sole was still there, and so strong? Did he want to know how, earlier today during her shift, when a twelve-year-old girl wanted to buy the same cheap, linen-scented perfume that Ana always used to wear, Jessica sat in silent judgment of the girl's thin, mouse-brown hair and chapped lips and too-wide eyes, as if some little girl was too weird and too unattractive for a four-dollar plastic bottle of perfume? Or did he want to know about how, while Jessica was having sex with John in the back seat of her car the other night, she started crying so loudly and violently that she'd tricked him? John had thought they'd been cries of passion, what he'd been able to pull from her depths, but they'd had nothing to do with him. Her cries were from grief and rage. She'd bitten John hard, on his shoulder, desperate to cause someone else pain.

Jessica resumed scanning. "I don't feel anything. I'm sort of numb about it."

"What about your dad? Is he doing any better?"

"He gets in these moods," Jessica replied, echoing what

her father had said earlier that morning. "I can't really blame him for some of the things he does."

"I remember when Ana died," Peter said. "It was . . . it was *awful*. Your dad's allowed to have a bad day about it. *You're* allowed to have a bad day about it."

Peter was just trying to be nice—Peter *was* nice—but that didn't make his timing any less terrible or his words any less infuriating. Jessica wanted to wail like a fucking banshee because *this* exactly was the problem: Her entire neighborhood knew all the details of her miserable life. Peter knew. Peter's friends knew. Peter's friends' grandparents knew. Mrs. Rivas from earlier today probably knew. Her fucking cat Hudspeth probably knew. They knew about Jessica's dead mother, her dead sister, her alive but destroyed sisters, her total disaster of a dad.

Jessica's phone chimed, and she pulled it from her back pocket to read a message from John.

hey babe! come get me and lets go somewhere! xxoo.

It was 1:06 a.m. Jessica's shift had been over for six minutes.

"I'll finish all this," Peter said, gesturing to the shelves. "It's no big deal. I've got all night."

"Thanks," Jessica murmured.

She turned and rushed down the aisle toward the break room, where she'd stored her keys and her wallet in her locker. She couldn't wait to be alone in her car, to feel the sticky outside air and to drive with her windows rolled down.

Rosa
(early Tuesday, June 11th)

NIGHTTIME WAS PERFECT for listening. There were birds. Mockingbirds. There were dogs. They all howled together even though they were in separate yards. Mostly, there were crickets. It was hard for Rosa to imagine a single cricket's heart, what it looked like or how fast it beat. Dozens of crickets must fill a backyard on a summer night, all with hearts that thump or whoosh in different rhythms. All those hearts fuel all those legs that scrape together. They scrape together to create a song that will bring them a mate.

Rosa was outside, sitting in her chair and listening to the crickets. A new moon, a perfect white circle, was perched just above the telephone wires, and the air was thick. There were probably going to be storms again. Rosa's hair was puffed around her head, and her bare feet sank a little into the still-damp ground. She felt buzzy and full of static.

Something landed on Rosa's shoulder. She opened her eyes and saw a firefly. She watched it launch off her arm, disappear, glow, disappear, glow. She stood and chased after it, which was something she hadn't done in years.

Another firefly blinked, off to Rosa's left. She spun toward it, but then another caught her eye. And then another. The yard was alive with dancing light. The fireflies pulsed and swooped, so silently. It was dizzying, delirious. Rosa didn't know where to turn. She burst out laughing, feeling lost.

Another firefly lit up right in front of Rosa's face, and when she clasped her hands together to trap it, she could feel the insect's wings flutter against her palms. When she released her cupped hands, Rosa watched for a moment as the firefly blinked away in the direction of Concepcion Park, where the news had said the escaped hyena had first been sighted. Was this a sign? She decided it was. She dragged her chair to the back porch and went inside the house.

Iridian was in the bedroom they shared. She'd fallen asleep with one of her notebooks open on her chest. She did that a lot. The digital clock on the nightstand read 1:16 a.m. Rosa grabbed a backpack from her closet, put on a pair of rubber boots, and left.

Down in the kitchen, she gathered up a half-eaten bag of potato chips, an apple, and a granola bar. She filled a thermos with cold water. She noticed that someone had left the freezer door open slightly, so all of the ice had melted and formed a giant puddle on the floor. A couple of flies were bouncing across the puddle's surface, taking sips from the still-cool water. After throwing down dish towels and scooting them up closer to the bottom of the fridge with the toe of her boot, Rosa left through the back door.

The street her family lived on was just four blocks from the San Antonio River and ran parallel to it, so the walk to Concepcion Park didn't take very long. The closer Rosa got to the water, the more the night sounds started to change. The crickets multiplied. There were thousands of them it seemed like, all of them trilling, but there were also the croaks of frogs. Some birds were chirping, but mostly they rustled in the leaves of the trees that lined either side of the river.

The neighborhood was dark and quiet. Only a few houses had their lights on.

Rosa walked up and down the soggy banks of the river and waited for more signs. She hoped to hear the hyena's laugh, or at the very least, a quick huff of its breath. She hoped to see the flash of a glassy eye, something she could follow. It wouldn't have been as bright and clear as the glow of a firefly, but it might be enough.

The water in the river was a rushing murmur, but

occasionally there were pops and plunks, like twigs breaking and falling into the murk. Speakers from a car somewhere out in the neighborhood went *boom, boom, boom.* Rosa couldn't hear the music, just the *boom, boom, boom.*

The perfect circle moon was high overhead when Rosa finally stopped to sit on the ground near the riverbank. She opened her backpack and started eating her apple. Once she was done, she pitched the core into the water and lay down on the driest patch of grass she could find. Resting her head on her backpack, she stretched out and gazed up at the sky. There weren't many stars in the heart of the city, but there were some.

Rosa believed in signs, but she didn't believe in coincidences. It was no coincidence, for example, that the anniversary of Ana's death came on the same day that an animal escaped from the zoo. Maybe other people wouldn't see those two things as linked, but Rosa liked to think that she was more attentive than most people.

She just wasn't quite sure of *how* or *why* those two things were linked yet. She had to be patient and let the answers come to her. Patience was key.

Something buzzed in Rosa's ear, probably a mosquito.

What, she wondered, went on in a mosquito's heart?

Rosa closed her eyes and curled her fingers into the grass. It felt a little bit like fur.

Jessica

(early Tuesday, June 11th)

RAFE HAD A rule against boys in the house, and John shared a bedroom with his brother and his cousin, so Jessica's car was usually the only place where she and John could be alone together. Sometimes they sat in her car outside of John's house. Other times they went to a park or the empty lot of an office building. Sometimes they made out. Sometimes they talked. Sometimes, they made out *then* talked.

For now, they were parked a couple of streets over from Jessica's house, across from the high school. They weren't making out. Or talking. They were just sitting. It was three-something in the morning. Thunderclouds were rolling in, and Jessica was waiting for John to tell her to drive him home.

It had only been a little over two hours since she'd run out of the pharmacy and plunked down with a contented sigh into the front seat of her car. She didn't feel content anymore.

"Aren't you tired?" Jessica asked.

John shifted, angling in. "You're trying to get rid of me?"

John usually smelled like his house, which smelled like his kitchen, which smelled like the yeasty bread his grandmother liked to bake. Tonight, he didn't smell like that. He smelled sour. Not sour like yeast, but sour like sweat, like he'd been out under the sun for hours, sweating then cooling, sweating then cooling.

"Of course I'm not trying to get rid of you." Jessica slouched in her seat. "I'm just tired. I was at the store forever, and I have to get up early tomorrow and go back again. Hey, speaking of that . . . I've been thinking about asking my manager about transferring."

What Jessica said next came out in a rush.

"It wouldn't be for a while. I'd have to make sure my family was set up alright, and I wouldn't go anywhere too far, just like to Austin or Galveston. It's a good time for a new start, you know? You and I—we can get a cheap little place together, but still be close enough to visit home when we wanted."

It took a while for John to respond. "The last time you tried to run away it didn't work so well."

Jessica scoffed. "It's not *running away* if I'm sitting here telling you about it. I'm asking you to come with me."

"I love you, Jess," John said. "But I'm not leaving San Antonio."

"But do you *want* to?" Jessica urged.

"It's not about wanting to or not. I won't leave. My family needs me."

Jessica held in a snicker. John's family needed him for what, exactly? He'd never had a job. His mom spoiled him rotten, and since his car broke down in the spring, all he'd been able to say he'd done this summer was stay home and fix his little cousin grilled cheese sandwiches for lunch every day.

What did John know about a family that needed him? Jessica's dad had turned from a man into a puddle the other day and would've stayed there, sobbing on the street, for God knows how long, if Jessica hadn't literally hauled him off the ground and begged him to walk. When he wasn't having a public meltdown, Rafe required nonstop words of love and loyalty. He also required food, so Jessica had to carve out money from her paycheck each month to keep the fridge stocked. She also had to make sure Iridian didn't fossilize under the covers of her bed and that Rosa didn't do something weird like sprout wings and fly off into the sky.

Speaking of Rosa.

Up ahead, a familiar form wearing a long dress and

rubber boots was crossing the street. As Rosa passed under a streetlight, Jessica noticed she was eating something. Beef jerky? A candy bar?

"Is that . . . ?" John asked.

Jessica honked her horn.

Rosa stopped and turned. She waved and then waited as Jessica started her car and drove up the block.

"What are you doing?" Jessica called out the open window as she pulled up alongside her sister. "It's about to start raining."

Rosa turned toward the black sky pulsing behind her, and as Jessica stuck her hand out the window, she could feel the humidity breaking and giving way to cool, pre-storm winds.

"I know," Rosa replied, taking a bite of what Jessica could now see was a granola bar. She stepped closer to the car, and Jessica saw blades of grass sticking to the fabric of her sister's dress, and mud caking her boots. Rosa was also, for some reason, wearing a backpack. "I was on my way home."

"On your way home from *where*?" Jessica demanded.

"The river," Rosa said, simply. "I was looking for the hyena."

John barked out a laugh.

"Of course you were," Jessica replied. "Just get in the car."

The Day Jessica Torres
Attacked a Priest

HECTOR'S PARENTS, BEING good Catholics, opened their home after Ana's funeral so that the neighbors could gather, pick at potluck dishes, and express their condolences to the thoroughly distraught Torres family. The girls were there, of course. Rosa was wandering around in a somber daze. Iridian was wide-eyed and stunned, and Jessica was looking . . . lost. It was so unlike her. She just shuffled from room to room, her gaze pinned to the floor. She was wearing Ana's lipstick, a dangerous shade of near-hot pink, as well as a bluebonnet-blue sundress that used to belong to her older sister. It was several sizes too big and it swallowed her up.

We were there, too, of course—forced by our parents

to wear our church clothes and to stay downstairs with everyone else and not hide up in Hector's room. That was okay because we were on a mission. We started out in a cluster at the base of the stairs and then fanned out from there. We hovered, eavesdropping, seeking more details about Ana.

On the night she died, we'd all fallen asleep watching television in Hector's room and had woken up to a sound—at first, Jimmy thought it was a gunshot; Calvin said it was more like the hard, sharp beat of a snare drum—followed by a girl's strangled cry. That cry was followed by the hard snap of a tree limb breaking, which was followed by the squeal of tires against the asphalt as a car tore down the street. We tumbled over one another to get to the window. The first thing we saw were Ana's curtains, flapping gently in the summer wind. Her window was open—no, not open, *broken*. Someone must've thrown something through it. We watched a piece of glass the size of a hubcap dangle from the frame, then fall. Then, Ana's sisters appeared in the window. They were screaming.

They were screaming because there, facedown in the yard, at the base of the oak tree, was Ana. Her body was not twisted, her legs and neck not kinked at strange angles, but her long dark hair was fanned out across the dried-out patches of grass, and she wasn't moving. A flip-flop was on her right foot. Its mate was on top of a nearby bush. Clutched in Ana's right hand was a branch from the oak tree, as if she'd tried, at the very last second, to reach out, take hold, and break her fall.

After that, everything happened so fast: Ana's sisters kept screaming, but now they were out in the yard. The ambulance came; the cops came. Rafe was sitting on the porch step with his head in his hands. The neighbors had to run into the yard to console the Torres sisters because it was clear Rafe wasn't going to do it himself.

The official word was that Ana was in the process of sneaking out her window when she lost her footing and fell. As much as we'd wanted to be Ana's heroes and take her away to wherever it was she wanted to go, there were other guys who played that role for her. Several nights a week, various guys—*older* guys, older guys *with cars*—would ease to a stop a couple of houses down the street, turn off their lights, and wait. Eventually, Ana would open her window and climb down the oak tree. She'd run to the car and be off and gone for a couple of hours, and when she'd come back she'd be in a state of sort-of undone: Her skirt would be a little twisted, the hem of it not quite lined up right. Her hair would be ratted in the back.

But there were other theories about Ana's death: she leapt, intentionally, after a fight with her father; she leapt, intentionally, after learning she was pregnant and that the baby's father was an older married guy; she leapt, intentionally, because she was a sad girl trapped in a sad house.

At Hector's, it was hard to watch the Torres girls shuffle

from room to room and politely receive various words of sympathy because we could see the pain in their faces—the pain of their loss and the pain that comes along with forcing small smiles and pretending that kind words from their neighbors made any kind of difference.

In other parts of the house, there was the usual stuff whispered in corners about Rafe being a tragedy of a man. He'd never been the same since his wife, Rita de la Cruz, had died shortly after giving birth to Rosa. He'd become a shell, helpless. He couldn't make the most basic decisions, like what to get for takeout or which shirt to wear to church. For a while, he'd taken up with an older widow from the neighborhood named Norma Galván, and after that had fizzled out, he'd been involved with various other women. He wanted them to take care of him; they wanted to take care of him. Unfortunately, none of them lasted for longer than two months, and, in the end, all he could truly rely on, or so he said, were his girls. In this life, family was all there was.

We heard that he'd told his daughters that if they got jobs, the money would have to go to the family—for groceries, bills, house repairs, stuff like that. Once the girls graduated and if they decided they wanted to keep going to school, it had to be at one of the nearby Alamo Colleges, close enough for them to commute from home.

The weight of Rafe's neediness was heavy enough to crush all four of the Torres sisters, but Ana, being the oldest in a motherless household, bore the brunt of it. She packed her father's lunches for him in the mornings, made sure his Negra Modelos were poured into frosted mugs when he got home, and went to neighbors' houses to try to smooth over bitter feelings after Rafe borrowed money he couldn't repay.

The women gathered in the Garcias' kitchen on the day of Ana's funeral shook their heads—pitiful, they said, patètico. Some said it wasn't his fault, the way he was.

"He was born out of God's favor," Kitty Bolander's mom claimed. "Anda mal. The clouds, they follow him. He walks outside, and it starts to hail."

Father Canty, who'd led Ana's graveside service, hadn't arrived yet, but three other priests from the local parish were there, pinching small paper plates in their large sausage fingers while shoveling down heaping forkfuls of Calvin's mom's famous King Ranch chicken.

The priests didn't notice us lurking nearby. We watched as they spilled sour cream down the front of their robes and dabbed at the little white blurs with their napkins. One of them burped and didn't even say excuse me. The things they were talking about to each other were like the things we heard people say in mobster movies. One said that Rafe was in a *bad spot* and that he owed someone named Edgar Rivera Lopez—we'd never heard of him—a *boatload* of money. The situation had gotten so bad that Rafe was living in a perpetual state of fear. He was *marked*.

Another priest said, "He will be forced to leave San Antonio and go back to Crystal City."

Another added, "He cannot hide forever."

For a moment, the priests were quiet. One of them put his empty plate on a side table and took a long drink from his plastic cup. Then he sighed. "Rafe is overwhelmed," he began, "and was never equipped to raise four daughters on his own. It doesn't help knowing now how rebellious Ana was. It's possible she was also a liar. It's all because she has no mother."

The first priest shook his head and muttered something we couldn't really hear, but by then we weren't listening. Our attention had shifted to Jessica, who'd suddenly and silently appeared in the doorway. From the expression on her face—blanched white with anger, a familiar sight—it was obvious she'd heard everything the priests had said. She opened her mouth to speak just as her dad came up from behind her and gently gripped her shoulder. Iridian and Rosa were behind him. He leaned down, said something into Jessica's ear, and started to steer her away. It was time to go. Jessica left with her words unspoken.

The gathering went on. There was still food to be eaten and rumors to be spread about Rafe's no-good luck and his problems with money and women and life in general, but, in other corners of the house, talk had shifted to the upcoming basketball season and concerns about the neighborhood: rising taxes, petty fines imposed for minor code violations, and families who'd lived in the same house for decades being bought out by developers. There were For Sale signs on almost every street now.

Father Canty finally arrived and joined the huddle of priests. They were on their third helping of King Ranch chicken when Jessica returned. She stormed in through the front door and then right past us, the massive folds of her blue dress swishing around her legs. She smelled like sweat and lawn clippings. She was sisterless, fatherless, alone.

She stopped in front of the group of priests, waiting for them to notice her. When they didn't, she reached out and tugged on the sleeve closest to her. It belonged to the one who had referred to Ana as "rebellious."

That priest turned, and the others did the same. Collectively, they wiped the corners of their mouths with their napkins and shifted their expressions to ones of well-practiced sympathy.

"You didn't know Ana!" Jessica shouted. She spun toward Father Canty. "You didn't know her, so don't talk about her like you did!"

If Father Canty was stunned by the confrontation, he didn't show it. Instead, he stepped forward and bent at the waist so that he was eye to eye with Jessica.

"My dear," he said tenderly, "I know this is a very difficult time for you, but you are a young woman, and as such, you have to consider that there are many things in life you do not yet understand."

Jessica lunged. With an open palm, she hit Father Canty in the face. Then she screamed and raked her nails across his cheek.

Hector's dad rushed forward. He pulled Jessica away, hoisting her into the air, where she continued to kick and thrash, her dark braid whipping around her head. Her dress rode high, exposing the length of her brown legs. Father Canty pressed a napkin against his face and seemed surprised to see, when he pulled it away, that the girl had managed to draw blood.

Jessica was almost through the door of the room when she threw out her hands, gripped the frame, and braced herself there.

"Don't tell me I don't understand!" she screamed. "Ana was not a liar! You're the liar, old man! You!"

Hector's dad was pulling hard, but Jessica wouldn't budge. She turned her head and spit in his eye. She tore the paint from the doorframe the same way she'd torn the skin from the priest's face. Finally, brave Mrs. Bolander went over and pried Jessica's fingers from the doorframe one by one.

"I hate you!" Jessica yelled, as Hector's dad tossed her over his shoulder like a bag of lawn fertilizer and carried her through the front door. "I hate you all!"

We watched through the window, mouths agape, as Jessica Torres was carried across the street to her house. The whole time, she kept kicking and screaming.

If anything, once outside, her screams got even louder.

Jessica
(Tuesday, June 11th)

JESSICA STOCKED BIRTHDAY cards, lip balm, bags of little chocolate bars, whole milk, skim milk, almond milk, soy milk. She worked the register for an hour, and people kept coming in, one right after another after another. She tried to guess what they would buy, and she was right about forty percent of the time. When it came time for her lunch break, Jessica sat in the back room, humming to herself, eating some nearly expired deli meat and cheese she'd bought from the refrigerated section and drinking a cherry Diet Coke. It was all very normal.

● ● ●

At six-thirty, half an hour after her shift had ended, Jessica was in the parking lot of the pharmacy, sweating through her clothes and staring at the engine of her car. The battery was dead. Her phone was buzzing nonstop in her back pocket. She didn't even need to look to know it was John. She'd told him earlier she'd swing by his place after work to pick him up, and now she was late.

"Oh, *come on!*" Jessica yelled.

"Need a jump?"

Jessica spun around, and there was Peter Rojas, backlit by the sun, looking like a saint holding a pair of jumper cables.

"Yes. A jump. Please. Thanks. We have those at the house, but I always forget to get them out of the garage."

"No problem," Peter replied.

Peter jogged over to his truck to pull it closer. He kept the engine running as he opened the hood and attached the cables, positive to positive and negative to negative. Jessica noticed a bead of sweat trickling down from Peter's hairline to the outside edge of his eyebrow, and she had the strange, sudden urge to swipe it off with her finger.

Once he was done, Peter straightened. He was so tall he blocked out the sun, and Jessica had to tilt her chin up to look him in the eye. For a while, Peter said nothing as he peered down at Jessica with that slightly perplexed expression people get when they're trying to figure out what to say or if they should say anything at all.

Jessica's phone buzzed again. Sweat was pooling at her lower back. She was ready to get this show on the fucking road.

"What?" she urged.

"Nothing."

"No, not nothing. What?"

Peter shifted his weight to lean against the front bumper. "Do you still sing?"

Jessica coughed, thrown by the question.

The answer was *no*, and Peter knew that. Jessica had stopped singing with the school choir the fall after Ana died. Peter had stayed on.

"Why would you ask me that?" she asked.

"It was just a question." Peter shrugged. "I heard you in the break room the other day singing along to some song. It reminded me of when we were in choir together."

"So you were spying on me?"

"We work together, Jessica," Peter replied, deadpan. "I was in the break room. You were in the break room."

"So, you were spying on me."

Jessica understood why everyone liked Peter. Really, she did. He was the epitome of a good egg—the kind of person who carried jumper cables in his truck and helped strangers and was patient with old people. Jessica was a terrible, terribly judgmental, rude and selfish person, and, because of that, Peter and Peter's kindness made her feel even worse about herself than she already did.

"You know what?" Peter said. "Forget it. Forget I said anything."

Jessica snorted. "Right."

Peter gestured to the battery. "You want to get in and give it a try?"

Jessica said nothing as she climbed into her car and twisted the key in the ignition. After a series of sputters, the engine finally caught. She sagged with relief as Peter unfastened the cables and slammed down her hood.

"Crisis averted." He swiped his brow with the back of his hand, leaving behind a smudge of grease. One of the old ladies in the store would spot it later and make a big production of wiping it away.

"Thanks," Jessica muttered through the window.

"You're welcome."

"See you later."

"Great."

"Great."

"Cool."

They were talking like robots now.

Jessica wished Peter would just walk away, but there he was, still with that slightly perplexed expression on his face. Surely he wasn't going to ask her more questions about singing. It was possible he was going to try again to ask some version of the very worst question of all—*How are you doing?*—and Jessica wasn't sure she'd be able to handle it.

"Is everything okay?" Peter asked.

"God, Peter. Everything's *fine.*"

By now another little line of sweat had tracked all the way down the side of Peter's face. A bead was hanging there, right at the edge of his jaw. Instead of reaching out and swiping it away like she still wanted to, Jessica began tapping her fingers against her steering wheel.

Peter looked down. The bead of sweat dropped from his jaw to the asphalt and then vanished.

"Okay, well." Jessica shifted her car into reverse. "Thanks again."

Even before she'd pulled all the way out of her parking space, Jessica's phone buzzed, immediately buzzed again, and then started buzzing nonstop. A call was coming in. She ignored it.

When she was about halfway to John's, Jessica pulled over but kept the car running on a side street. She tilted her head back against the seat and started to sing. Just to herself—along with nothing. She began softly, but then got louder and louder. The singing turned to shouting, and Jessica became vaguely aware of a woman walking her dog—one of those pequeño dogs, but neither a Yorkie nor a Chihuahua—who had slowed and kept glancing her direction.

Jessica's phone buzzed again and, finally, she grabbed it. Without even reading the message, she typed out a reply.

Sorry. On way. Manager made me stay late. xo

Jessica hesitated, trying to think of a better way to lie or not-quite lie. She couldn't come up with anything, so she just hit send. She pulled away from the curb, still belting out a song to no one but herself.

What a question: *Do you still sing?*

Peter would never know her secrets.

Rosa

(Tuesday, June 11th)

ROSA'S SEARCHING AT night hadn't yielded any results, so she thought the daytime might be better. It wasn't. She'd spent hours out in the heavy humidity and had found nothing. When she was on her way back, and just a block from her house, she stopped to watch two cardinals swoop through the branches of an oak tree in a neighbor's yard. The birds were spinning in circles, diving into each other, knocking leaves loose. They were a happy tangle of flapping and chirping. Eventually, one of them landed on a branch so thin that it couldn't support its light, hollow bones. The branch snapped. The bird fell. Rosa expected the cardinal to stop itself, do a graceful mid-air pivot, and resume playing with its bird-friend. Instead, it plummeted all the way to the ground and landed without a sound, in the grass. Rosa looked up the street and then down to see if anyone else had noticed, but aside from Teddy Arenas checking his mailbox a few houses away, she was alone. The other cardinal, on a high branch above, waited for a moment, let out a couple of mournful chirps, and flew away. On the ground, a red wing fanned above the blades of grass, motionless.

She'd never seen anything like that before.

Iridian
(Tuesday, June 11th)

IRIDIAN WAS STARING at herself in the mirror. The midday light was good. She was tilting her head—left, right, up, down—to catch the shadows, and putting her fingers on her skin to mash it around. When Iridian was younger, she'd stick Scotch tape all over her face to pull the corners of her lips up or down or to try to flatten out her sharp nose.

She was practicing at becoming invincible. Every day, she'd stand in front of her bathroom mirror and come up with insults to hurl at her reflection. She practiced keeping her expression blank and worked at dodging and deflecting.

"Beakish," she said to herself. "You look like a fucking bird."

It had taken a long time and a lot of practice, but Iridian had gotten pretty close to convincing herself that her face—with eyes set too wide like a lizard's, a nose like . . . well, like a beak, and lips so thin that when she puckered they looked like a wadded-up gum wrapper— had *character*. Most of the books she read had girls in them who weren't beautiful, but whose faces had *character*. This just meant that the things that made them *them* were on the inside. In those stories, it may take a while, but eventually a person would come around who admired those girls for their giant hearts or their razor wit or their unbendable will.

Iridian was leaning forward, her nose practically grazing the mirror, when a thump on the wall behind her caused her to jolt.

"Rosa?" Iridian called.

Her sister didn't respond, so Iridian stuck her head out into the hall. The door to their bedroom was slightly open. There were no lights on, but the sun was shining in through a gap in the curtains. Maybe it was nothing. Maybe there was a squirrel in the attic.

Iridian went downstairs. She sat on the counter and ate cereal for the second time that day. After she was done eating, she rinsed her bowl, went back to her room, and brought one of her notebooks from her hidden stacks into her bed. She picked up a pen and opened to a page in the middle. She'd been making progress on her witch-vampire love story. The plot wasn't really there yet, but she'd been brainstorming some good scenes.

I want him, Iridian wrote. *But above all, I want him to want me. I want him to want me so badly that he'll bury his teeth into the flesh of my arm and tear off a piece of it.*

I like to watch his hands and the way he grips his pen when he scribbles a note to himself, or how, when he sleeps, his fingers still seem to move, knowingly, tapping lightly across the covers. I reach out with my own hand, mimicking the movements across his skin, and he twitches. Sometimes he startles awake.

I want to float into him, for him to absorb me, for him to eat me up.

Iridian wrote and wrote and wrote.

After a while, she heard the sound of her sister's light footsteps coming up the stairs. She looked up to see Rosa standing at the door.

"What's up?" Iridian asked.

"Dad's home."

It was the second time in two days he was home when he shouldn't have been.

"Okay."

"He doesn't look good."

Iridian paused. "And?"

Rosa didn't reply.

"Where's Jessica?" Iridian asked.

This was what *she* did: dealt with Dad.

"Still at work, I think."

Iridian made a big show of throwing down her notebook before following her sister downstairs.

Rafe was on the couch in the living room, bent over and gripping the sides of his head. Rosa was right: He didn't look good. He was grimacing, pressing his fingers against his temples so hard that the tips were going white.

"He's drunk," Iridian said to her sister.

Rosa gave her head a shake. "I don't think so."

Iridian knelt down in front of her dad. He didn't smell drunk, but he sure looked it. He was still folded in half, so Iridian pushed him up to where he was sitting semistraight. His hands fell limply into his lap, and Iridian's gaze fell to his wrist, around which was a piece of yellow string. Three beads were threaded on it: a white one, a blue one, and a black one. Even though Iridian hadn't seen that bracelet in probably ten years, she recognized it immediately. Ana had made it one day in elementary school, during art class. God only knows where Rafe had found it—probably shoved in the back of a kitchen drawer. Iridian made a noise—sort of like a cluck or a gurgle—and had to look away. She felt sick, actually nauseated, by the sight of a little girl's bracelet on a grown man's wrist.

Rafe coughed a couple of times. He didn't cover his mouth. Usually when he was drunk his face would turn punch red, but this was different. His skin was pale, mottled like a TV-show corpse. He coughed again, then wheezed. He unzipped his jacket partway, revealing the white V-neck shirt beneath. His chest heaved as he struggled to get breath down into his lungs.

"Are you okay?" Iridian asked. "You don't look so great, Dad."

"Too warm," Rafe said.

The AC was blasting, and the ceiling fan was directly overhead, whipping around at what seemed to be a dangerously high speed.

Rafe turned his head and mumbled something to his youngest daughter. Rosa left the room and went into the kitchen, where Iridian could hear the creak of a cabinet door opening, followed by the whoosh of water running from the tap.

"Hey." Iridian poked her dad in the shoulder. "If you're sick I can call Jessica and have her bring something home from the pharmacy, yeah?"

Rosa returned and placed a glass of ice water in her dad's hand. None of the family's glasses were part of a matching set, and some were so old they used to belong to the girls' grandparents. This one once had white-and-yellow flowers painted on it, but by now all the flowers had practically smudged off from years of use.

Rafe took a shaky sip of water, then cleared his throat to get Iridian's attention. When their eyes met, Iridian braced herself for her dad to tell her she was like a disease, or something else equally awful.

He croaked out, "Ana," and then erupted into a coughing fit. Rosa snatched the glass away so that he wouldn't spill and placed it on the coffee table.

Ana. Ana, Ana, Ana.

"Dad, I know—" Iridian started.

"Iridian," Rafe said, interrupting. "I can't breathe . . . my head."

Iridian sighed. Which was it? His lungs or his head?

"We'll call Jessica," Rosa offered. "She can come home and take you to one of those twenty-four-hour clinics."

"I don't need a clinic. No doctors." Rafe groaned and pushed himself to standing. He was up, but wobbly. He placed his hand on the back of the couch. There it was again: that little string bracelet.

A series of soft sounds—a click, a plunk, and a thunk—caused Iridian to turn. The glass Rosa had just placed on the table had tipped, spilling water and ice across the wood surface and down onto the carpet.

"I must've bumped it," Rosa said, rushing to the kitchen for paper towels.

Rafe hobbled into his room and closed the door. Iridian was still on the floor in the living room, sitting on her heels. By then, both of her feet were asleep. Her thoughts went to her closet, to her books, then to her bed, and to her notebook. All she wanted was to spend the rest of this day with those pages.

"I'm going back upstairs," Iridian called out to Rosa. "If he does this again, don't come get me."

Jessica
(early Wednesday, June 12th)

STONES PLUNKED AGAINST Jessica's window. At first, she had one of those moments when dream and reality merge: She was at the pharmacy, opening boxes in the stockroom. Peter Rojas was there with her, and he kept picking up and dropping the same heavy box on the concrete floor over and over again.

Then Jessica was awake, but not all the way. She vaguely realized she was in her bed with the covers pulled up over her head. Her breath caught, and her eyes flew open. She tossed off her comforter, hurled herself across the room, and pulled back the curtains. John was there with his arm cocked back like a baseball pitcher. He grinned as he let a stone fly at Jessica's window. Behind him, idling at the curb, was Jenny Sanchez's Buick.

Jessica hadn't gotten much sleep in the last few days, so she wasn't in the mood for whatever this was. She knew, however, that she couldn't just leave John out there. She held up a hand, telling him to wait, and after wrestling on some clothes—cutoffs, a T-shirt, flip-flops—she crept downstairs.

"What are you doing here?" Jessica whispered to John once she was out in the yard. "What happened to your phone?"

"Dead," John replied. "Come on."

John led Jessica to the car and held the door open. Jessica slid into the back seat, bracing herself for the reek of stale cigarette smoke. John climbed in next to her. Jenny's Buick was a hand-me-down of a hand-me-down. It used to belong to Jenny's brother, and before that, to Jenny's uncle. Its color was a nearly iridescent pale sky blue, and what was left of the original interior—what wasn't patched up with black electrical tape—was royal blue leather. It reminded Jessica of a big metal blue jay.

"Hi, Jenny," Jessica said.

"Hey, girl." Jenny flicked the ash of her cigarette out her open window and reached up to the steering column to shift the car into drive.

John threw his arm around Jessica's shoulders.

"Seriously," Jessica urged. "What are you doing here?"

"C'mon, Jess." John brought her into an embrace that was just a little too tight. "Where's your sense of adventure?"

Jenny drove north, into the heart of downtown San Antonio, and then parked her car on an empty side street. From there, John led Jessica across a large, empty square toward the Cathedral of San Fernando. This was Rosa's church, and the family's church back when they pretended to be Catholics. It wasn't just a church, though. It was more like a monument, an architectural marvel, a mammoth thing built hundreds of years ago with towers and arches and spires and bells that rang to mark the hours.

As Jessica neared this church-monument, she could hear whispers and hushed laughter, but she couldn't yet see who was there. She could only make out dark, body-shaped clouds and phone screens and the glowing tips of cigarettes.

"Hey," Jenny called out. "Sorry we're late."

Heads turned. People said hey back. At this point Jessica could see that the group was made up of people from school or friends of friends, maybe a dozen total, including, of all people, Peter Rojas.

Peter was standing on the fringes, next to Calvin, another one of the boys who was always at Hector's house.

It was weird to see Peter there, out of his element, wearing normal clothes—army green shorts that came just past his knees and a white T-shirt—and without a name tag pinned to his chest. His shoes were the same, though: off-white canvas sneakers, not that Jessica would admit to noticing. Their eyes met, and Peter gave Jessica a small nod before looking away.

"So what's going on?" John asked.

"Okay," Jenny said, pausing to light another cigarette. "We're playing sardines in the church. Someone hides, like in hide-and-seek. The rest of us wait out here for five minutes, then go in. When you find the person who's hiding, you hide with them. The point is for the group of hiders to get bigger and bigger until there's just one person left running around the church wondering where the hell everyone is. So." Jenny looked around, took a drag from her cigarette, and exhaled a puff of smoke into the dark night. "Who's hiding first?"

"Me," Jessica said. "I'll go."

John cocked his head. "Really?"

"Really." Jessica smiled. "Here's my sense of adventure."

"Okay," Jenny said. "Good luck. You have five minutes."

Jessica skipped quickly up the stone steps that led to the entrance of the church and kicked off her flip-flops so they wouldn't suck and slap against the tile. It took both of her hands to open the giant wooden door and shut it behind her, and once inside, she waited for her eyes to adjust to the darkness. Directly in front of her was the font of holy water, and beyond that were the doors that led to the cathedral proper. On either side of her were more closed doors that led to hallways, offices, more rooms—all good places to hide, for sure. The cathedral, though— that's where Jessica wanted to go.

It was dark there, except over to her left where the red glass candles glowed in staggered rows. Jessica remembered the church smelling like blown-out matches and incense, but that night it didn't smell like that. If anything, it smelled like Rosa: clean, comforting, and faintly like dust. Jessica padded down the center aisle, the tile ice cold under her bare feet, and turned down one of the rows.

She could've sat or reclined on the pew, but instead she shimmied beneath it so that she was flat on the floor. The wood of the bench was inches from her face, and just above the tip of her nose was a gray, penny-sized circle of chewed and flattened gum. She took a big breath in and then out and then waited.

It seemed like longer than five minutes before the front doors of the church opened. There were whispers, followed by a bright, loud laugh. Jessica heard everyone go off in different directions, some into the hallways that extended off that front room, others up stairs. The cathedral doors creaked open. Someone was heading over to the side, in the direction of the confession booth. At least a couple of people were coming down the center aisle. Eventually, Jessica saw a pair of beat-up black Adidas coming her way. They were John's. She pushed back deeper under the pew, causing it to squeak. John stopped. He shuffled his feet and turned in a circle. He didn't see Jessica, didn't realize she was there. She could've reached out and touched him. She could've scraped her nail against his rubber sole. If she'd had a pin, she could've pricked the skin of his ankle with it.

"Jess," John hissed, not down to where she was, but out to the whole room. "Jess, babe. Where are you?"

Jessica covered her mouth with her hand. How funny that John thought she would respond to him. He *actually* thought that she wanted him to find her, just like he thought she wanted him to wake her up in the middle of the night and force her out of bed, but he didn't know how thrilled she was to be left alone in the cold dark. Now that she had that thrill, she wanted to hold on to it, coat it in sugar and chew on it.

John whispered a curse and then took off down the row toward the center aisle. Back at the door, he stopped and called out again. Jessica didn't respond. She still had her hand over her mouth. Eventually, the doors opened, John's footsteps faded, and the cathedral was quiet. Jessica exhaled and laughed to herself.

The quiet didn't last very long. Little by little, the cathedral filled back up with sound. Pipes started to bang.

The floorboards up in the organist's loft creaked as if someone was slowly pacing back and forth across them. Voices rose up from other sections of the church, the sound seeping through the cracks of the stone. There were echoes and the click-clack of shoes against tile.

Jessica could explain away the creepy sounds. The banging noises could be from an old boiler. The groans could be from the centuries-old foundation continuing to settle. That or rats. What sounded like ghosts talking to each other was most likely wind or the voices of Jessica's not-really friends being carried through the pipes.

Jessica had never been afraid of the dark, or silence, or weird night sounds, but back when Ana was alive, she'd pretend to be afraid of thunder just so she could pad down the hall to her big sister's room. Ana had this habit of going to bed early, like at nine at night, but then she'd wake up a couple hours later and stay up until three or four in the morning. She once told Jessica she liked feeling that she had not just the whole house but the whole neighborhood to herself.

When Jessica had gone to Ana's room during thunderstorms, Ana would usually be awake, wearing just her white underwear and a ratty old shirt. She'd be on her phone or painting her nails, sometimes both. She'd glance up from whatever it was she was doing, and even if Jessica was interrupting, she wouldn't act put out. She'd ask if Jessica was scared because of the thunder and if she wanted to hang out for a little while. Jessica would nod. Her little girl's heart would be beating so, so fast.

Usually, Jessica would pretend to fall asleep on Ana's floor, just so she could stay in the room longer and listen to her sister do all the things she did. Ana would experiment with eyeliner, put on face masks, and flip through weeks-old magazines. Sometimes she'd go into the bathroom, open the window, and turn on the vent. Jessica would open her eyes just enough to watch her sister pull out a cigarette and a matchbox from behind a stack of mismatched towels in the cabinet. Ana would sit there on the edge of the sink, wearing hardly anything, staring into the night, blowing clouds of smoke out the window. The girls' grandpa smoked, and the bitter smell always lingered on his breath, his hair, his hands, his clothes. Ana, though, always somehow smelled like her perfume, like linen.

John shouted Jessica's name. He was far away now. Jessica could hear some of the other people, too, shouting and laughing up in the choir loft. Someone screamed, scared by something or nothing. Someone else laughed. John shouted Jessica's name *again*. Then he barked it out, like he was angry, like he was through, like he didn't want to play this stupid game anymore.

Jessica's phone buzzed. She reached in her pocket to turn it off completely, and then continued to lie there, barefoot and with her ankles crossed. She interlaced her fingers on top of her stomach, listening.

She'd nearly fallen asleep when she heard the door to the cathedral open and footsteps come up the aisle. When she opened her eyes, she saw Peter Rojas's scuffed-up off-white sneakers approach and then come to a stop. Then Peter sat on the pew, right above Jessica.

"What are you doing?" Jessica whispered.

"I found you," Peter said. "I'm supposed to hide with you."

"Shouldn't you be at work?"

"I called in sick tonight."

Jessica clucked, mildly impressed that Peter had it in him to lie about anything. "You called in sick for *this?*"

Peter didn't reply, just shifted in his seat. Jessica waited. Peter didn't move.

"Go away," Jessica said. "Please."

"I don't think that's how this game works."

Jessica returned her gaze to the coin-sized wad of gum above her face, and when it was clear that Peter really wasn't leaving, she sighed.

"So," she asked. "Do you still sing?"

"No." Peter laughed. It sounded nice, had rhythm, like a stone skipping across water. "Not really."

"Why not?" Jessica asked. She couldn't help herself. "You used to be really good at it."

She was teasing, but she wasn't lying. Peter had been in the show choir, a group that went to nursing homes and

Jewish community centers to sing pop standards and show tunes for old people. Jessica knew that Peter's friends gave him unending amounts of shit for it, but he never seemed to care.

"That's kind of a long story," Peter replied.

The wooden pew squeaked as Peter again shifted his weight, and if she'd been a kind person, or even a normal person, she would've asked to hear the long story. It's not as if, in that moment, either of them had anything else to do, and Jessica found herself genuinely curious. If someone had enough musical talent to make people listen and clap along, what would it take to stop? That was a good question, but it never made it even close to the tip of her tongue. The question buried itself deeper and deeper inside her, the words more and more unsaid and unshared. Seconds ticked by, and pipes continued to bang somewhere in the depths of the church. The silence stretched out, but it wasn't awkward because Jessica didn't believe that any silence was awkward.

However many minutes later, the cathedral doors opened.

"Game's over," Peter said quietly.

Voices exploded into the cathedral, ricocheting off the stone, so loud and wrong-sounding that Jessica winced. She scooted out from under the pew but stayed sitting on the tile floor.

"Holy fuck!" Jenny cried out when she saw Jessica. "There you are. We were seriously about to leave without you."

Everyone was there, including John. Jessica gave him a bland smile.

Peter stood. "I just found her. Just like, a minute ago."

"Well, good." Jenny threw up her hands. "Game over. Let's get the hell out of here."

John asked Jenny to wait while he walked Jessica to her door. During the ride back, John had said nothing about how Jessica had ignored him in the church when his feet had been inches from her face. Instead, he'd just sat in the back seat of the Buick, with his arm slung across Jessica's shoulders, and shot the shit with Jenny. Was her brother still dating that girl? Did he like his new job? That's cool. That's cool.

It wasn't until Jessica was reaching for her keys that John finally spoke.

"Were you thanking Peter Rojas for saving you the other day?"

Jessica froze, her fingers grazing the door knob. "I . . . What?"

"Do you think I'm stupid?" John leaned in. Jessica felt the heat of his breath, oily and unwanted. "Did you think I wouldn't find out about that?"

"There's nothing to find out about," Jessica replied. "My car needed a jump, and he helped me out."

"You should've told me."

Jessica was all of a sudden very, very tired. It was late, and she thought that maybe the lack of sleep was making her hallucinate. There were fireflies in the yard. They flashed and dimmed, flashed and dimmed—in a rhythm, in time with one another. Like a song.

"You shouldn't hide things from me," John added.

Jessica was so worn out she thought maybe John was right. She could stand to be more open. It would hurt: to crack open her chest and pour out what little was there. But she was feeling bold, deliriously optimistic.

Jessica spun around. "Have you ever heard me sing?"

She went on before John could interrupt: "Before my sister died, I used to sing. I was in choir and pageants and stuff. I was really good. My teachers would tell me I was a natural."

Jessica mustered a smile, and in that bizarre, hopeful moment, she believed in the impossible. John had never heard her sing, not really. The only times he would've had the chance were in the car, along with the radio, or if she was listening to something on her headphones and thought she was alone.

John had glitter-gold eyes. He was beautiful when he wanted to be. A couple of nights ago, she'd asked him to fly away with her. It wasn't too, too hard to imagine them together in their little studio apartment. They wouldn't have furniture, but they would have each other. He would listen to her sing.

John said nothing, and Jessica realized he didn't know how to answer. She'd made a mistake. She'd wanted to give him a sliver of something rare and good about herself, and, instead, she'd backed him into a corner. She wanted her rare goodness to be a gift, but her timing was all fucked up.

Jessica knew her timing was all fucked up because John finally replied by asking, "Are you making fun of me?"

"What?" Jessica balked. "No. *No.*"

"John!" Jenny called out from the idling Buick. "John. Let's go!"

John held up his hand, silently commanding Jenny to wait. His gaze remained pinned on Jessica.

"Did you think I wouldn't find out about what happened with the car?" he asked, steering the conversation back. "With Peter?"

"Nothing *happened* with Peter," Jessica insisted. "You know I wouldn't do that to you. My battery was dead, and I needed help."

Help. The word tasted like shame, bitter like ash ground between her molars. She looked across the street at Hector's. Peter's truck wasn't there. There were no lights in the upstairs window. In her yard, the fireflies had stopped flashing.

John reached out and grabbed Jessica's wrist. He knew how to do it so it looked like a gesture of affection. He pressed his long fingers into her pulse point, then past it to where the tendons scraped against the bone.

Jessica winced, grinding her teeth. She didn't want to give in. She didn't need to apologize for this. She hadn't done anything wrong.

John pressed harder.

"I'm sorry," Jessica gasped. "I didn't tell you because I knew you'd be mad. It was a mistake. I'm sorry." She glanced over her shoulder toward the Buick, but Jenny was looking down, focused on her phone. Then she glanced to the house, to her upstairs window. Something—a fuzzy flicker of darkness behind the curtain—had caught her eye. It was barely there, then gone.

"Please," Jessica said. "I'm sorry, and I'm very tired."

John released his fingers, and then brought Jessica's wrist up to his lips. This was what mothers did: kiss away the hurt. He was disgusting. Jessica was ashamed that she'd ever wanted to give anything of herself to him. Her nails were so close to his face. She could tear across his skin, into his eye.

"I'll see you tomorrow."

John made his way across the yard and climbed into Jenny's car. Jessica could still feel the slickness of his saliva on her wrist. It felt like a violation, like she could wash and wash and the spit would always be there.

• • •

Minutes later, Jessica was standing in the rising steam of her shower, letting the water run through her hair. Out of the corner of her eye, she saw a shadow pass on the other side of the clear plastic curtain. Assuming it was just Iridian coming in to borrow a shirt or something, Jessica closed her eyes and dipped her head back. She liked to run the water as hot as possible for as long as she could, liked the challenge of standing beneath it until the feeling on her skin went from scalding to soothing. She'd started humming another old song from the pharmacy's playlist when she got the sense that something was . . . off. Her voice wasn't echoing in the same way. It felt like the space—the shower, the entire bathroom—had gotten smaller.

Jessica opened her eyes, and there, in front of her face, through the veil of steam and on the other side of the curtain, was a hand. Its dark palm was facing her. Its fingers were spread. The hand was so clear, Jessica could see the blurry swoop of a lifeline and the horizontal slashes on skin that marked the division between each individual finger bone. The hand pressed inward against the plastic, stretching it tight. Jessica jolted back, nearly losing her balance against the slick surface of the tub. She caught herself by smacking a wet hand against the tile. Then she did the only thing she could think to do: She stared straight at the hand and pushed her own hand against it. It was solid and fleshy. Jessica let out a garbled cry, then ripped back the shower curtain. There was no one. Nothing there.

Dripping wet and gulping down desperate breaths, Jessica grabbed a towel, ran into her bedroom, and then dashed down the hall to her sisters' room. Iridian was asleep in her bed. Jessica started to call out Rosa's name, but then clapped a hand over her mouth and collapsed back against the wall.

"Shit," she mumbled. "Holy *shit*."

She gripped the towel tighter around her chest.

"You're fine," she told herself. "Everything's fine."

Jessica found her balance on two shaky legs and went back into her bedroom, leaving behind her a trail of wet footprints. In the bathroom, she turned off the water in the shower, dried herself off completely, changed into a fresh pair of underwear and a shirt to sleep in, and started brushing out her long hair. It was all normal. Totally normal. The bristles of her brush caught on a knot. Jessica yanked and yanked, bringing tears to her eyes and snapping the strands from her scalp. She tried humming to herself again, but it was nothing, just a bunch of nonsense notes.

"You're fine," she told her reflection. "Everything's fine."

She braved a look back at the shower curtain, and saw, there in the condensation, the outline of a hand, perfectly centered, with beads of moisture dripping from its edges.

She dove toward the toilet and threw up.

Rosa

(Wednesday, June 12th)

ON WEDNESDAY MORNING, Rosa decided to search for the hyena in shifts. She left the house early and was heading back in the middle of the day to use the bathroom and refill her thermos when she felt the shift in the wind.

The day had been bright and hot and humid, but then, all of a sudden, it wasn't. The entire eastern sky was dark, the color of pigeon feathers. That dark sky pushed a wall of cool wind right into Rosa, blowing back her unbound hair and the fabric of her long dress, blowing back the leaves on the trees. Rain was coming.

Rosa took off into a jog, ignoring how the jolting movement caused the stiff leather of her shoes to scrape against her heels. The thermos in her backpack bounced hard against her spine. The pigeon-colored sky was now all around. The wind was blowing so hard that loose leaves and bits of trash were tumbling down the street. A cup from a fast-food restaurant skittered and spun on the asphalt. The dogs in the neighborhood—both inside houses and out in yards—took up yipping and howling. The rain started to fall, leaving circles the size of checkers on the concrete sidewalk. The drops were so big, they felt like pennies when they hit the top of Rosa's head.

When Rosa rounded the corner, she saw Jessica's car a little ways down, parked in front of their house. Wednesdays were her days off from the pharmacy. Despite the rain, Jessica's arm was hanging out her driver's-side window, and her middle finger was tapping against the door.

Rosa got closer, approaching the car from the back. There was a jolt of movement, and it took her a split second to process what she'd seen: John had reached over and taken hold of Jessica by the neck. Jessica's hand, the one that was extended out the window, tensed and then smacked the outside of her car door. Jessica's head jerked to the side, like she was trying to pull it away.

Rosa gasped, froze briefly, and then started running. When she reached the car, she could see John gripping Jessica's chin. Her sister's neck looked painfully twisted, and she shouted something—*stop* or *off*—at which point Rosa whacked her palm against the closed passenger-side window. John immediately released Jessica and spun around.

"What's going on?" Rosa demanded through the glass.

"Nothing." John's voice was muffled. "We were just talking."

"Yeah." Rosa glanced at her sister, who was staring straight through the windshield, her jaw clenched. "Looks like it."

John opened his door so quickly that Rosa nearly tripped over her own feet as she backed away.

"I'm walking home," he said. "See you later, Jess. Later, Rosa."

Neither sister responded. Rosa watched John make his way down the sidewalk, slouched forward against the rain and with his hands in his pockets. She looked at the street, then over to Hector's house. The front door was open, and just the storm door was closed. A single lamp was glowing in the depths of the darkened living room. She looked up to the second-floor window and what she knew was Hector Garcia's room. A light was on in there, too. A shadow passed behind the curtain. Hector and his friends were there, watching. They thought they were protectors, which was a silly thing all boys thought.

Jessica kept sitting in her car, staring through the rain-blurred windshield. Only after John had turned down a side street a block away did she finally get out and head toward the house. She passed right by Rosa as if she wasn't there.

"I don't like him," Rosa called after her. "Has he done this before? Why haven't you told any—"

"Don't start," Jessica snapped. "He's just in a bad mood."

"He's *always* in a bad mood, Jessie."

They stopped together at the front door, under the shelter of the awning. Rosa could see the pink marks on Jessica's skin from where John's fingertips had dug in. This wasn't the first time Rosa had told her sister how she felt about John, and it wasn't the first time Jessica had gotten defensive about it. If Rosa pushed, Jessica would tell her that she had *no idea* what it was like to be in a relationship, that Rosa shouldn't *dare* act like she knew what went on between a girl and a guy in love because Rosa hadn't even been kissed yet or had anyone touch her. That last part, about the kissing and the touching, wasn't true, but Rosa never said anything about it. She had the right to her own secrets.

Still, though. This was different. Rosa had always known that John was mean and that Jessica always jumped when he said jump, but this was the first time she'd seen evidence of him touching her sister in an aggressive way. Had there been signs? Had she missed them?

"Don't tell Dad," Jessica said, as she unlocked the front door.

"Alright." Rosa's heart broke a little. "Of course. If that's what you want."

"I've been telling him I want to leave," Jessica said. "That's why he's in a bad mood."

"Leave *him*?" Rosa asked, startled. "Like, break up with him?"

"No." Jessica paused. "Like, leave San Antonio."

"Oh." Rosa shook a drop of rain from the tip of her nose. "Where would you go?"

Jessica shrugged. She looked tired. Her mascara was flaking off. There were little specks of black around her eyes, and her lipstick was smudged. There was a blur of dark red on her jaw, from where John had pulled the color away from her mouth.

"Austin, maybe? Maybe the Valley to stay with Aunt Francine. Anywhere but here. I asked him to come with me, but he doesn't want to."

"You should go by yourself," Rosa told Jessica. "If that's what you want to do."

"It's not that easy." Jessica pulled her key from the door and faltered, like that little flick of her wrist had exhausted her completely. "You wouldn't understand."

Jessica turned, and Rosa wondered if her sister's weary appearance was due to something more than what had just happened with John. It seemed like an older weariness, like one that had tidily tucked itself inside her. Rosa didn't ask *Are you okay?* or *Did something happen?* because it was clear that something *had* happened and Jessica was *not* okay.

"Do you think . . . ?" Jessica crinkled her nose, like she did when she was uncomfortable but didn't want anyone to know she was uncomfortable. "Do you think there's something wrong with the house?"

Rosa didn't know how to respond. All sorts of things were wrong with the house. Pick a room, pick a cabinet in a room. Open the door, and there were reminders of dead women. Look at the floor, look at the wall. There were scuffs and scratches of lives lived. Was it possible for a house to be abandoned and still have four people living in it?

"What do you mean?" Rosa asked.

Jessica's teeth dragged across her bottom lip, pulling the color off even more. There *was* something wrong, something really wrong.

"Nothing," Jessica replied. She opened the door. "Forget I said anything."

Rosa knew it was a lie, but what could she do? It was impossible to force the rain to stop falling. It was just as impossible to force the truth out of her sister when she was determined to keep it locked up tight.

Rosa was a searcher, though. She was determined and had ways of finding things.

Iridian
(Wednesday, June 12th)

IRIDIAN'S NOTEBOOK WAS down at her feet, open and with the pages spread wide. She must've kicked it there while she'd been napping. She fumbled in her blankets, trying to find her pen, but it wouldn't have been the first time one of them had been lost for days in the folds of fabric or wedged tight in the space between her bed and the wall.

It was raining outside, pretty hard from the sound of it. Iridian could hear the whoosh of wind and the drums of drops against the windows and the roof. It wasn't night, just the middle of the afternoon according to the clock on her nightstand, but her entire room was in shades of gray. It was dreary and wonderful. She would've stayed in bed for hours more if she hadn't needed a glass of water.

Iridian stepped into the hall and then stopped. The hall, the house—everything—smelled like oranges. The air conditioner clicked on and blew out orange-scented air. She closed her eyes and could picture herself back at Francine's place in South Texas, out in the dry air and the orange trees. She took another step and yelped as the bare sole of her right foot landed on something hard and thin. She looked down, and there it was: her pen. It must've gotten caught up in her waistband and then fallen out as she walked from her room. As she bent to pick it up, a mark on the wall—scrawled there in blue ink on the white paint, just an inch or so from the baseboard—caught her eye. It started off as a series of broken lines—light tick marks— but then those marks started to merge with curves and loops. The loops turned into letters. The letters formed words. The ink became darker, the lines thicker, as if the hand holding the pen had become more sure of itself.

I want him   I want him to want me

A hard breath burst from Iridian's lungs.

"Ana," she whispered.

Those words were Iridian's words—from the story she'd just been working on. The writing, though— especially the letter *a*'s, handwritten in the typed-out style, with the little umbrella-curl on top—was Ana's, without a doubt.

Iridian didn't know how long she waited for her sisters to come home—minutes? an hour? She also didn't really remember going downstairs. Mostly she remembered sitting on the couch, her spine too straight, and being haunted by the smell of oranges—so strong it was making her sick.

When her sisters did come home, Rosa rushed to Iridian's side. The fabric of her dress was soggy from the rain, and Iridian gripped it tight, squeezing out water. Jessica stood by the end of the couch. Her hair was in a ponytail, but it didn't look right. It was lopsided, puffed, like she'd been running through the woods and branches had snagged her long locks. A dark splotch the size and shape of a peanut shell stood out on her cheek.

"My words," Iridian told her sisters. "Ana's writing. Upstairs."

"I'll go look," Rosa said.

While Rosa was upstairs, Jessica just stood there, doing nothing and saying nothing. Iridian gazed at the blank television screen. She tried to swallow, but it felt like her tongue was a wad of cotton.

"I saw her hand," Jessica eventually said.

"It smells like oranges," Iridian said. "Do you smell it?"

There was a pause. "No," Jessica replied.

"Why is she doing this?" Iridian asked.

Jessica didn't respond.

After a while, Rosa came back downstairs.

"I taped up a piece of paper," she said. "You can't see it anymore."

That was a fine fix, but Iridian knew it would be a long time before she went upstairs again. She was under attack, and the only thing she knew to do was hide.

The First Time Ana Torres
Came Back as a Ghost

SOME NIGHTS, BEFORE Ana would undress at her bedroom window, she'd go out into the street. Wearing white Keds, a long T-shirt, and short shorts, Ana would march under the light of the street lamps. She was practicing to be a majorette, which was something we'd heard her mom had done back when she was in high school.

We'd watch Ana hurl a silver baton into the dark sky, and then spin around with her gaze up. Over and over. Ana could spin. She had that down. She could march. She could toss her baton so high it nearly grazed the telephone wires, but the problem was, she could hardly ever catch it once it came back down. Something about her aim was bad. Her fingers always grasped but never caught. The baton would ricochet off her hand, bounce against the asphalt, and skitter away. Ana never gave up, though. Again and again, she'd snatch up the baton and head right back into the middle of the street. Once there, she'd tick up her chin, press one fist against her waist, cock out her elbow, and prepare to lead the vast, invisible band behind her.

We were the first people to witness Ana come back as a ghost, and we considered ourselves lucky. She died in June, and we saw her again in August. It happened at night, when hauntings typically happen. We were in Hector's room. It was late, way past midnight, when we heard thumps at the window—not like rocks being thrown because that sounds like *ping, ping*—but actual *thumps*, like the soft knocking a knuckle makes on wood. This was particularly weird because Hector's bedroom was upstairs.

Calvin was closest to the window. He crawled up on his hands and knees and slowly pulled the curtains back. There was no one on the other side, of course, just the night sky and the light coming in from the street lamps. He looked over his shoulder and laughed.

"You're all such pussies," he said.

Just as he was about to release the curtain, Calvin turned back to the window, this time looking out and down, toward the street. His expression spun from humor to horror, and for a moment he was frozen. He made a choking sound and then fell backward.

Jimmy vaulted over Calvin to get to the window. He yanked the curtain back and also froze, just for a second, but then his face broke out into a smile. His eyes grew wide; they started to glisten. He reached out and put his palm on the glass pane, gently.

Deep down, we all knew the one thing—the one *person*—that could make Jimmy's face light up with that amount of joy and awe. We flew from our scattered places around the room, pulled a pale and still-stammering Calvin up from the floor, and huddled behind Jimmy. We looked out the window and down.

It was Ana. Of course it was Ana.

All things appear ghostly under the weak light of street lamps, and so that was how Ana appeared. We knew it was her because she was standing with her back to us. How many times had we seen that back, the swoops of those shoulders and hips? Even though the ghost of Ana Torres was wearing an oversized white T-shirt that came down to mid-thigh, we knew that body beneath. It was seared into our minds. Ana wasn't in her room, though, and she wasn't undressing. She wasn't in the street with her baton, either. Instead, she was in her front yard. Her pose, in a way, mirrored Jimmy's. She was facing the window of her dad's first-floor bedroom, with her hand up, but instead of pressing her palm flat to the glass, she was knocking against it with her knuckle.

The ghost of Ana Torres continued her steady knocking, and up in Hector's room, we could hardly breathe.

Eventually, the porch light at the Torres house flicked on. Ana's ghost turned its head slowly toward it. The front door opened, then the screen door, and then out came Rafe. We pushed back from the window and closed the curtain, leaving just an inch-wide gap for us all to peer through.

"Who's that?" Rafe shouted into the night. He was shirtless, wearing baggy jean shorts and holding a baseball bat. He took a couple of steps out into the yard, heading in the direction of the window.

Ana, though, was gone. We don't know how it happened. We never saw her fade out, evaporate, twitch like static and then disappear. She was just . . . gone. There, then not.

We watched Rafe stalk around the yard for a bit, calling out, making threats into the quiet night while smacking the bat into his open palm. He finally went inside, but the porch light stayed on. We drew back the curtains again and waited, staying up until dawn, hoping beyond hope that Ana would come back, but she never did.

It was Hector who finally broke the silence: "So what do we do now?"

Watching Ana undress and watching Ana twirl her

baton were our secrets to keep. But this—this felt too big and too *not ours* not to share with the Torres girls.

"We should leave Rosa a note," Jimmy said. "In her tree."

So that's what we did.

Several years ago, Rafe had tied a thick rope to one of the larger branches of the old oak tree in the front yard, and then fixed a knot at the bottom of the rope to serve as a foothold. It was a swing. Rosa was the only one who ever used it. She'd be out there for hours, pumping her knees to take herself higher. She'd cry out with joy, content with entertaining herself.

There was also a hollow in that tree. It faced away from the street, and we used to watch Rosa store things in that hollow—little things she'd find in the neighborhood like feathers or small stones or shards of colored glass. That hollow was the best place we could think to leave the note. The mailbox was out of the question. Did any of the girls have a cell phone? We had no idea, and if they did, none of us knew any of their numbers.

It took us most of the morning to get our message just right. We wanted it to be short and to say the right thing and to not have any major misspellings.

Calvin had the best handwriting, so he wrote it, in blue ballpoint pen on paper torn from a composition book. Hector volunteered to run over and put it in the tree.

We never saw Rosa retrieve the note, but a couple of days later, Hector's mom called us from downstairs saying that a letter had been left in the mailbox addressed to "Hector & His Friends." We ran downstairs, took the letter into the backyard, and crowded around as Hector unfolded it.

Rosa's writing, in pencil on heart-shaped stationery, was so light. When the sun hit the paper, the words were nearly invisible.

Thank you for telling me about my sister, she'd written. *I hope she comes back. If she doesn't, I will go out and try to find her myself.*

Rosa

(Wednesday, June 12th)

ROSA HAD TO wait almost an hour before she could speak with Father Mendoza, so once she took her seat in front of his wide oak desk, she placed her hands into her lap, leaned forward, and got right to the meat of the thing.

"Good afternoon, Father," she said. "I'd like to know what Catholic doctrine has to say about ghosts."

Father Mendoza was a tall, thin man originally from the Rio Grande Valley. Rosa thought he looked like he was made of sticks, and he always smelled somewhat brittle, like dry kindling about to catch fire. It was true that, shortly after arriving at San Fernando, Father Mendoza, in his attempt to counsel Rafe when they'd come across each other in the grocery store, had gotten punched in the face. Father Mendoza had then promised Rafe he'd leave the Torres family alone, but Rosa wouldn't have any of that. Nearly every week since Ana had died, Rosa had sat right there—at that oak desk, with her hands folded in her lap—and asked her priest questions about faith and kindness and doubt and death. The marks Ana had left on the wall hadn't scared Rosa, hadn't made her wild-eyed and twitchy like they'd made Iridian or pale and mute like they'd made Jessica. When she'd first seen them, and traced the blue ink lightly with the tips of her fingers, she'd smiled. Her heart had bloomed like the big white petals on the magnolia trees in the park. With one beat, it had tripled in size. Her sister had come back. Within seconds, though, that smile faded. Ana's marks on the wall were so broken, and the lines were so wobbly. Ana may have been back, but something was wrong. If the lines were broken and wobbly, then Ana's spirit was broken and wobbly, too. Rosa was worried.

"Well." Father Mendoza put his hands in his lap and leaned forward in his chair just as Rosa had done. "Unfortunately, church doctrine isn't completely clear. There's a lot on demons, but less on ghosts. Basically, we view them as souls lost in purgatory, stuck between heaven and hell because they need to make amends or atone for something. Some of them are harmless wanderers. Others are angry and play tricks." The priest sat quietly for a moment. "Why do you ask?"

Play tricks, Rosa repeated to herself. And then she said, out loud, "I think my sister Ana has come back."

Father Mendoza didn't smirk or snicker, which Rosa appreciated.

"Have you seen her?" he asked.

"No," Rosa replied. "But others have. And she's doing things."

Rosa looked away from Father Mendoza's light brown eyes and stared off into the corner of the room, thinking. She liked this room. She liked the walls, which were painted stark white—white like the blossoms on a magnolia tree. She liked the fact that nothing hung on the stark white walls except for a cross and a small ticking clock. The room was always clean. She could do a lot of good thinking in a room like this. The only thing that broke the perfection of the clean, white room was the row of sugar ants marching up the wall behind Father Mendoza's chair.

Ants sought shelter indoors during the rain, when their home in the ground outside got too wet. That made sense. Living creatures want to be comfortable, dry, and safe in familiar territory. If Ana was a spirit trapped in purgatory, she must've been very uncomfortable.

"I can tell you this," Father Mendoza went on. "If God has willed Ana's spirit to return, and if God has willed you and your family to bear witness, you must be accepting and receptive to her and whatever that message might be."

Father Mendoza then cleared his throat and glanced up at his clock. Rosa knew there were other people out in the hall who had come after her and were waiting to speak to the priest, but still, she'd been in his office for barely ten minutes.

"Do you have any idea what your sister's message might be?" the priest asked.

"Not yet," Rosa replied. "But I'll figure it out."

On her way out of the church, she came across Walter Mata blocking one of the hallways. He was up on a ladder, changing a light that had burned out. The sight of him caused Rosa to stop short. Her breath came out in a single, strange pop. She knew that, in addition to being both a grade ahead of her in school and her ride to church every Sunday, Walter worked at the church a few days a week, doing odd jobs. He'd fix leaky toilets, change air filters, sweep, mop, empty trashcans, whatever anyone needed him to do. In order to change the light, Walter's right hand was raised toward the ceiling, and the muscles in his arm were twitching as he screwed in the new bulb. Rosa liked the look of that arm. She thought, *Huh.*

"Hey," Walter said, noticing Rosa.

"Hi," Rosa replied. Then she scooted past the ladder legs and went on her way. There were other things to think about right then aside from the unexpected shock-delight of Walter Mata with his arm raised, changing a light.

• • •

Rosa's own room wasn't a very good place for thinking. It wasn't wide open like the yard or good and clean like Father Mendoza's office. Her room was a mess, but she'd never dream of going into Jessica's room, which was an even bigger mess and where she wasn't sure she'd be able to find a cleared-off space to sit.

So, for a while, Rosa sat on the floor of her mess of a bedroom. She sat and waited. She listened. She sniffed at the musty air, hoping to pick up on Ana's cottony scent. She sat through several cycles of the air conditioner clicking off and on. Downstairs, she heard voices coming from the television. Iridian was down there. She was on the couch, burrowed under a blanket and watching soap operas. The volume on the television was turned almost all the way down. The voices of the characters were just murmurs rising up through the floor, but the sound of them still tugged on Rosa's nerves.

She relented, and went down the hall to Jessica's room, but just to pass through to get to the window, and then to the oak tree outside the window. After shoving up the sash and sticking her head into the humid night, Rosa saw a spot on the trunk of the tree, a fresh blond oval that stood out against the darker strips of bark. It was a scar. A year later and the tree was still healing from the night when Ana had put her trust in a branch that couldn't hold her weight. Rosa could relate to the tree. She knew what it felt like to have a part of her snapped off, leaving her with a big, raw hole that might heal but would never heal right.

Rosa was careful with her footing. The recent rains had made the bark soft and slick. First she climbed out, and then she climbed up, hooking a leg over a branch above, pulling and twisting until she was on top of that branch, belly down. She shimmied forward, knocking loose leaves and small branches, until she could latch on to the gutter in front of her and pull herself onto the roof. She'd only gone up to the roof a few times before, and every time she'd ended up with oak leaves in her hair and scrapes along her forearms from pulling herself along the gritty tiles. It was always a fight.

Rosa much preferred being on the ground to being in the sky. She liked having a connection to the earth, and was comforted by the thought of miles and miles of life beneath her feet. But the sky reminded Rosa of her sister: Ana, who wanted to fly away from Southtown. Ana, who seemed to always stand on the tips of her toes as if she *could* fly away from Southtown.

From up on the roof, Rosa couldn't hear the television, but of course there were other sounds. There were shouts from backyards, from kids playing before dinnertime. Garage doors opened and closed. A couple of streets away, a construction crew was finishing up for the day, and she could hear the last few rapid-fire punches of nails from their guns. Above Rosa's head came the roar of airplanes, taking off from or coming in to the nearby airport.

Rosa had just found a place to sit near the peak of the roof when she heard a rustle from the oak tree. The leaves then shook, but it was too small a shake to have been caused by a squirrel. Rosa took a step back down toward the tree. It was dim in the twilight, but she swore she could see dark red deep in the tree. Her first thought was that it was the wing of a lonely bird.

Rosa took another step and lost her balance. There was no traction between the sole of one of her shoes and the roof tile, so her right foot slid forward six inches. She fell on her left knee and caught herself in an awkward split. Rosa closed her eyes and let out a breath. Another airplane flew overhead. When she opened her eyes she saw the red again, deep in the leaves. Crouching, Rosa leaned forward as far as she could. She didn't look down.

"I'm here, I'm here," Rosa said, pressing the palms of her hands into the roof tiles to gain as much traction as possible. She wanted to be ready for anything. Then she said, "Play tricks."

Iridian
(Friday, June 14th)

THERE WAS NOTHING like standing in the middle of the orange groves in the summer in South Texas. The scent hung so heavy it wasn't even necessary to really breathe it in. It was there, always—that oily bite, that sting of citrus.

Iridian had only stood in the middle of the orange groves—the ones down in Mission that belonged to her aunt Francine—at two points in her life. The first time was when she was just over a year old and had walked without having to hold her mother's hand. Of course she didn't remember that. The second time was three years ago, the summer when she was thirteen, when Francine had come up to San Antonio to take Iridian and her sisters for a long weekend over the summer. There had been four of them.

Ana had been alive then. The long weekend had turned into a week had turned into a week and a half.

Iridian remembered the smell of oranges most of all, but also the feel of the wind, in particular how that wind would blow dust that would then get caught in her hair— all the way from her scalp to the ends. She'd liked the gritty feel, and would go days without taking a shower.

Iridian also remembered the day Rafe came. There was no wind that day. The girls had just finished breakfast when they heard his truck approaching, rattling like a sick person. While Iridian and her sisters had stayed seated at the table, Francine went to meet Rafe at the door. There had been shouting. Iridian had plucked out a few of Rafe's words: *kidnapped, mine, no right*. Ana had looked to her sisters and then had taken a bite of buttered toast.

"Don't worry," she'd told them, smacking crumbs from her lips. "We'll come back."

"We'd better," Iridian had said.

In the truck, on the way back to San Antonio, crammed between Rosa and Jessica, Iridian chewed on the end of her braid, sucking up the dust and the bitter smell of oranges.

She wasn't a writer then, or even that obsessive a reader, so she didn't yet know the pure joy that came along with smelling the pages of books, how a new book smelled like chlorine or how a used book sometimes smelled like cigarettes or tangy breath. All she loved that summer was being coated in dust and the smell of oranges.

And now, it made Iridian mad thinking about how much she once loved being outside. It made her particularly mad on a night like this one, when she was on the couch in the living room, covered up by a crocheted blanket and pretending to be asleep. She had been clamping her jaw shut for so long that a headache had taken root and bloomed behind her right eye. She was angry, but she was also scared—angry at herself for being so scared. She couldn't help it. The house had been making sounds all night. Windowpanes in the kitchen were shifting in their sashes. The refrigerator kept clicking. Ice cubes were falling from the door to the floor and shattering, one every half hour or so. The sounds then got closer. The ceiling fan above her head creaked. Something—a fly maybe—buzzed around her head, but then it stayed in one place, and the buzzing got louder and more persistent. Maybe she was making that up. Maybe it was just a symptom of her headache.

Then, Iridian heard the click and fizz of a soda can being opened. She tossed the blanket aside and sat up, knowing exactly what she was going to see: Jessica holding a Diet Coke. She didn't have any makeup on—not even the faintest flick of mascara—and she was wearing red plaid pajama bottoms and a blue-striped tank top. Her socks didn't match. There was a ragged hole in one, at the big toe. It was jarring—the clashing patterns, the bare face. Iridian hadn't seen Jessica look so un-put-together in a long time.

"Hey," Jessica said. "Do you know where Dad is?"

"What are you lurking around for?" Iridian demanded. "What time is it, anyway?"

"After three." Jessica slurped her soda. "Dad should be home by now."

"Why don't you just call him?" Iridian asked.

"He's not answering his phone."

Didn't they just have this conversation?

Iridian waited, then waited some more, but Jessica just kept standing there. Finally, Iridian rolled onto her side, burrowing her face into the cushions of the couch.

"You can't stay down here forever, you know," Jessica said.

"I can try!" Iridian shouted.

If she closed her eyes and thought about it really, really hard, she could feel the fibers of the cheap, scratchy couch and those of the cheap, scratchy crocheted blanket weaving together with the hairs of her arms and unshaved legs. Those fibers poked into the skin of Iridian's face, trapping her there, pincushion-style. She would become the furniture. The furniture would become her.

Iridian had been downstairs for two days now, camped out on the couch. This was her haunted life. She slept whenever—it didn't necessarily have to be night. When the seemingly never-ending storms weren't causing the power to blink out, she'd watch the channel on satellite that showed only soap operas, one episode after the other after the other. She was vaguely aware of her dad and her sisters coming and going, passing behind the couch on their way to and from the front door and the kitchen. Jessica was going to work or to John's. Rosa was going to church or to look for her hyena. Rafe was maybe going to work, maybe going to the bar, maybe going to sad Norma Galván's house a couple of blocks away.

Iridian hadn't changed her clothes. She hadn't taken a shower. Eventually, Rosa had warmed Iridian a can of tomato soup and brought down a toothbrush and some toothpaste from upstairs.

Iridian mourned the absence of her books. She'd find herself reaching for them, involuntarily. She missed the feeling of paper against her fingers. The loss was painful. The pain wasn't in her heart, but in her throat, where words come from.

"I keep waiting for something else to happen," Iridian said. "Every little sound makes me want to jump out of my skin." She paused. "Have you seen anything?"

"What are you watching?" Jessica asked, sitting on the edge of the couch. She yanked on the corner of the blanket to try to gather enough to cover her legs. "Anything good?"

"Go away." Iridian swatted at her sister's arm. "There's no room."

Jessica took another noisy slurp of soda, and the sound caused Iridian's headache to pulse.

"That lady has a weird mouth," she said, nodding toward the screen. "Seriously. These actors are so ugly. Where do they find these people?"

Jessica scooted her butt back, squashing Iridian's feet into the cracks between the cushions. "Get your giant-ass crane legs out of the way," she said. "You should write for soaps. You'd be good at that, right?"

"I . . ." Iridian hesitated. "Maybe?"

What was happening? Iridian stared at the side of her sister's face, which was lit up by the flashing screen. Who was this alternate, compliment-bearing version of Jessica? It wasn't the sneering version, the one who talked to Iridian as if she didn't have a brain in her head or a heart in her chest. It wasn't the hard and silent version, the one who wanted everyone to believe she was made up of wires and cold plates of metal, welded together tight.

This version of Jessica was just hanging out, sucking on a Diet Coke, seeming totally absorbed in a scene on low volume between a middle-aged woman wearing a slinky designer gown pointing a gun at another middle-aged woman wearing a slinky designer gown. Everything seemed so *normal.* Jessica hadn't said another thing about Ana or Ana's *hand* or the writing on the wall.

With her gaze still on the screen, Jessica pulled more of the blanket toward her, tucking it up and under her chin. Iridian was left with a corner that only covered her from the waist down. She was sort of cold now, but it actually wasn't that bad: two of the Torres sisters sitting together on the couch, watching soaps.

"This blanket smells," Jessica eventually said.

"*You* smell," Iridian replied.

Jessica cracked a smile, and Iridian ate it up.

Jessica

JESSICA HAD ONLY two memories of her mother, but they were both so old she didn't know if they were real or if she'd invented them. The first was simple. It was of her mother standing outside, backlit by the sun. Her bare legs were copper-brown, and there was a crease of sweat behind each of her knees. Her nails were short, round, and not polished. She was wearing three gold rings that Rafe had given her on three separate occasions, all stacked up on one finger. Aside from those rings and a small gold cross that hung around her neck, she wasn't wearing any other jewelry.

The second memory Jessica had of her mother was of them in the car together. Ana was also there. This memory Jessica was almost positive she'd made up, because she would've been only four years old and strapped in a car seat in the back when it had happened. Ana was in the front, even though Jessica knew now that her sister would have been too young to be riding shotgun. It was cold outside. Ana was wearing a puffy pink coat that was dirty around the wrists and had probably been bought secondhand. The heater wheezed. After easing through a stop sign, Jessica's mom reached over and took Ana's hand.

"Hold your breath," she'd commanded.

They'd been driving through a graveyard. It was on both sides of the car, as if the cemetery had been there first and the street had later been plowed through it. There were tall iron gates and tilted stones. Most of the writing on those stones had been rubbed smooth. Names and the dates of long or short lives had dissolved along with the bones below. The graves went on and on. Jessica's eyes were starting to water from holding her breath for so long.

Finally, after they'd driven through to the other side, Jessica's mom dropped Ana's hand and told both of her daughters a story. It was about how, when she was a girl, she went to her uncle's funeral. She didn't have a good coat, so she stood there shivering throughout the graveside service in a long-sleeved wool dress. Once she got home, she stood in front of the radiator until the sun went down, but she couldn't get warm. At dinner, she ate chicken soup that turned cold when it hit her tongue. After dinner, she took a hot bath, but she was still freezing. She put on a bunch of clothes, heaped blankets on her bed, and climbed into it. Still, she shivered. Nothing like this had ever happened to her before. She told her mother she thought she was sick. Her mother—the girls' grandmother—brought her hot licorice tea and told her that, no, she wasn't sick. She was just unlucky. Some of the dead people in the graveyard, her mother said, release mal aires, which enter a living person's body through the holes in their heads, like their nostrils and their mouths. It can happen any time of year, but especially in winter, when the ground is frozen and the corpses are uncomfortable.

"That's what happened," Rita Torres told her daughters.

During the funeral, mal aires had worked their way into her body. They wrapped around her bones and fastened themselves to her muscles. They dug in and gave her chills. They wanted her to know what it felt like to be dead. Rita's mother told her the feeling would pass in a day, and if it didn't, she'd take her to a lady who knew how to deal with these kinds of things.

The feeling didn't pass. It got worse. Jessica's mom woke up in the middle of the night with aches in her ears. By morning, one of her eardrums had burst. Fluid started leaking down the side of her neck. There was something in her head, pushing against skull bones, and it wanted something—it wanted to get out, or it wanted *her* to get out and make more room.

Jessica's grandmother drove her mother across town to some lady's house. That lady had just finished making ham sandwiches for her young sons when they'd arrived. She washed her hands and led her mom into a back bedroom. Once there, she rubbed alcohol on Rita's head, pressed her thumbs across her eyebrows, and whispered a short prayer. She told Rita to go home and take baths in hot salt water, twice a day.

The next morning, Rita was still a little chilly, but better. The day after that, she was back to normal.

Many years later, long after their mother had died, Ana asked Jessica if she remembered this story. Jessica said she did—she remembered sitting in the back seat, looking at Ana's dirty sleeves, and watching their mom reach over and grip her small hand.

"So you held your breath?" Ana asked. "That whole time?"

Jessica nodded. "I still do—every time I go past a graveyard. What about you?"

"I never even tried," Ana said, with a flash of a grin. "So who knows how many angry spirits I've been carrying around with me all this time."

Jessica
(Friday, June 14th)

"SIGN PETER'S CARD?"

Jessica looked up from her dinner of caramel corn and chocolate milk. Her manager, an older lady named Mathilda, was holding out a red envelope and a pen. Jessica was confused.

"What?"

Mathilda gave the envelope a little shake. "Peter's card. Everyone's signed it but you."

Jessica was still confused. "Is he sick?"

Peter didn't look sick. The last time she'd seen him was yesterday when they'd passed each other between shifts. She'd been in the employee bathroom for nearly half an hour, clipping her fingernails and then shaving her armpits over the sink. When she'd finally come out, there was Peter, leaning against the wall, waiting. He'd smiled and said hey, like it was no big deal that Jessica had hogged the bathroom for way too long. Even under the harsh fluorescent store light that made everything it touched look bleached and corpselike, he appeared easy, relaxed, like he was outside waiting for the bus on a warm spring day. Peter was infuriating.

"Are you kidding?" Mathilda asked, her smile crooked. "His last day is Sunday."

"Sunday?" Jessica replied. "As in, two days from now?"

"Well . . . yeah."

Jessica blew past Mathilda and charged out into the store. Her shift had been over for almost half an hour, so she'd changed out of her work shirt and into a gray V-neck that used to belong to John. She still had her khakis on, though, and the fabric swished when she walked. A Celine Dion ballad was blasting through the store speakers. It was the ironic soundtrack of her life.

Jessica found Peter in the candy aisle, up near the registers, where he was stuffing handful after handful of chocolate truffles into display boxes.

Peter heard the harsh swish of Jessica's khakis and glanced over his shoulder. Nope, he didn't look sick. He looked pretty great in that too-tall, easy-breezy way of his. If anything, Jessica was the one who looked sick. She'd stopped showering at home and was now practically living out of the store and out of her car. As a result, her hair and makeup had suffered. Jessica made excuses for herself—*to herself*—claiming the light was just too bad in the store's bathroom, but really she'd stopped caring.

"Oh, hey," Peter said.

"Mathilda told me you're leaving," Jessica blurted. "She asked me to sign your card."

"Oh. Nice. A card. Thanks for telling me."

"Where are you going?"

"College," Peter replied. "Up in San Marcos. But I'm going to visit family in Mexico for a couple weeks before that." He scooped up another handful of truffles. "What are you still doing here? I thought you'd be long gone by now."

"You didn't tell me that," Jessica snapped. "I didn't know that. About you leaving." She paused. "You're just a junior. You can't leave yet."

"I've been taking dual credit," Peter said. "Besides, I . . . didn't think you'd want to know."

Peter waited for Jessica to reply, which wasn't happening because Jessica didn't know how to reply. Did she really care about the details of her coworker's life? She had enough going on in her own life, in her *own house*. And, oh crap, Peter had that look on his face again, brows creased, mouth slightly puckered with concern, like he was about to ask Jessica how she was doing. She dreaded hearing that question—or some variation of that question—so much that she started to shift up onto the balls of her feet, preparing to turn and break into a sprint. Peter didn't ask that question, though. He didn't say anything. Instead, he plucked one of the chocolate truffles from the pile, unwrapped it, and then popped it into his mouth. He unwrapped another and held it out to Jessica.

Fast like a whip, Jessica snatched the chocolate from Peter's fingers and tossed it in her mouth.

"Holy shit, you're a thief." Jessica chomped on the chocolate as fast as she could to get rid of the evidence. "Peter Rojas, I would've never expected. What would your abuela in Mexico say if she knew?"

Peter licked the chocolate off his fingers. "I've never done that before."

"Sure."

"You're a bad influence."

"The worst."

Jessica crouched down and took her keys from her pocket, poised to dig into a strip of tape. "Do you need help or anything?"

"Yeah, sure," Peter replied.

For nearly an hour, Jessica and Peter restocked almost the entire candy aisle. Jessica opened boxes of peppermints and cinnamon chews and those puffy things shaped like peanuts. Occasionally, Peter left to help with the registers, but, for the most part, they worked together, largely in silence, which Jessica appreciated. She of course knew all the words to all the songs that came through the speaker, but she didn't sing along. She caught herself humming once or twice but cut that off quick.

"Are you going to be at the block party tomorrow?" Peter eventually asked. He was across the aisle, with his back to Jessica, rearranging price tags.

Jessica paused, dropping a pack of Swedish Fish in her lap. She hadn't gone last year because the party had fallen on one of the days immediately following Ana's death. Or maybe the neighbors had canceled the party out of respect. She couldn't remember. That time was always a little fuzzy.

"I don't know," she said. "I work Saturday mornings. I could be there later. What about you?"

"You aren't picking up your phone."

Both Jessica and Peter turned at the sound of John's voice. That voice—Jessica had never thought much about it before, but now it grated. It felt itchy, itchy and cold like a ghost in her bones. Jessica realized she was wearing John's T-shirt, and she was tempted to strip it from her skin. She plucked at the fabric, shook her shoulders a little bit.

John had already apologized for what had happened the other day in the car, bought Jessica some roses—wilted pink ones from the grocery store—and took her out for soft serve. He'd do better, he'd said. Jessica had forgiven him but not really. She'd said the words *it's okay*, but she hadn't meant them. Every day in the work bathroom, she inspected the little bruise on her cheek, watched the colors change, watched it fade. She imagined all the ways she could leave bruises of her own.

Did she say anything, though? *Do* anything? Of course not.

"My battery's dead," Jessica lamely replied.

It was a bad lie. John would know. The word *dead* sounded fake, cracked in half.

"I asked her to stay and help," Peter said, rising to stand.

"Let's go," John commanded, ignoring Peter altogether. "What's wrong with your hair, Jess?"

Jessica was still holding the plastic bag of red candy fish. It was the perfect, stupid prop for this scene—this one scene of her entire, stupid life. She closed her eyes, willing the doors inside her to all bang shut. It was time to play dead. Tonight, after they left here, John would get pissed, then probably want to have sex with her, and she'd probably let him.

After dropping the bag of candy, Jessica stood. John approached her and reached out to brush his hand across her cheek. Jessica looked at Peter, and saw his gaze jumping from the bruise on her cheek to John's thumb. He didn't even try to hide his open staring. The muscles in Peter's jaw twitched as he noticed how they matched—the size and shape of John's thumb and the size and shape of the mark on Jessica's face. Jessica turned away and grasped John's hand in hers before Peter could catch her eye or say anything. She didn't want be on the receiving end of his rage or his pity. She didn't want anything from him. She didn't care if he was leaving in a couple of days, and she wasn't going to sign his fucking card.

But then Jessica did something she couldn't really explain. On her way down the aisle, she grabbed a couple of chocolate truffles and stuffed them in her pocket. She hoped that Peter had seen her. Maybe he'd take it as a reminder that she was a bad influence. Or maybe she wanted him to know that, in a way, she'd be carrying a little piece of him in her pocket for a while.

The Night Jessica Torres
Made Out with John Chavez
in Front of Everyone

IT WAS THE first party we'd ever been to.

That's not true, of course. We'd been to plenty of birthday parties, block parties, baptisms, but this was different.

It was the first party we'd ever been to where we'd walked in, stood among the kids we went to school with, and felt like the smallest people in the world. Not small in stature, but small in spirit. We'd done everything, of course, to try to make that not be the case. We'd planned it to where we walked into Evalin Uvalde's house on that Friday night in the early days of September, three months after Ana had died, like a pack, like a gang, with blasé-sneering expressions on our faces, intentionally two and a half hours late, dressed in our coolest clothes and wearing too much cologne. The goal was to make an impression while pretending like we didn't care about making an impression. When we walked into Evalin's house, however, we made absolutely no impression. None. People may have looked at us, but they didn't see us. They looked *through* us. We were wallpaper.

The very first thing we saw when we walked into Evalin's house was Evalin herself. John Chavez had her pressed up against the wall of the entryway—right inside the front door—and they were really going at it. Behind them and around them were tons of people drinking, laughing, and shout-talking into each other's ears. All those people were acting like it was no big deal that John had one hand up Evalin's shirt and was full-on groping her boob. Honestly, it kind of looked painful for Evalin, like John was squeezing the way someone might furiously juice an orange. And the sounds their mouths were making were so weird and loud. There were people laughing and shouting, there was music playing, but even still, over all that, we could hear the squish and slide and suck of lips and tongue. None of us had *that* much experience with making out—Hector claimed to have gotten to "third base" with Faye Gutierrez after the block party two summers ago, though Hector was very often full of shit—but what was going on between John and Evalin seemed super unromantic.

We were grossed out, but that didn't mean we could

stop staring. Eventually, Calvin elbowed Hector. Hector blinked and elbowed Jimmy. It was time to snap out of it and move. We turned ourselves sideways and started inching through the crowd. Of course, we knew that if we were in any way as cool as we had hoped we'd be, the crowd would've parted for *us*.

The last time we were in such a full house was when we were at Hector's on the afternoon after Ana's funeral. We'd been on a mission then: to gather up precious bits of information about Ana. This party at Evalin's wasn't at all the same, and we had a completely different, three-part mission: to convince the people we went to school with we weren't total losers, to get tipsy on cheap beer, and to maybe talk to some girls. We kept our ears open, though. Maybe people were still talking about Ana; maybe she was still, in a way, alive to these people—like she was for us— in the swirls of stories and rumors.

For sure, Ana would've been in this house, at this party, if she'd been alive. She would've snuck out her window to get here. All the kids from school would've stopped what they were doing the moment she came through the door. They would've turned and looked. The noise level would've lowered. The crowd would've parted for her as she moved through it. There seemed to be a big, black hole in the middle of Evalin's house where Ana should've been.

Did anyone aside from us think that? For sure, John Chavez didn't.

See, there's something else about John—something big, something we learned later from the other kids at school. John was the guy who Ana had been sneaking out her window to see on the nights leading up to her death. John was the guy who Ana had been sneaking out her window to see on *the* night of her death. John had watched Ana slip, Ana fall, Ana hit the ground. And he'd *driven away.* He wasn't the villain in our story because villains typically have spines. He was lower than that—the ultimate, ultimate unrepentant coward.

From what we'd just witnessed in the entryway, John had very clearly moved on, and we didn't understand how. That was a huge part of why we couldn't stop staring when we'd first walked in. We were sort of transfixed, but we were also really, really pissed—even though John was known far and wide to be a grade-A dick, the more we thought about it, the more it made us slow-burn angry how he'd moved on, and with Evalin Uvalde of all people.

Evalin had a long-standing reputation for being really mean. Jessica Torres was also mean, but the two were mean in different ways. We'd always thought Jessica was mean because she was so full of life that it chafed at her from the inside out. She was always simmering, and it reminded us of a pot of stew on a stove. She contained so much beneath her skin, and when she got heated up, all those things tumbled and boiled. Evalin, on the other hand, was colder, crueler. She'd say and do mean things just to say and do mean things. Evalin was the type of person who would trip a kid to watch them cry and then deny ever having done anything—and then tell the kid it was *their* fault.

Less than ten minutes after we'd arrived at the party, Jessica Torres finally showed up. We ran into her when she was in the kitchen, by herself, pouring Sprite and vodka into a red plastic cup. She was wearing Ana's clothes—a black denim skirt that didn't fit quite right and an oversized blue T-shirt—but she was always wearing Ana's clothes those days, so that wasn't surprising. The cup she was holding was shaking because her hand was shaking. Her hair was tied back, and we could see pink splotches on her cheeks. She was about to pop. We'd seen her look that way, at Hector's house, right before she attacked Father Canty. If Jessica had come in through the front door, she would have seen what we'd seen: John Chavez swallowing Evalin's face like a desperate fish.

"Hey, Jessica," Calvin said, trying to sound cool and casual. "Are you okay? Do you need anything?"

Jessica's gaze flashed up, and Calvin winced. He actually cowered a little, as if the rage on Jessica's face caused him real pain.

"What the fuck did you just say?" Jessica snapped.

"He just wanted to know if you're okay," Jimmy chimed in. He waited a couple seconds before adding, "Are you?"

For a few terrible moments, Jessica studied us, and we waited for whatever insults she would spear our way. We braced ourselves. We were ready. It would be okay. We'd welcome those insults because we knew whatever pain they would cause us would be temporary and would pale in comparison to the pain that constantly tumbled and boiled through Jessica's organs.

The insults never came, though. After a moment, Jessica let out a sound—like a breath or a grunt, a noise that indicated we weren't even worth the effort of forming a word—and then she tipped her head back to expose the length of her throat, chugged her drink, and reached back to the bottles perched on the kitchen counter to pour herself another. She took great care to fill her cup up to the very tip-top, and then walked out.

We followed Jessica through the crowd of people, and, to her credit, she managed not to spill more than a couple of drops of her drink. She was headed to the entryway, to where John and Evalin were still doing their thing and John *still* had his hand squashed against Evalin's boob.

Jessica was mad, and when she was mad she created something like a force field of anger. People stopped talking and turned in her direction. They made space for her as she slid by. We heard someone whisper, "Oh shit," and just as Evalin tore her swollen lips away from John's mouth, Jessica threw—overhand threw like a baseball—her cup straight at Evalin's face. The plastic and ice and clear liquid exploded against Evalin's nose. The cup bounced off John's shoulder.

"*What the fuck, bitch?*" Evalin screeched, as John just backed off, eyes wide, shaking himself dry and lifting the edge of his shirt to wipe the side of his face.

We tensed, waiting. All around us, others did the same. Jessica was going to do something. She was going to either say something brutal or strike out violently, like the way she'd done with the priest or the way she'd done with Muriel Contreras and the pencil. We watched, not caring anymore about being cool, but wanting to know how Jessica was going to avenge her dead sister. We silently cheered her on.

Evalin wiped her face with her hand. She lunged off the wall and shoved Jessica in the shoulder.

"I said, *What the fuck?*"

Do it, Jessica, we urged. *Make things right.*

Jessica drew in a sharp breath, and then she did . . . nothing. More like, she shrunk. All of a sudden, her body seemed to get much, much smaller. Her eyes stopped glowing with rage and went dull, out like a light—*click*. We'd always known Jessica Torres as a fighter, but that night we watched her lose that fight. Something in her just gave up. Evalin shoved Jessica again on the shoulder, and Jessica lazily swiped Evalin's hand away. Evalin, obviously embarrassed, screamed in Jessica's face about Jessica being pathetic, about Jessica's *family* being pathetic, and that new version of blank Jessica stood there, staring first at the wall just over Evalin's shoulder and then over to John Chavez.

It was one of the many times we could have said or done something and, instead, we said and did nothing. One of Evalin's friends eventually came over, straightened Evalin's shirt that was still all bunched from having John's hand up it, and started to pull Evalin into the other room.

Jessica was still staring at John, with that cold dullness in her eyes, and John was now staring back. The side of his mouth quirked up. Jessica took a step forward. She then pressed herself flat against John's chest and took hold of both sides of his face. From the other room, Evalin could see what was going on. She shouted out, enraged, as Jessica stood on the tips of her toes and crushed her lips against John's.

She was the one who then pressed John back against the wall of the entryway, and *she* was the one who put her hand up *his* shirt. Their lips and tongues slid and smacked against each other.

"What the hell?" Hector whispered.

Jessica and John have been together ever since.

Jessica

(Saturday, June 15th)

A SCREECHY LAUGH from across the street made Jessica flinch. That laugh, so piercing and distinct as to rise above a big crowd, belonged to Norma Galván, Rafe's date to the block party. As Rafe flipped burgers at a portable grill set up in the Garcias' front yard, Norma laughed at every single thing he said. And, as Norma laughed, she had to fight to keep her balance because the high heels of her strappy sandals kept sinking into the lawn. In between bursts of laughter and trying to stay upright, Norma took sips from a can of Tecate and picked at her flower-printed blouse in an attempt to separate the fabric from her moist skin. Jessica watched as Rafe leaned down toward Norma and nuzzled his nose at her temple. Norma gazed up, smiling all loopy.

Jessica was standing next to John in the shade of an oak tree, wondering if she'd ever looked at him all loopy like that. She also wondered why her father was hanging out with Norma Galván again. Possibly, it had to do with money, given that Rafe had asked Jessica the other day to "borrow" two hundred dollars. Norma was known to keep rolls of cash stashed all over her house, in places like coffee cans and hollow porcelain statues. Rafe had said he needed the money for a truck payment, but Jessica was pretty sure his truck had been paid off for years.

Jessica then heard a different laugh—gentle like skipping stones—and she knew exactly who that laugh belonged to because she'd heard it dozens of times from across the store, from aisles away. There, behind a couple of folding tables covered with foil-wrapped dishes, was Peter. He was helping Mrs. Garcia pour tea into red plastic cups and was grinning at a little boy who was not-so-sneakily trying to steal three cookies off a plate.

Next to Peter was Calvin Ortiz's mom, who was fussing over things, making sure everything was all set, that there were enough paper plates, napkins, forks, and spoons. She smacked the boy's hand away from the cookies, but laughed while she did it. In a nearby yard, Kitty Bolander and her friends were having a Hula-Hoop contest. The girls were laughing so loud, they sounded like they were screaming, like their joy took up so much space in their bodies it was physically painful.

It was a bright, beautiful, non-rainy day, and there was laughter everywhere. No one knew that the ghost of Ana Torres had caused Iridian to freeze in place on the downstairs couch, or that Jessica hadn't slept any more than eight hours combined over the course of the last three days. Jessica was surprised no one could see how badly she was starting to warp. Everything—her vision, her attention span, her ability to sort change into the register—felt like pencil marks that had been half-heartedly rubbed out with an eraser. Like everything was as blurry as the letters on old, slumped tombstones or like the shadow outline of a hand against a shower curtain.

No one in the neighborhood knew anything about this—about Jessica, about the things happening in Jessica's house. Jessica didn't really want anyone to know. She cringed. She felt like she was under assault.

Teddy Arenas's new dog, a sand-colored, big-pawed puppy, bounded up to John and started pulling on the end of his shoelace with his tiny, determined teeth. John smiled and crouched down. He made cooing sounds and let the dog lick him on his hands and his nose, even on his lips. Eventually, the puppy rolled onto his back and gazed all goo-goo-eyed at John the way Norma was gazing at Rafe across the street.

Jessica told herself: John is a good person because he likes dogs. Good people like dogs.

But then Jessica realized she was still cringing. The expression was stuck on her face. Just as Teddy came up to reclaim his dog, Jessica heard Peter's stone-skip laugh again, and turned to the sound. She knew she didn't smile, but it was possible that her expression had softened.

"I'm going to get something to drink," Jessica said before heading over to the table where Mrs. Garcia and Peter were still setting up cups of iced tea. John had seen it: the way Jessica had reacted to Peter's laugh. She knew because even though she hadn't asked John to follow her, she could sense him close behind, and she knew what he'd do before he did it. He reached out and took hold of Jessica's wrist, stopping her mid-step. He squeezed so that his fingers dug into the place right at Jessica's pulse point, and her whole arm tensed. She winced as a ribbon of pain shot up to her elbow.

"Time to go," John said, without raising his voice.

Jessica let out a huff but stayed rooted. Behind her, Kitty Bolander and her friends were still shrieking their joy. Again, Jessica looked over to her dad and Norma.

Norma was stroking a hand up and down Rafe's arm, lightly. She then threaded her fingers with the ones on his free hand and leaned in to rest her cheek against his shoulder. Norma gave Rafe a kiss on his temple, so tenderly it nearly made Jessica gasp. She was transfixed. She couldn't stop watching this woman, her neighbor yet a stranger, offer comfort to her father.

Jessica was jealous. She wished she had someone who would hold her hand in a gentle way and lean against her shoulder. She even wished she was a dog so that John would take her face in his hands and gaze at her like she was the sweetest thing in the world. Instead, John was still gripping her wrist with so much force her fingers were starting to go numb.

"Did you not hear me?" John asked. He tugged her wrist, down, and Jessica felt her shoulder jerk out of joint. "I said, it's time to go."

Jessica watched a squirrel drop an acorn into a tiny hole at the base of a tree in a neighbor's front yard. She wished she was at work, under the freezing-cold air-conditioning, stocking candy and humming along to ballads. She wished she was alone in her car, singing at the top of her lungs. Jessica said nothing, and pretended her silence was a revolutionary act. She then realized how sad that was.

"I fucking heard you," Jessica muttered.

She ripped her hand from John's grip and continued toward the tables. But John reached out again, grabbing her by the elbow this time. He was trying to get her to stop, of course, but also to turn and face him.

Jessica didn't do that. She didn't look over her shoulder at John because she had the buzzy feeling of being watched. She turned her head slightly and locked eyes with Peter. He was still behind the folding table. Only now, he wasn't filling cups. He was holding one, though, and Jessica watched the plastic buckle under the strain of his grip. His gaze moved from Jessica's eyes to her elbow—and to John's hand there. A muscle twitched at the narrow edge of his eyebrow.

John squeezed tighter, and Jessica sagged a little from the sudden hit of pain. She knew that John had seen Peter looking at Jessica. He knew what Peter saw, and that's why he'd squeezed harder. In the past—like, a couple of days ago—Jessica would've been scared. She would've anticipated anger and then pain, and it would've made her weak with fear. Not today, though. Not on this bright and beautiful day. Peter's eyebrow twitched again, and Jessica sucked in a breath.

She didn't know exactly what would happen next, but she had an idea. She lifted her free hand to cover a smile.

"What the fuck are you looking at?" John sneered at Peter.

Peter leapt over the table, knocking over several cups and sending their contents splashing. He shoved John, not on the shoulder or on the chest, but on the face—like, he put his *entire hand* on John's face and pushed it backwards, chin to sky. John stumbled but recovered, and then quickly landed a punch on Peter's left eye.

Hector and Calvin were sprinting across the street— to do what, Jessica had no idea. This amazing fight didn't need to end, and Peter didn't need any help. A line of blood was trailing down the side of Peter's face—just like that line of sweat from a few days ago in the parking lot—but Jessica didn't have the urge to go up and wipe it away. She liked it. Liked the way it started at his brow and traced his cheekbone. She also liked it when Peter grabbed John by the front of his shirt and punched him in the nose. The resulting crunch was loud and oddly inhuman, like a grunt a dog makes when it launches itself into a bowl of food. John landed hard against one of the folding tables. Plates and serving bowls flew, and the table itself crashed to the ground.

It took a moment, but when John stood, he was covered in a swirl of food and blood. His white T-shirt was smeared with red but also something brown—chocolate cake, maybe—and a deviled egg was stuck, yolk-side, to his upper arm. John lumbered toward Peter, fists clenched. The blood on Peter's face had reached his chin. Then it dripped—so perfectly—right onto the toe of Peter's off-white sneaker. Peter didn't notice. He didn't blink, didn't back down, as John lunged.

Peter ducked. He elbowed John in the stomach, and when John doubled over, Peter punched him underhand. Again, blood sprayed, Corvette red, into the grass and onto Peter's sneakers. John straightened, and Jessica noticed the skin around his eyes was already turning colors.

And what was Jessica doing all this time? She was just standing there. She wasn't trying to pull John away or yelling for them to stop or anything. Ice and iced tea had sprayed onto her at some point, but she'd made no effort to wipe it off. Her hand had moved from her mouth, her fingers splayed across her nose and her eyes. She was doing that thing, faking horror, watching while pretending not to be watching. But if someone were to take a closer look, they'd see her cheekbones hiking up and gentle crinkles around the corners of her eyes, like she was smiling and trying to cover up her glee. Like she was *laughing*.

And where was Rafe? He was still behind the grill, watching. Norma was huddled up against him. A spatula hung from one hand. Jessica glanced his way and thought he looked kind of limp, kind of frightened, like the last thing he'd ever want to do was leap into the fray and break up a fight between two young men. That's the kind of man Rafe Torres was—the kind who would cling to a spatula in a time of crisis. Even Hector and Calvin had finally decided to step in and were now attempting to pry John and Peter away from each other.

Jessica couldn't hold it in anymore. She laughed. The sound burst out of her, and it sounded harsh and mean, like a row of grackles squawking on a telephone wire. She didn't think she'd ever laughed like that before. Clearly, she was losing her mind. She laughed and laughed.

Calvin and Hector were pulling John away from Peter, and John kept yelling, "I will fucking kill you!" which somehow made Jessica laugh harder. There were tears in her eyes. Her vision blurred. She started hiccupping. She doubled over, clutching her stomach, and eventually landed on her knees in the grass. The sun was still shining on this bright, cloudless day. It was hot, but the grass was cool, and the ground beneath was soft.

Jessica collapsed onto her side, and it was like she was a tiny bug peering through the tall blades of grass. She felt as if she could laugh there forever.

Rosa

ALMOST EXACTLY TWO years ago, Rosa and Ana had been sitting together on their back porch, doing nothing special, just drinking iced tea on a warm summer night. Even if they never had anything to talk about, since they were so far apart in age, Rosa had always liked being alone with her oldest sister. She liked that they shared an appreciation of the dark sky, and she liked the way Ana's long hair was always wavy and dynamic, like it was caught on a breeze even if there was no breeze at all.

There had been fireflies that night, blinking at the edges of the yard, and as time passed, the fireflies had multiplied. There were still some in the distance, but others were lighting up just inches away from Rosa's face. Ana had been reaching out and lazily trying to grab them. More and more had started blinking—so many that they'd played tricks with Rosa's vision, leaving tracks and trails, the way fireworks do.

"Are you doing this?" Ana had asked Rosa, and in the next moment, the yard went dark. The fireflies had blinked out, all at the same time, but Rosa could still feel them there, hovering in the heavy air. She could hear the hum of their little wings.

"You *are*," Ana had said, and then the yard had burst with light, so suddenly that it made Rosa gasp. The fireflies had lit up, all together. Then, a long moment later, they'd gone back to their regular, irregular blinking.

"I didn't," Rosa had said. "I'm not."

"I've always known there was something special about you," Ana had replied. She'd said it sternly, like a schoolteacher. "Now we know."

No one had ever said anything like that to Rosa before. It would've seemed like a tacky, bad-luck thing to say. Rosa had never thought there'd been something special about her. In fact, she'd thought there'd been something very sad about her. Her life was the cause of someone else's death. She'd been born, and her mother had died. It was a simple and terrible fact.

"Listen," Ana had said. "You're different than everyone

else. You're blessed. I mean, God has gifted you with something. I don't know what it is, but it's something. I hope you figure out what it is. I hope you can make the fireflies do that again."

Rosa

(Saturday, June 15th)

ROSA WAS WALKING to Concepcion Park when she heard shouting, followed by the crunching and crashing of things colliding. She hustled back toward home and saw that Peter Rojas and John Chavez were fighting. People had gathered around. Jessica was in the grass, on her back. She looked like she was convulsing. Rosa ran to her sister and saw that Jessica wasn't convulsing. She was laughing.

"Girls?" Mrs. Bolander asked, tentatively approaching. "Is everything alright?"

"We're fine," Rosa said, putting her hand on her sister's shoulder. "Jessica? What happened?"

Jessica couldn't respond. She was gripping her stomach, hardly able to breathe, overcome by her cackles.

The shouting and crashing and crunching continued just a few feet away. Rosa didn't look, but she could hear the sound of flesh thwacking against flesh, followed by stupid John telling Peter he would kill him. Jessica laughed harder.

Rosa glanced up just in time to see Peter punch John in the eye. The blood was so red as it left John's body. Red like the feathers of the cardinal that had fallen from the tree.

Iridian
(Saturday, June 15th)

IRIDIAN HADN'T UNDERSTOOD the sunlight at first.
She'd woken up on the couch after a nap of hours or minutes, licked her dry lips, and stretched out from fingertip
to toe before she'd noticed the long rays of light seeping in
through the curtains. The light caused her to sit straight
up, and that's when she saw the notebook on her lap. It was
new. She could tell without even opening it. The cover was
yellow plastic, but it had a paper half-cover on top of that,
one that boasted the brand name and page count. Iridian
knew it was a gift from Jessica because when she picked it
up, a receipt from the pharmacy showing a twenty-percent
employee discount fell out.

Iridian held her new notebook for a moment before flipping through the crisp, blank pages. Some were stuck together. They smelled beautiful, fresh like ink and chemicals.

Laughter from the block party outside filtered through the walls of the house. Iridian's sisters had suggested earlier that she get out, if just for a little while, if just for a hot dog and a piece of Mrs. Bolander's famous buttermilk pie, but Iridian would rather stay inside with a ghost than go outside with actual living people and animals and who knew what else. She went to the kitchen to grab a snack and maybe even make herself a cup of tea. Even though she spent most of her time indoors, Iridian could appreciate a nice day. The sun was shining after several dreary days of rain. There were breezes. Iridian couldn't feel them, of course, but she could see the leaves and the branches of the trees swaying, and she watched a squirrel chase another squirrel across the abandoned frame of the trundle bed in the dirt yard. It was all very simple. Bad things didn't happen on a day like this, when the sky was bright and people were outside laughing.

As she smacked on her chocolate puffs, Iridian surveyed the kitchen—the cracked and stained linoleum floor; the loud, whining appliances that had probably come with the house back in the 1970s; the fridge that randomly released ice cubes from its door; the food-spattered range.

It made her think: This house isn't good enough to be haunted. There weren't any libraries with old, cryptic notes shoved between the yellowing pages of dusty books. There weren't winding staircases with polished banisters. There weren't wood floors that were warm and worn from the soles of many generations of family feet. There weren't any gables or widow's walks or turrets. There weren't any rooms that were a little bit colder than the others, or rooms that were kept locked up "just in case." The walls didn't moan when the wind blew. The Torres family wasn't entangled in some generational curse like the Mayfair witches. They had no important heirlooms, just a banker's box full of their mom's old stuff that their dad kept on a shelf in his closet. It contained a couple of button-up blouses, a pair of red flat shoes, a bundle of crepe-paper flowers, a recipe book that used to belong to Grandmamá de la Cruz, and a postcard their mother had once sent home from a trip she took to see family in Morelia, Michoacán.

There were piles of dirty laundry in the closets and unwashed dishes in the kitchen sink. The faucet in Iridian's bathtub always dripped, and there was a ring of rust around the drain. Jessica didn't even have a real shower curtain, just a plastic liner that was once clear but was now streaked with layers of mineral deposits and grime. Everywhere, the carpet was old and dirty. Some of it was buckling, wrinkled like waves on water. Not a single bed in the house was made. The furniture was practically all from estate sales. The house was just some crappy old house, not in any way ghost-worthy.

Iridian knew that if she died on the couch or from falling down the stairs, and had any kind of choice in the matter, she would never, ever stick around this place.

Again, laughter rose up from outside. There was the shrieking of little kids doing something like chasing each other around. Then Iridian heard a woman's gleeful *whoop*, followed by a man shouting *Hey!* to someone.

People were happy. They deserved their nice party. If Iridian were there, things would only get worse. She'd be forced into talking to someone. She would probably say the wrong thing.

The spoon Iridian had been using to eat her cereal slipped from her fingers and fell with a clang into her bowl. The milk tasted acidic. She gagged, nearly choking on mushy chocolate puff.

Even now, a year later, she could still feel the sudden, vibrant shame she'd felt after saying the wrong thing to Ana, just hours before she died. It felt like a full-body rumble, an *oh shit* shock followed by the intense desperation of wanting to scoop words back into her mouth and eat them.

The day Ana fell from her window, she and Iridian had fought. It started when Iridian went into Ana's bathroom to borrow some shampoo. At the time, Ana had been downstairs in the kitchen with Jessica—Iridian could hear them both laughing, followed by the sound of one of them mashing the buttons on the microwave. As Iridian had been leaving with the shampoo bottle in hand, she'd seen that one of Ana's drawers was open. Normally, whatever was crammed in a drawer wouldn't have caught Iridian's eye—decades' worth of anything and everything filled every corner of the Torres house—but what she'd seen made her heart plummet.

It was a pregnancy test. It was new, unopened, safe in its box. But still.

There were footsteps on the stairs, and Iridian heard her sister—Ana—call out her name.

For a moment, Iridian considered acting like nothing had happened and nothing was wrong. She could slide the drawer all the way closed and Ana would never know about her snooping. But Iridian didn't want to act like nothing had happened. Of course, she knew Ana snuck out her window all the time to meet boys, but she never would've guessed her sister would be so careless—so *stupid*—as to get herself pregnant, or in a situation where she might even *think* she was pregnant.

It was a nightmare. Iridian saw it all unfold. She knew Ana would have the baby. It would be a little girl because this was a house full of girls, and all Iridian's plans of running away with her sisters would be ruined. They couldn't run with a baby. Ana couldn't be both their leader and a mother. None of the rest of them could be the leader. Iridian wasn't brave enough—not brave like girls in books.

Jessica could make a decision but could never follow through with anything. Rosa would just lead them in circles.

Iridian had sucked the end of her braid into her mouth, hoping to taste the faint tang of the dirt from the South Texas orange groves. Instead, she'd tasted oil and sweat—it wasn't the same at all.

Iridian took the box from the drawer. She held the tragedy in her hand, and when Ana finally reached the top of the stairs and found her, Iridian said, "You said we'd go back. You *told* us."

"Go back where?" Ana asked. Her gaze fell to the box in Iridian's hand. "Iridian, wait."

Iridian didn't wait. Instead she hurled out the ugliest thing she could think of—a thing that was not true, but true in that moment. "How could you do this to us, you dumb whore?"

Ana slammed the bathroom door shut and leapt forward.

"You're going through my stuff?" Ana demanded, all up in Iridian's face.

Iridian waited—to get smacked, to be yelled at, for Ana to get defensive and then apologize and apologize again—but Ana just crumbled. She fell back against the closed door, covered her eyes, and sobbed. Eventually, Ana slid all the way down to the ground and tossed the pregnancy test across the bathroom. Iridian was trapped.

All she could do was stand there, mortified, radiant with shame. She did swallow, a couple of times, as if trying to gulp down her sour-tasting mistake. At last, Iridian took a step toward her sister, but Ana held up a hand, silently commanding Iridian to stay back.

"I was so scared," Ana hiccupped. She wiped her eyes roughly. "But it's nothing. It's fine now. *You're* fine now, Iridian. Alright?"

Again, Iridian took a step forward. She reached out, but her sister smacked her hand away.

"No," Ana said. "You fucked up."

Ana stood and left, and those were the last words Iridian ever heard her sister say.

The laughter continued outside as Iridian spit out her half-chewed cereal, rinsed out her bowl, and put it in the overstuffed dishwater. The front door opened, and there was a new sound—gaspy and raspy, a sort of hysterical giggling. It belonged to Jessica. When was the last time Iridian had heard Jessica *giggle*? When had she *ever* heard her do that?

"What's going on?" Iridian asked, stepping into the living room.

"There was a fight," Rosa replied. Jessica was collapsed against her little sister, gripping Rosa's shoulders to keep from falling over. She was wet, like someone had tripped and spilled a drink on her shirt. "Between John and Peter Rojas."

Jessica laughed harder.

Iridian looked to Rosa to explain, but all Rosa could do was shrug and shake her head. After a few seconds, Jessica managed to get herself together enough to head toward the staircase on her own.

"Are you sure you're okay?" Iridian asked.

Jessica hiccupped. "I just need to change clothes." She hiccupped again.

Jessica got halfway up the stairs, and then spun toward her sisters. Her head had swiveled so fast, it looked like she'd been hit in the face. She wasn't laughing anymore.

"Wh—?" Iridian started.

She couldn't finish the question because she didn't want the answer. There had to be something else, some new terrible thing—phantom steps on the stairs, a misplaced, girl-shaped figure in a doorway, or more writing on the walls—more *I wants*. Iridian reached back to grip the couch and dug her nails into its scratchy fibers.

Jessica shook her head and tapped her ear.

That meant: *Listen.*

There was still the sound of laughter coming from outside, but new laughter had joined it. It was different: joyful, rising like a cluster of bubbles, but also sort of cruel and breathy and gleeful. It was the sound of someone who'd just been told a good-bad secret. It was as familiar as the handwritten letter *a*'s on the wall. It was Ana's laugh, and it was coming from upstairs, in the direction of Jessica's bedroom.

Jessica spun again and then ran down the stairs. Halfway down, she tripped over an old tear in the carpet and was thrown into a waiting Rosa.

The laughter continued, and Iridian cried out. She turned and braced herself—her hands and her forehead—against the back edge of the couch. She pressed hard. She was trying to get *in*.

"Stop!" Jessica commanded. *"Shut up."*

The laughing stopped. There were still the squeals coming from the little kids outside, but the house was quiet. Iridian stayed where she was, scraping her face against the couch. She felt her sister—Rosa—reach out and put a cool, small hand on her back. The three Torres sisters waited. Outside, a couple of birds chirped, thrilled about the sunshine.

Iridian heard Jessica swallow hard and then say, "Ana?"

There was a creak, like a foot being placed on the top step, followed by a drawn-out, hungry inhale, the type that someone would take after having held their breath underwater for a long, long time.

Iridian yelled, then yelled again. She kept yelling, over and over—long, loud, incoherent, non-word cries. She was yelling because she didn't want to hear what came after that inhale. She wanted the sound of her yelling to rise up and swallow the sounds of her sister's spirit. She wanted to drown out the world with noise.

Jessica
(Saturday, June 15th)

JESSICA LEFT THE house—she bolted out the door and was gone. The maniacal laughter that had felt like big, big waves crashing against the walls of her stomach, pressing against her rib cage, had been replaced by dead-cold nothing. She was a void. Iridian was yelling with her face smashed against the cushions, and Jessica didn't want to hear that. Rosa would take care of it.

Jessica found John right outside, leaning against her car, holding a cup of ice to his beat-up face. Peter was nowhere around, and his truck wasn't parked outside Hector's anymore.

"Where'd you go?" he asked.

"To change," she replied.

John looked to the front of Jessica's shirt, which was still speckled with light brown drops.

"Come on," she said, unlocking the door.

Jessica could do these easy things: walk out of her house, unlock her car door, drive to the pharmacy, buy first aid supplies to fix up John's face. These things were simple, as opposed to going back into her house and listening to her dead sister laugh with her or *at* her or whatever the fuck that was.

John waited in the car while Jessica went into the pharmacy to buy antiseptic and cotton balls. After that, she administered first aid in the parking lot. The cut on John's lip was crusted with blood, and she could tell from the bruising it probably still smarted. She repeated the simple process: slosh a cotton ball with antiseptic and press to John's lip. Eventually, John bucked his head back and hissed. He reached up and grabbed Jessica's wrist, forcing her to stop and meet his gaze. She tried not to stare at the one eye that was swollen nearly shut, the bruising around it nearly black. The seam of that eye, all along his lashes, was moist, weeping like a cut blister.

"You're pressing too hard," John said.

"Sorry," Jessica muttered.

She wasn't sorry.

Rosa

(Saturday, June 15th)

AFTER WARMING UP some leftover chicken fried rice
Jessica had brought home the other day, Rosa eventually
coaxed Iridian into the kitchen. They ate together at the
table, and then Rosa led Iridian to the couch in the living room. She clicked on the lamp. The television was still
on. Rosa sat down next to Iridian and started telling her
about her searches for the hyena and her trips up and down
the river and out to Concepcion Park. She described the
sounds of frogs and wind and crickets.

As Rosa started in on all the birds she'd seen recently—
cardinals, bluebirds, crows, little warblers—Iridian's
eyelids started to flutter closed.

She waited a few minutes to make sure Iridian was asleep, turned off the television, and then went upstairs to grab a box she kept under her bed. When she was younger, Rosa used to collect all kinds of colorful things. She liked tiny racecars with missing wheels, swirled-glass marbles, and bird feathers. She'd find objects around the neighborhood and hide them all over: in a plastic grocery bag that hung on a hook in her closet, in the hollow of the oak tree outside, in an old sour cream container she'd buried under the bushes in the backyard. Over time, she'd narrowed her collection down to the most important objects, and those objects were in a single shoebox.

Rosa pulled that box onto her lap and sifted through the contents. Her fingers skimmed a fake pearl button and a couple of Fiesta pins, and then landed on the note she'd received last July, a little over a month after Ana had died, from the boys across the street. One of them had written it, printing in very neat letters on a piece of a rounded-edged page from a composition book, the kind Iridian had always used. It was dark in the room, so she couldn't read those neat letters, but she didn't need to read it. She knew by heart what it said.

We saw Ana last night. She was standing in the front yard tapping on your dad's window. We thought you'd want to know. P.S. This is not a joke. We are serious.

She'd believed the boys, figuring they didn't have a reason to lie. They'd never been the mean types. She'd never heard about any of them playing pranks on other kids at their school. They didn't come right out and say they'd seen a ghost, but they didn't have to. She knew that's what had happened. But she couldn't understand why Ana would appear first to Hector and his friends, as opposed to her and her sisters.

There had to be a connection, Rosa thought, between Ana and the hyena and the cardinals. There just had to be. Rosa decided she needed to search again, and she needed a better, or quicker, method than on foot. She needed a car, or someone with a car. There was no way Jessica would take her around, or her dad, but maybe there was another option.

Rosa tucked the boys' note back in with the pearl button and the pins and the rest of her most important treasures. She guided the box to its hiding place, and then went into the hall to grab the receiver to the landline. She tried the church first, but Walter Mata wasn't there. He picked up on the second ring on his home phone.

"Hi, it's Rosa Torres," she said. "Do you think you can borrow your mom's car for a while?"

Rosa was wondering if she'd made a mistake. Cars were different from feet. Obviously. She was too removed from the ground. The car's muffler was sort of broken, making *huff-huff* sounds. Being a cautious driver with only his recently acquired learner's permit, Walter was diligent about using his turn signals, so in the background there were always these little *click-clacks*. The radio was on, playing the doo-wop oldies his mom liked. It was low-volume, but still. Rosa didn't like those kinds of sounds.

"Why do you want to find this hyena so badly?" Walter asked.

"It might need my help." Rosa was looking out the open window. She'd trained her eyes to see in the dark. She could make out distinctions in black shades and shapes and could tell a possum from a cat from a football field away.

"How can you help it?" Walter asked.

"I don't know," Rosa replied. "I'll know when I find it."

She'd had Walter drive her up and down the streets closest to her house first, and they'd fanned out from there. Closer to downtown, just a few streets away from hers, things were changing. Where, a few weeks ago, a small house had sat, there was now an empty lot. Where, a few weeks ago, an empty lot had sat, there was now a new, bigger house, or a small row of condos, or a bar with a cute, cursive neon sign above the door. Several of the houses that were still there had For Sale signs out front, even though those houses were occupied and Rosa could see lights on inside.

"I think it has something to do with my sister," Rosa said. "The hyena, I mean."

"Which sister?"

"Ana."

"Oh. As in, her spirit?"

"Yes." Rosa swiveled in her seat. "You think that makes sense?"

"I know a thing or two about spirits," Walter replied. "I spend a lot of time in an old church, remember?"

Rosa turned again to face the window. "Father Mendoza spends a lot of time in an old church, too, but he hasn't been particularly helpful or encouraging."

"To clarify," Walter said, "I spend a lot of time in the *basements* and *abandoned rooms* of an old church. I have a different perspective."

Rosa smiled out into the night. Maybe, she thought, this trip wasn't a mistake after all.

"Let's try the park again," she said.

Walter clicked on his turn signal.

For almost an hour, Rosa and Walter walked through Concepcion Park. The night wasn't hot, but the air was thick. Rosa was sweating inside her rubber boots, and her dress was sticking to her skin. It turned out to be not a very good night for searching. There were too many distractions. People were out late, playing baseball under the harsh lights. Cars took up almost all of the spaces in the lots. Some of those cars had windows that were steamed up—or smoked up, Rosa couldn't tell. Walter wasn't a distraction, though. Sometimes he tagged along beside Rosa, and sometimes he went his own way. Whenever she looked, Rosa noticed a firefly flash above Walter's right shoulder. She was sure this was a sign, a good omen. She needed a good omen.

"Are you scared?" Walter asked. "About your sister?"

"No," Rosa replied. "I just want to know what she wants. Are *you* scared? Of the spirits in the church?"

"Oh yeah." Walter laughed. "But not enough to quit my job, right? It's funny. I sort of like being scared."

Rosa didn't think it was funny at all. She thought it was wonderful.

They were making their way across a field when Walter stopped and went into a crouch. He'd found something. Rosa squinted, but she couldn't see what it was. Walter straightened, and there, pinched between his fingers, was the tiniest snail shell. It was a perfect coil, and without a single chip. As he turned it, its iridescence gleamed in the moonlight.

"Do you want this?" Walter asked, holding the shell out to Rosa.

"Yes," Rosa replied.

She knew exactly where she'd keep it.

Iridian

(Saturday, June 15th)

ON THIS NIGHT, when Iridian wrote, she was alone in a dark house. The first thing she did was turn the television back on so she could take comfort in the glow of other people's fake lives, and the second thing she did was grab her new notebook. Using a blue pen Rosa had fetched from upstairs earlier, Iridian filled all the lines of the first page with two words: *I'm sorry.*

They were, of course, for Ana—for what Iridian had said a year and a week ago. Apologies and forgiveness were rare and did not come easy in the Torres house, because rarely did anyone deserve them.

Iridian hated emotions because the one she felt the most was shame. It never left, or when she thought it was gone, there it was again, like a hard tap on her shoulder or a sudden stomach cramp or the sound of her name being called when she was sure no one was around. Iridian knew she didn't deserve forgiveness, but Ana deserved apologies. And Iridian would give them to her until her fingers bled. Ana would see them because she had eyes enough to read and then write on walls.

Jessica

(Saturday, June 15th)

AFTER DROPPING JOHN back at his house, Jessica sat in her car in her driveway. It was late, but she still didn't want to go back into her complicated house. Remnants of the block party littered the street. A red plastic cup was wedged in the opening of a storm drain. Several napkins were half stuck to the asphalt, waving feebly in the dull breeze.

Jessica's left arm was draped out her driver's-side window, and she was tapping a beat on her car door. Across the street, the light was on in Hector's bedroom, and she wondered if the boys knew she was out there. Finally, close to midnight, she saw Peter's truck round the corner and pull to a stop in front of Hector's. As Peter killed his engine and opened his door, Jessica whisper-shouted his name and climbed out of her car.

Peter stopped, his eyes narrowed. He looked up and down the darkened street and tossed his keys in his hand, as if he was testing their weight and was ready to use them as a weapon.

"It's just me," Jessica said. "I swear it."

Peter came forward, and Jessica saw the short, neat cut between his left eye and his brow. Aside from that, the eye didn't look so bad. It wasn't swollen shut and oozing fluid, though the white part was shot through with streaks of red, like some capillaries had burst. She quickly scanned the rest of his face. The light from the street lamps was dim and hazy orange, but she couldn't see any swelling at his jaw or bruising at his temple. Jessica wished he would smile one of his easy smiles so she could check if he'd chipped any teeth.

"Here to survey the damage?" Peter's question was an icy snap in the warm night.

"I was worried about you," Jessica replied.

"Why?"

"What do you mean *why*?" Jessica ran her fingers through her humidity-puffed hair and then motioned to the street. "Because of what happened."

"Why would you be worried about me, Jessica?" Peter urged. His face was uncharacteristically stony, nearly eerie under the street lamps. "I'm just someone you work with."

Jessica looked to the street, her eyes landing on what used to be a piece of white frosted cake. It was by the curb, smashed and covered with ants.

"I'm sorry." It was the second time Jessica had said those words that night, but the first time she'd meant them.

Peter stepped closer, and Jessica lifted her gaze from the street just enough to see his hands hanging by his sides. There were bruises on them, across the ridges of the knuckles. Peter flexed his hand, and Jessica wondered how much those knuckle bones still stung, and if anyone had bent over them and cared for them, dabbed gently at them with a cotton ball.

Just inches from Peter's bruised knuckles, a firefly flashed.

"For what?" Peter said. "Sorry for what?"

Jessica startled and looked up. Peter was angry, but he was giving her a chance. She knew that whatever she said next would ruin something. It would either ruin something for her and John, or for her and Peter. She had to make a choice. It wasn't simple. Or, it was too simple.

"Do you want to come inside?" Jessica asked. "We can talk inside."

She could go inside again, if he came with her.

Jessica half expected Peter to glance over his shoulder at Hector's window, to check to see if his friends were watching, but he stayed focused on her.

Did his expression soften, or did Jessica just imagine it?

"Alright." Peter nodded in the direction of the front door. "Sure. After you."

Rafe had always had a rule against boys in the house, but Jessica didn't care about rules right then. Besides, her dad wasn't even home. He was probably out with Norma, spending the night at her not-haunted house. Jessica led Peter through the dimly lit living room, past the flashing television and a sleeping Iridian huddled under that stinky old blanket, and then up to the second floor. On the staircase, Peter slowed to look at the photos in frames that hung on the wall.

"Your mom."

Peter pointed to a photo of Jessica's mother. She was sitting in a lawn chair at a pool party, wearing a forest green bikini and large black sunglasses. Her long brown hair was parted down the middle and hung over her shoulders. Jessica was ready for Peter to ask about her, about how much Jessica remembered about her, and Jessica would have to shrug and say not much, which was the disappointing truth.

"She looks like Rosa," Peter said.

"She does."

Jessica unlocked and opened the door to her bedroom, realizing too late it was an embarrassing wreck of trash and clothes and dirty sheets. Her face turned hot as Peter

did a quick scan, taking in the sorry sight of damp towels tossed into corners and empty tubes of lip gloss and
mascara that littered the carpet. Nothing in his expression
gave away what he might've been thinking until he went to
the window, pulled back the curtain, and looked out into
the night.

"This used to be Ana's room," Jessica said.

"I knew that." Peter let the curtain drop and then
turned toward Jessica. "We used to watch her from
Hector's." He dropped his head and shook it. A blush
spread across his cheeks. "That sounds creepy. It *was*
creepy. We were creeps."

"What did you see?" Jessica asked, genuinely curious.

Peter lifted his head and crinkled his brow.

"When you would watch her," Jessica clarified. "What
would she do?"

"She would sneak out," Peter replied. "Climb down the
tree. A couple hours later, she'd come back and climb *up* the
tree. Most of the time, though, she would just stand here
and look out. Not to the street, but to the sky." He paused.
"You don't do that. Stand at the window and look out."

Jessica should've been angry. Peter was giving her
proof of his and the neighborhood's prying eyes. She
wasn't angry, though. There was a difference, she realized,
between being spied on and being noticed. She wanted to
be noticed, and Peter had noticed her. It gave her a buzzy,
soft-edged feeling her hard self wasn't used to.

"Did you see her fall?" Jessica asked.

"No. We heard the glass break. And a car drive away."

"It wasn't John," Jessica said automatically. "He said it wasn't him."

She winced and then scrubbed a hand across her face. It was like those terrible words had actually stung as they came out of her mouth. She'd always known John was there, even if he denied it. The boy who had tasted and touched every centimeter of Jessica's skin had seen her sister die and had driven away.

"I'm sorry," Jessica said. "I'm sorry I just said that."

"You should stop apologizing," Peter said.

Jessica snickered. "Well, I've got a lot to be sorry for, so . . ."

Peter cracked a smile. It was so small, but so perfect. "You weren't the one who decided to fight me."

"All I do is fight you."

Peter opened his mouth to speak but was interrupted by a tapping at the window. The sound wasn't a hollow *ping* made by thrown stones, but more like a softer thud.

A ripple of fear went all the way down Jessica's right arm, from her shoulder and out through her fingers. She closed her eyes and waited for the hard cluck of Ana's laughter.

"The tree?" Peter asked.

Jessica shook her head. "Too far away."

The tapping continued. It was rhythmic and controlled—not like branches being tossed against glass by the unpredictable wind. Jessica opened her eyes and saw that Peter didn't seem scared. He hadn't blanched, and his eyes weren't wide. He went over to the window and pulled back the curtain. The tapping stopped. Peter looked down, to the lawn and to the street, and then turned to face Jessica.

"Ana," she said.

"What does she want?" Peter asked, in an echo of the question Iridian had asked the day before. When Iridian had asked it, Jessica hadn't answered. She hadn't answered because she didn't have an answer. She still didn't.

"I don't know." Jessica sat down on the edge of her unmade bed. "We don't know. It started when I . . . I saw her hand. Then she wrote on the wall. Today, we heard her laughing. I don't know what it means. All these little tricks. It's like . . . why would she do this to us?"

"Do you think she's sending a message?"

"Yes. Maybe. I don't know." Jessica cocked her head. "Do you really believe all this?"

"Sure," Peter said. "Why wouldn't I?"

The way Peter was acting—the way he was standing all easy-like with his hands in his pockets and without his shoulders all tense and hiked up around his ears—it was strange. He'd just been in a street fight and had just been told the room he was standing in was haunted, but some-how that was all no big deal, water off his back.

How, Jessica wondered, can a person not absorb all the cruel and painful and scary things about life? How did Peter not itch every day? How was that possible?

"I haven't told John," Jessica said. "I don't even . . . I don't even know where to start."

Peter didn't respond. Maybe it was because of the men-tion of John's name.

For a long moment, it was quiet. There was nothing, not the tapping against windows or the rushing hum of the air conditioner. Jessica thought maybe she heard some-thing from downstairs, like Iridian snoring faintly, but then that stopped, too.

"I can't believe you're leaving," Jessica said.

"You can leave too, you know." Peter leaned against the side of Jessica's dresser. "Not many people would choose to stay in a haunted house."

This is what Jessica had wanted: someone to tell her to fly away. And now, here she was, recycling the words that John had spoken a few days ago that had sent her heart plummeting. She was nothing but a mimic.

"I can't leave Southtown. I have a job. My family."

Peter pushed off the dresser and came forward. Jessica wanted so badly to lean forward and do something sim-ple, like lift the edge of his shirt and kiss the skin of his stomach.

"I don't know what it's like to live in this house," Peter said, "and I'm in no position to tell you how to live your life."

"But?"

"But . . ." Peter began. "If I was the ghost of someone who had always, in life, looked out her window with an expression on her face like she was desperate to escape, and I had come back to send a message, it would be to tell her sisters to get out of this house and never look back."

Jessica waited—for the sound against the window to return more urgently, for the light bulbs in her room to burn bright then blow out, for anything big and bold to tell her Peter was right.

"There's one more thing," Peter went on to say, "and I don't care if you repeat it to your boyfriend."

"I won't tell—"

"I don't care if you tell him," Peter said, interrupting. "There are two huge tragedies here. The first is that you are legions better than John Chavez, and he doesn't deserve you."

Jessica's hands balled into fists.

"And the second?" she urged.

"The second is worse. You know you're better than him, but you refuse, for whatever reason, to do anything about it. I have no problem fighting him. I'll do it over and over again, but you should figure out a way to fight him, too. You don't have to do it alone, but you have to do it."

The words were on the tip of Jessica's tongue: *You don't know me. You don't know what you're talking about. Things aren't so fucking easy.*

But also these words: *I still sing. I do it when I'm alone in my car in empty parking lots. My voice is better than it's ever been.*

Jessica closed her eyes, and her ears tuned in to the wheezing rattle of her dad's truck, coming up the street. Soon there was the sound of a steel door slamming shut, followed by a wet, uncovered cough. Jessica opened her eyes, and Peter was there, still hovering in front of her.

"My dad's home," she said. "You should probably go."

Jessica walked Peter out of the house in silence, but once they were out in the yard, Peter stopped and turned.

"I can't hear," he said.

"What?"

"I can't hear anymore," Peter replied. "Not like I used to."

Jessica realized he was answering a question she'd asked when she'd been flat on her back on the floor of a church: *Do you still sing?*

"I was in a fight," Peter said. "I was drunk, and I picked a fight with my sister's boyfriend over nothing, and he hit me in the ear and broke some bones behind my eardrum. I can't find pitch anymore."

"I never heard about that," Jessica said.

"I'm glad." Peter looked out to the empty street. "It's not exactly my proudest moment. And I don't want people thinking I'm a violent drunk, which apparently I am."

Jessica didn't know what to think. She didn't drink, but she knew what it was like to blow up and lash out and pick pieces of other people's skin from beneath her fingernails. On the other hand, she was getting really, really sick of sharing space with boys who were also capable of blowing up and lashing out. She was just so tired of pain. But what she wasn't tired of, and what she was just starting to get a taste of, was honesty. Peter had shared something hard and true with her, and for that she was grateful.

"I'm sorry about your ear," Jessica said.

Peter shrugged. "I deserved it."

"Maybe," Jessica replied, smirking. "Too bad you won't be around for me to teach you how to sing again."

When Jessica came back inside, her dad was sitting at the kitchen table, in the dark, nursing a bottle of Negra Modelo.

"Boys aren't allowed in the house," Rafe said.

Jessica didn't reply. She was too busy humming a little tune to herself.

"There are rules here," Rafe added.

Jessica kept ignoring her father as she made her way back to the staircase. She'd just placed her hand on the banister when Rafe called out her name again. There was something, a pleading sadness in his voice, that made her stop—stop walking, stop humming.

"Anything about that two hundred dollars you were gonna let me borrow?" he asked. "For the truck?"

Jessica should've been mad. Her fingers should've gripped the banister with more force, but she just started up the stairs again and continued to hum.

Iridian
(Sunday, June 16th)

THE ROUTINE ON Sunday was simple. Iridian ate chocolate puffs up on the kitchen counter while Rosa sat in the backyard and tried to talk to the animals. Jessica eventually strolled in wearing her work clothes, but this Sunday she didn't look perfectly perfect. Her hair was thrown up in a clip, and her only makeup was a dash of mascara. She smelled weird, too sharp and sterile, like Lysol or air freshener.

"Dad's asleep in his room," Iridian said.

Jessica grabbed her keys off the kitchen table and left without a word.

Rosa came in just as the Matas' car outside started honking its horn.

"See you later," she said, hustling toward the front door.

Iridian finished her cereal, put the bowl in the dishwater, and then went back to the couch. Once there, she wrote and wrote, page after page after page. She started with another page of *I'm sorry I'm sorry*, but then she tried to write down everything she could remember from her old notebooks upstairs into her new one. She wrote in the margins, in curves around the corners, in between the spiral holes, until her pen started running out of ink.

Eventually, Iridian fell asleep there, with the television on mute and her notebook open on her chest and pen dangling from her fingertips. She woke up a couple of times—once, briefly, when the air conditioner clicked on and she had to pull the blanket up tighter around her shoulders, and again when she heard soft thumps on the stairs and then in the rooms above her head, and she'd assumed that her little sister had come home from church and was trying not to make too much noise.

"Rosa," Iridian croaked. She shifted on the couch so that she was facing the ceiling and watched a spider spin a strand of web between two blades of the unmoving fan. The air conditioner clicked on once more, which was followed by the sound of more footstep-thuds coming from the stairs. The air, Iridian thought, smelled a little like oranges.

Iridian called out her sister's name again, but there was no reply.

"Dad?" she whispered.

Bracing one hand against the side of the couch, Iridian pushed herself to seated, peered toward the staircase, and made a noise—a strained little groan.

Scattered down the staircase were the books—Iridian's books, Ana's books—that had once been stacked neatly in Iridian's closet with their spines facing the wall. They were now spread out, some with their pages yawned open, and some with the pages *missing*, torn out and tossed around. There was paper *everywhere*. The cover of *The Witching Hour* was there, right in Iridian's eyeline. Iridian's notebooks—also once stacked neatly in her closet—were there, too, scattered. Like the books, some were still intact, but just barely. Some were in pieces, ripped—*shredded*. Others were spread open, hanging half on, half off the stairs, like mouths, like big mouths with jaws unhinged from screaming or laughing.

Iridian tumbled off the couch just as she heard someone outside, in the front of the house. There was heavy breathing, grunts, the sound of someone rooting around in the earth by the bushes and bumping against the side of the house.

Rafe, she thought.

It was another bright day, and maybe he was outside doing yard work. That seemed possible. Iridian never ran to her dad in search of safety, but in this instance she didn't know what else to do. She yanked open the front door, pushed against the screen door, and ran out barefoot into the grass.

Rafe wasn't out there doing yard work. What was there was an animal, crouched low on four bent legs. Those legs were black, but its body was spotted, black on tan. A strip of fur all the way down the length of its spine stood taller than the rest. Its dark muzzle was smeared with blood. And there, pinned under one of its front paws, were the remains of a squirrel. The dead animal's bushy tail fluttered in the light breeze, the sunlight shining off its red fur. Iridian watched—still breathless, close to fainting—as that crouched-low animal opened its mouth and its throat started to bob. A sound came out—not a grunt, not breath. A laugh. Hyenas, they laugh like that. They sound like cruel people doubled over and cackling.

Iridian started to shake—not just her hands, but her entire body. The tremors were so violent they caused her teeth to rattle.

"Rosa," she pled feebly.

Rosa did not come, but the animal did. It abandoned the squirrel and stalked forward, its dark eyes pinned on Iridian. It stepped to the side and cut off the path to the front door, as if it somehow knew that Iridian's escape was always inward, never outward.

Iridian looked to the street for help, but she was alone.

"It's fine," she whispered to herself.

It was *not* fine. She was still shaking. The hyena, still laughing, took another step forward, and Iridian let out her own scream. It was a low guttural howl from the back of her raw throat that was like nothing she'd ever produced before.

Again, Iridian looked to the street. Peter Rojas's truck was parked in front of Hector's house, along with a couple other of Hector's friends' cars. The front door to Hector's house was open, but the screen door was closed. All Iridian could think was that she needed to get inside. Inside, anywhere.

The hyena stepped forward, and Iridian took a matching step back. She stepped back again. And again. Light-headed, she gulped, forcing air down into her lungs. The cool grass crunched under her bare feet as she moved— this was good. She just needed to keep moving. She was on the sidewalk and then on the slick asphalt of the street and then on grass again, in Hector's front yard. When she reached the house, she didn't ring the bell, just pulled at the handle. The door was open, and Iridian stumbled inside. Hector's mom was in the living room, sitting on the couch, doing something on her computer with her headphones in.

"Iridian," Mrs. Garcia said, trying to hide her surprise. "Is everything alright?"

Iridian didn't know what to say, so she didn't say anything.

This was a nice house, so different from hers. She'd noticed that when she was here before, last summer. It wasn't dusty. The furniture mostly matched. There was a shelf full of sports-related trophies, and everywhere—on the walls, on side tables—were pictures in frames of Hector and his older sister. They were together, posing and smiling. They were by themselves, posing and smiling. What a nice family.

Iridian flew up the stairs, keeping her gaze on her feet. There was a blade of grass stuck to her big toenail. Pebbles from the road were wedged between her toes.

She could hear the boys even before she reached the top of the stairs. The door to Hector's room was slightly open, and Iridian could see Hector and four of his friends sitting on the floor at the foot of Hector's bed, in front of an old television set. They were passing around a box of cornflakes, scooping out the dry cereal with their hands and shoveling it into their mouths.

Jimmy was closest to the door, so he saw Iridian first, and froze, mid-chew. He nudged Hector, who ignored him. It was only when Iridian pushed open the door fully and stepped into the room that Hector turned his head and saw her.

"Oh . . ." he said. "Uh . . ."

The other boys—Calvin, Luis, and Peter—also turned to face Iridian. They said nothing, just stared.

"There's something outside my house," Iridian choked out. "By the window."

The boys reacted as if they'd suddenly been set on fire. They sprang up, leaping over one another to get to Hector's window. Calvin's hand latched on to the curtains, but he lost his grip when Luis elbowed him in the face. Cornflakes flew from the box, scattering across the bed and floor. Hector tackled Luis, and then tossed him backward. Finally, it was Jimmy who stepped over his pile of friends to reach the window first. He yanked back the curtain and pulled the cord to raise the blinds. He held his breath, looking out and down.

"She's not there," he said. "There's nothing there."

Hector, Luis, and Calvin crowded around him to look.

"There's nothing fucking there, Iridian!" Hector shouted, spinning around. "What the fuck?"

Iridian just stood there, mute and trembling. This was a mistake, a huge mistake. She shouldn't have come here, and she had no idea why Hector was yelling at her.

"Iridian," Peter said.

He was the only one who hadn't wrestled his way across the room. He was standing at the foot of Hector's bed, and the first thing Iridian noticed was how tall he was, taller than Iridian had remembered. He was dressed for work at the pharmacy, wearing a blue collared shirt and khaki pants. There was a small bruise above his eyebrow, and Iridian remembered how Rosa said he'd been in a fight with John.

"Are you okay?" Peter started to reach for Iridian, but thought better of it and withdrew his hand. "What was it? What was there?" He glanced down to Iridian's dirty feet.

"The hyena," she said.

"No way," Hector sneered.

"It was there," Iridian insisted. "In the yard. It was right there."

"There's nothing there," Jimmy whined. Both of his palms were spread out against the glass, and the tip of his nose was squashed flat against the pane.

"I swear it," Iridian said. "I heard something. I thought it was my dad, but when I went to check . . ."

Iridian's voice cracked. What a stupid thing to be doing, crying in a room full of boys she hardly knew, hardly ever spoke to, who she knew thought she was an awkward freak.

"I believe you," Peter replied, turning to face her. "Alright? Just ignore them. They thought it was—"

He paused. Hector, Luis, and Calvin all turned, nearly in unison, away from the window.

"You thought it was *what*?" Iridian asked.

Peter glanced to Hector. "Ana," he said. "We should probably tell you something."

Iridian listened to a story from a year ago about Ana standing outside, tapping on a window, and then Rafe stalking around the yard with a baseball bat. It wasn't the best, most dramatic ghost story she'd ever heard, which is how she knew it was true.

Ana had returned—for her dad, for Iridian and her sisters, for all of them.

"It's true," Iridian said to the boys. "Ana *is* back, but she's not the same anymore."

The Day Iridian Torres Walked Away from the Tenth Grade

IRIDIAN TORRES NEVER went anywhere without three things: a worn-out paperback copy of *The Witching Hour* by Anne Rice, a black-and-white composition notebook, and a peacock blue ink pen. She carried *The Witching Hour* and the notebook with her, from class to class, stacked on top of whatever textbook or binder she was required to have. She always sat in the back row. If there was a window in the room, she'd sit in the desk closest to that. Her spine was always bent way forward, and her legs were folded underneath her on the hard plastic seat. Iridian didn't really talk to people after her sister died, and people didn't really talk to her. But even in mourning, Iridian managed to make pretty good grades, so the teachers gave her a pass when, instead of taking notes, she'd just write in her composition book with her blue ink pen or open up *The Witching Hour* in her lap. Everyone—teachers, other students, staff—figured it was best to leave her alone, not because she would snap at them like Jessica, but because when someone puts up that thick a wall around themselves, you just respect it.

We didn't have uniforms at our school, but Iridian had created her own. She wore white slip-on sneakers, narrow-legged and high-waisted jeans that made her already skinny body appear skinnier, a short-sleeved T-shirt of some kind (always a solid color; never with a graphic), and a jean jacket. The jacket had a patch on it, on the back, over her right shoulder blade. It was of a nopal cactus with a couple of pink flowers in bloom.

We imagined that if some stranger had walked into one of the classrooms and had seen Iridian there, in her uniform, writing in her notebook, they would have thought, *That girl is lost in her own world.* But that wasn't it at all. Iridian wasn't lost, and she was the furthest thing from being in her own world. In truth, Iridian was very aware of the real, *actual* world. The way she sat at her desk, with her long limbs folded up close to her body like an insect—she looked uncomfortable, like everyone else's breath was pressing too hard against her, making her smaller and more compact. She felt everything—*too much*. The world seemed so hard for her to live in.

Of course, we wanted to know what Iridian was writing in her notebooks. Jimmy thought it was some kind of burn book, a list of classmates Iridian felt deserved to suffer the way she clearly suffered. Calvin thought the burn book idea was overdramatic. The answer, according to him, was obvious: Iridian was writing about vampires because Anne Rice wrote about vampires, and if someone reads the exact same book over and over again, it's probably going to get stuck in their brain. That made a lot of sense until Hector pointed out Iridian always carried around *The Witching Hour*, which, by the very title, would seem not to be about vampires, but witches.

We really had no idea what we were talking about, but when we discovered the truth of what Iridian was writing about in her notebooks, it was a nightmare. There weren't any vampires or witches, but it was a nightmare all the same.

On a Tuesday in December, Iridian was in the cafeteria eating lunch alone. Right there, by her tray, like always, was *The Witching Hour*, her composition notebook, and her blue pen. Evalin Uvalde—the girl who was making out with John Chavez until Jessica threw a cup at her face—came up from behind Iridian and snatched her notebook. On instinct, Iridian whipped around and reached back, but Evalin spun out of the way, cackling. Evalin then hopped onto a nearby table and opened Iridian's notebook.

After scanning through a few pages, she landed on one that made her grin so wickedly wide.

This moment was important. It was the moment when the three of us who also had this lunch period, and who were sitting just a couple of tables away from where all this was happening, could've stopped what came next, or *attempted* to stop it and spin its trajectory on a different path. We could've saved Iridian Torres—it was so obvious she needed saving—but we didn't. We remembered what happened the last time we tried saving one of the Torres sisters. Our heroics had backfired in the worst possible way. So instead of doing *anything*, we just sat there, our curiosity burning.

Evalin cleared her throat, and we couldn't help it— we leaned toward the sound. Other students—almost the entire lunchroom—stopped talking and also leaned toward the sound. People hushed each other. Even the workers behind the counters got quieter, or so it seemed. The dings of the registers and the clanks of trays lessened, softened. That day, we were all hungry for nastiness.

"*I have a problem,*" Evalin read out loud, while Iridian curled into herself, shrank deeper into her jean jacket. "*I can write most of the parts, like the parts describing the characters, what they look like, or how it feels when one character wants another character so much their knees turn to jelly and their heart starts to beat all fast and jangled. I know what this feels like. I can write that. But what I can't write are the sex* scenes. *I have no frame of reference! I've never been with a guy or a girl. I've never even been kissed, and while I'm pretty sure I can fake those descriptions or borrow them from one of Ana's books, that would be . . . disingenuous. I'd feel like a fraud. The descriptions wouldn't be from the heart. It wouldn't be real, and I want it to be real.*"

Evalin read all this with a fake-earnest tone, and not once did she break character, even though her friends had their hands clasped over their mouths, their eyes watering from holding in their cruel laughter.

It got worse. Of course it did. Evalin looked up from the notebook and straight to where we were sitting.

"*I'm thinking about asking one of the boys across the street at Hector's for a favor,*" she said. "*I wonder if one of them will have sex with me.*" Evalin snorted. "*Just once. For research.*"

Evalin lost it. She doubled over, gasping and laughing, clutching the notebook to her chest. Her friends all lost it as well. They laughed these loud, full-throated, messy laughs. We could see past the tops of their mouths, to their tongues, to the bits of french fries or the remains of ham sandwiches speckled across those tongues. John Chavez, the biggest shithead in town, was there, hooting and laughing. Eventually, Evalin—still laughing, laughing so hard she was hiccupping—straightened up and put her hand in the air, palm facing forward, silently commanding everyone to wait.

There are two things that gutless boys do when they're being laughed at: They get defensive or they join in. The gazes of the people in the lunchroom that weren't on Iridian—who was still sitting, frozen at her table—were on us. In that moment, we hated Evalin and the evil pride shining in her eyes. We hated watching Iridian fold into herself. Most of all, we hated the fact that we—the ones who had wanted more than anything to be Ana Torres's heroes—buckled under the pressure. We sat there and started laughing, like cowards.

We laughed and laughed at Iridian, but later we talked about how much we hated that we just went along with it. We were sick with regret. It felt like a bunch of slick worms writhing around in our stomachs.

Regret. It's so useless so much of the time.

Evalin wasn't done. She'd needed a moment to compose herself, to shake out her shoulders and take a big breath, like she was some Olympic athlete about to run a big race, before she was able to continue.

She read on: *"I need to know what it feels like, how to do it. I'd like for it to be with someone who doesn't already have a girlfriend and someone who wouldn't feel the need to go tell everyone after it happened, and someone who wasn't a virgin, because it would be helpful if he knew what he was doing. That last thing, the virgin thing, is just a request though, not a requirement. Also, I will not form an attachment."*

Evalin snickered. She looked up from the notebook and tilted her head at us in a gesture of mock sincerity.

"*I promise.*"

There was still laughter throughout the room, but in some corners it had stopped. People with shreds of feeling in their hearts ducked their heads closer to one another, probably whispering about poor Iridian and cruel Evalin. Like us, they didn't do anything but whisper, though. The cash registers went back to their dinging, and the trays went back to their clanging.

One might think Iridian, overcome by embarrassment, would've run from the lunchroom and hid in the bathroom or the library or nurse's office for the rest of the day. She didn't do that. She just sat there, compact, staring straight down at the surface of the table. Her mouth was closed, but her lips were moving, twitching a little, like she was talking to herself.

Iridian's request was for sure a shock, but, when we think about it now, it wasn't totally bizarre. Iridian was the type of girl who was both withdrawn and hyperfocused. She saw things, and not in the dreamy, pseudoclairvoyant way Rosa saw things. Iridian was observant and keen in her own way. She was good with details, sharp like a knife. So it made sense that if she wanted to write something and make it true, she'd really want to *know* the thing she was writing about. She'd want to suck the thing up with her senses and then document it in her notebook.

Finally—*finally*—the bell rang. Iridian grabbed her copy of *The Witching Hour* and snatched her notebook from Evalin's hand, ripping a couple of pages in the process, and left the lunchroom. That was the last day we ever saw her at school.

Rosa

(Sunday, June 16th)

"IT CAME FOR you?"

Rosa was crouched in front of a bush in the yard, examining a bit of loose squirrel fur the color of red clay. At the same time, she was fighting down the strange urge to cause petty harm to her sister. It was like she wanted to tug out a strand of Iridian's hair or step down on her bare big toe. Rosa had never felt that way before.

"It didn't come *for* me," Iridian explained. "It was just here."

"How did it seem?" Rosa urged. "Like, how did it look? Was it sick?"

Iridian obviously didn't know how to respond to that, so Rosa's focus shifted from the fur tangled in the bushes over to Hector's house, where a jumble of boy-shaped shadows had appeared at the upper window. A bird cawed from a nearby tree.

"Come on," Rosa said, standing. "It's getting dark. Let's go inside."

"Wait." Iridian latched on to Rosa's arm, a little too hard. "Did you not hear what I told you, about the boys, about Ana? They said—"

"I know what they said," Rosa replied. "They told you about how they saw her ghost by the window last summer. I know. They sent me a note when it happened."

When Rosa looked into her sister's eyes, she saw a hunger there. Or like a *dis*-ease, a wildness. Maybe that wildness had passed to Iridian from the hyena. Iridian squeezed Rosa's arm harder, and Rosa's urge to tug a piece of Iridian's hair got stronger.

Everything was connected.

Rosa was on the bus on the way back to San Fernando. It wasn't the first time she'd been to church twice on the same Sunday, but there was a new kind of urgency to this trip. She supposed she could have tried to find Walter's mom for a ride—Walter was probably still at church, working—but she wanted to be alone before talking to Father Mendoza.

Sunday buses were usually empty, and Rosa's bus was no exception. It was just her, a woman in a uniform—a knee-length pink dress and tan-colored tights that made her seem like she worked in a diner—and the driver. Traffic was light, and the bus was only a couple of stops away from the church when the driver slammed on his brakes. Rosa flew—forehead first—into the seat in front of her. Dazed, she checked for blood, but there was no cut, just a tender spot that would for sure form a goose egg. The woman in the pink dress, though, was moaning from the floor. She'd been thrown completely out of her seat and was in a crumpled heap, bleeding from the mouth. There was a long run in her tights, all the way up her shin.

The driver got to the woman before Rosa could. He was trying to open a first aid kit and speak into his radio at the same time. He was saying something about an animal running out into the street, and how he'd had to come to a sudden stop to avoid hitting it.

"It looked sort of like a dog," he said. "Or like a real skinny wolf."

Rosa bolted out the side doors of the bus, first checking under the wheels and then looking frantically up and down the street. She thought she saw something—a flicker of a shadow low to the ground—on the other side of a parked car, and she ran toward it. There was nothing there, but then that same flicker caught her eye, this time as if it had just rounded the corner of a building up ahead. It was leading her closer and closer to the church.

This was perfect. This was just what she'd been hoping for.

Like last time, there was a line of people waiting to see Father Mendoza, but Rosa shoved ahead of all of them.

"I have another question," Rosa said, standing across from the priest's desk.

Father Mendoza's dry-kindling eyes were, as usual, patient and kind. His stark white office wasn't the type of room that Rosa expected would change much from day to day, but she hadn't expected it to be exactly the same as before. There were the same simple cross, the same simple ticking clock, and also the same line of ants marching in the same curve up the wall behind where the priest sat.

"Is it possible," she began, still slightly out of breath, "for the spirit of a person to enter another creature?"

"You're talking about possession?" Father Mendoza asked. "Like when a demon enters a person's body?"

"Not a demon, no. I'm wondering if the spirit of a person can enter the body of an animal." Rosa paused to look to the ants on the white wall. "Or an insect."

"Is that what you think has happened with Ana?" Father Mendoza asked.

"Yes," Rosa replied. "Maybe, yes. There were fireflies and a bird that fell. And the hyena. It escaped from the zoo on the anniversary of the day my sister died. It killed a squirrel on our front lawn." There was a little pinch in

Rosa's heart, and she pushed the palm of her hand against her chest. "I think . . . it may be close by."

Father Mendoza was quiet for a moment. Then he asked, "You think your sister is controlling these things?"

"Yes," Rosa replied. "Does this mean something?"

For a long time, Father Mendoza said nothing. He had to have known there was still a line of people waiting outside to speak with him, but he didn't look at his ticking clock. Rosa could see a spark in his eyes, like he was calling to mind a memory. He was off somewhere, in the room but not in the room. Rosa knew what that was like.

"Ever since you came last time, I've been doing some thinking," he finally said, "and I have a question of my own. Why is it Ana who is doing these things? Why isn't it your mother?"

Rosa suddenly felt very heavy. Over the course of the last year, she and her priest had talked for hours and hours about faith and death and the meaning of life, but they'd never talked about Rosa's mother. Rita de la Cruz was a woman who had grown up in the Rio Grande Valley, who'd met Rafe Torres when they'd both been in the ninth grade, and who'd died just hours after giving birth to Rosa. All Rosa knew was that, during the delivery, something had gone wrong. There was blood loss. Even the strongest heart can't beat without blood.

"I've never told you this," Father Mendoza went on, "but I knew Rita. I'm a couple of years younger than her, but we both grew up in Mission. It's a small place. Everyone knew everyone."

Father Mendoza's chair squeaked as he sat back and brought his fingers into a tent. His eyes were doing what dry kindling does when it heats up. They were smoldering. Rosa knew what was coming. Her priest was about to launch into a story. He probably thought this story, which would no doubt be about the young Rita de la Cruz down in Mission, Texas, was going to be a gift Rosa could then take home with her and cherish like a bird's bright feather or a perfectly coiled snail shell. Father Mendoza probably thought he was being kind and generous. But Rosa knew his story wouldn't really have anything to do with Rosa *or* her mother. She could tell by the warm glow in his eyes that, even if the story seemed on the surface to be about Rita de la Cruz, it was really about him.

"Our mothers had been friends since high school," he said, "but it wasn't until Rita was fifteen that we officially met. I was thirteen."

Rosa looked to the cross on the wall, and then to the clock. She closed her eyes and took a breath. Father Mendoza wasn't *listening*. She'd come to him with something specific and important, and he was turning it into something about himself. He was launching into this tale as if he had all the time in the world to tell it, as if it wasn't getting late in the day or if there wasn't a small mob of people still waiting outside his door for his counsel.

"You look a lot like her," Father Mendoza said.

Rosa felt even heavier. What a waste this was turning out to be. Jessica had always had a bad taste in her mouth when it came to priests, and now Rosa was beginning to understand why.

Just a moment earlier, Father Mendoza had said, "Everyone knew everyone." Rosa disagreed. No one knew anyone. Not really.

She wasn't there to argue that point, though, so she put up her hand, palm facing out, just like she'd seen Father Mendoza do hundreds of times while he led services. He'd hold one hand like that while the other rested on the opened pages of a Bible. The priest saw Rosa's hand, and he stopped talking.

"Thank you," Rosa said. "I'm leaving now."

Rosa found Walter outside, sweeping the steps. He was facing away from her and didn't know she was there. Rosa liked the look of it: Walter, a tall boy with strong arms, sweeping stone in the twilight. Still unaware of Rosa, Walter stopped his work and looked for a moment to the darkening sky, to the lightning flashes in the distance. She liked the look of that, too: a boy watching a storm.

"Walter!" Rosa called out.

Walter turned. "Everything alright?" he asked.

"After I figure all this out," Rosa said, approaching him, "about Ana, I'd like to go with you to the basement and abandoned rooms of the church."

"Okay." Walter laughed. "Of course."

Rosa reached for Walter's hand, and Walter let her take it. She didn't thread her sweat-damp fingers with his, but she held his right hand, palm up, in her left hand. Then she touched it. For what felt like a long time, she traced Walter's fingers across his rough fingertips and the blunt edge of each of his nails. She pictured these fingers holding hammers and light bulbs and ladder rungs. She pressed her thumb into the mound under his thumb. She spread his fingers wide to feel the webbing between them. This was a hand that did things. Rosa liked that. She liked that he wasn't a ghost, or a phantom animal. If she wanted, she could walk up to him and touch him.

Jessica
(early Monday, June 17th)

JESSICA AND JOHN had spent the last ten hours together, and she'd been half there for all of them. After her shift, she had gone to John's house because he'd told her to come to his house. They'd watched television. They'd driven around. They'd gotten burgers from a drive-through. They'd parked and eaten those burgers in the car and then made out a little even though John's mouth tasted like meat and Jessica wasn't really into it. Then they'd driven around some more. They'd talked. Well, John had talked. He'd talked about how his older cousin was never home anymore now that he'd enrolled in some classes at the community college, and because of that, John had to do more chores around the house. He may have talked about some other stuff, but

Jessica hadn't really been listening. For sure, she hadn't said anything back. He'd never asked her anything about herself or her job or her family. Eventually, Jessica pulled up outside her house, thinking that John would get the point. He didn't. The engine was off. The windows were rolled down. It was nearly five in the morning, and Jessica was so very over all of this. She thought back to when she was in grade school, in the choir. Her heart used to feel so full.

Jessica had a song stuck in her head, one she'd heard at work that day, probably seven or eight times. John was still talking as she looked out the windows and started humming to herself.

"Jess?" John urged. "What are you doing?"

Jessica closed her eyes and kept right on humming.

"Jess!" John grabbed Jessica's arm and shook her a little.

Jessica turned to hum in John's face, so close and so sloppy, spit flung from her lips to his. John blinked and leaned back.

"You've changed," he said.

The bruises around John's eye were still black and plum-colored, ringed with mucus yellow. It was sort of a masterpiece.

"You're making excuses to not see me," he added. "And you're acting all mean."

"That's not true," Jessica replied half-heartedly.

"It *is* true."

"Do you want me to take you home?" Jessica asked.

John said nothing. It was hard for Jessica to take him seriously, with his eye looking like that. She bit back a smile.

"So," she said, "I guess you just want to sit here and do nothing?"

"Fuck!" John shouted. Jessica recoiled and John leaned forward to press the tip of his nose into her ear. This time she felt *his* spit on *her* skin. *"Fuck!"*

"Stop," Jessica gasped.

"You stop!" John yelled.

"I'll just take you home." Jessica tried to twist her key in the ignition, but John stopped her.

"You're not listening to me! What's wrong with you?"

"Are you serious?" Jessica spun in her seat. "Are you *just* now realizing that something is wrong with me?"

Jessica opened her car door, but John reached across her and slammed it back shut. She grabbed frantically for her phone to call her sisters inside, but John snatched it from her hand and tossed it out his window and into the grass. He did the same thing with her car keys: yanked them out of the ignition and tossed them out the window. Then he took both of her arms, pinned them to her sides, and pressed his forehead against her temple. Jessica's whole spine rattled, and a scream rose up, which John cut off by pulling her forward then slamming her back against the seat. Her head bounced against the headrest, and for a second, Jessica saw stars.

"I worry about you," he grunted. "I'm worried you don't know how much I love you."

Jessica felt sick, but there was a little voice inside her chanting: fight, *fight*. She didn't know how to win a fight with John, though. She needed to think. She needed to buy some time.

"If you're quiet, I can sneak you up to my room," she offered. "Then I can take you home before I have to go to work."

"You're *not listening*." John pressed against her, skull to skull now. "Have you ever been scared, Jessica?"

What was John talking about? What *the fuck* did he know about being scared? How dare he ask her that, as if he knew the first thing about fear, about the blinding claustrophobia that went along with being trapped in a car, in a house, with a ghost, with a living person?

The worst fear of all, Jessica was coming to realize, was the fear of having no idea who she was. Jessica had become a ghost, and not a good kind of ghost like Ana or like the ones that maybe haunted centuries-old churches. She was acting like a small spirit. She was so mad all the time, but instead of striking out, she would do nothing or reach out with tentative, tissue-paper fingers. She had to do better. An angry girl was allowed to be angry. Earlier that day, in the pharmacy, Jessica had watched a girl her age screaming at her boyfriend in the allergy medicine aisle. The girl had kept yelling, "When were you going to tell me? When were you going to tell me, huh?" The boy kept trying to calm her down, but she wouldn't have it. Eventually, Mathilda came out with a security guard, and the girl had yelled, "Fuck this!" and then thrown a bottle of nasal spray at the boy's head.

Jessica had been transfixed. The scene had been so *inspiring.* Jessica had to start. She had to start scraping away the layers. This—this shit with John—was the first step, and, if she was honest with herself, it was the easiest because John was a total fucking loser.

"Get out of my car," Jessica said.

"Did you not hear me?" John asked. His disgusting meat breath poured into Jessica's ear, and she couldn't help it: She laughed. Then she pried one of her hands free and smashed down on her horn.

John was startled enough to allow Jessica to reach for her door handle again, but before she could fully open it, he grabbed her arms again, squeezing tighter. This time, it didn't matter that Jessica didn't know how to win. She fought anyway.

"Get out!" Jessica screamed, flailing against him. *"Get out!"*

She repeated those two words over and over again at the top of her lungs. The words stopped being words and became shrieks. Jessica stared straight into John's bruised eyes and continued to scream. For the first time, she wanted the whole neighborhood to be her witness.

Iridian

(early Monday, June 17th)

GIVEN THAT HER name meant "relating to the eye," it was ironic how selective Iridian's vision was. The things she wanted to see mostly lived in her head or in the worlds she created on paper. She could picture a character's skin in such vivid detail, she knew how it tasted. She knew so clearly—in her mind—the difference between eyes that sparkled with tears and those that sparkled with joy and those that sparkled with pride. The things she didn't want to see, she avoided. Instead of burying her head in the sand, she buried herself between book pages or under bedsheets or, now, into couch cushions. Rosa knew her sister well, so she'd known the solution to Ana's writing on the wall was to cover it up. She'd also known that the solution to Ana's destroying Iridian's books and notebooks was to simply pick everything up and put it back into the closet.

Iridian's new notebook was snug against her side, and the television was still on soap operas, still on mute. She wished she lived there—in the screen, in the beautiful houses on the screen where people spoke but you couldn't hear their muted words. At some point, Iridian fell asleep to that beauty. She woke when a lamp clicked on—more like, she jerked awake. Her long legs bucked against the tangle of her blanket. Iridian blinked and saw her father at the far end of the couch. With a dried crust of spittle at the edge of his mouth, he was the opposite of the beauty on the screen.

"What?" Iridian asked.

Rafe said nothing. A little knowing twitch played at the corner of his mouth, right next to the spit.

Iridian looked down and, there, clutched in her father's hand, was her notebook, the new one with the yellow cover. She exhaled hard and fast, and before she could even really think about it, Iridian launched off the couch. She collided with Rafe, and her notebook flipped open, its ink-covered pages fanning out. Iridian's nails dug into the skin of Rafe's wrist and the backs of his hands. Her attack worked—sort of. Rafe pulled away, but all Iridian was left with was a tiny scrap of paper with the word *ravage* written on it.

"This is what you think about?" Rafe demanded. "What kind of girl are you?"

"It's nothing," Iridian lied, because it was, of course, everything.

"It's filth! It's *trash!*"

Rafe waited for his daughter to respond, maybe to apologize, and Iridian waited for Rafe to do what he always did: say something terrible and then try to twist things to make it seem as if Iridian had been the one to force *him* into saying something terrible.

Rafe took a step forward, and, out of the corner of her eye, Iridian saw Rosa creep down the stairs. Iridian steeled her nerves, took a breath, and remembered how diligently she had practiced for this sort of thing. It was rare he could hurl an insult at her that she hadn't hurled at herself already.

"I know why you do this," Rafe said. "You're trying to make up for the fact that you aren't beautiful like Ana, talented like Jessica, or kind like Rosa. You are just . . ." He paused, trying to find the right words. "You are a nothing person. Not beautiful. Not talented. Not kind. I thought I raised you better, but I guess I was wrong."

Before, when this had happened at school, when her secrets had been plucked away and shared by and to her awful classmates, Iridian had been so humiliated she hadn't been able to move. She'd heard the jeers and laughter, but only over the white-noise roar in her head.

For a long, long time, Iridian had wanted to be completely inconspicuous, homebound, so introverted she was practically invisible. But *nothing?* Iridian didn't want to be nothing, and when she heard her father say that to her, she exploded like a star.

With a sharp cry, she lunged for the notebook again, but Rafe held it above his head, toward the overhead light and out of his daughter's reach. Iridian tried to claw her way up his arm, but Rafe pushed her hard—right in the center of her chest—and she fell back against the couch and then bounced onto the floor. Rafe started to flip through the pages, just like Evalin had done, like he was going to read from them. She couldn't bear the thought of her words coming out of his mouth, so she screamed. Still on the floor, she folded herself into the tiniest ball possible, closed her eyes, covered her ears with her hands, and screamed.

Rafe started reading. Iridian couldn't hear everything, but the worst/best phrases seemed to rise over her screams: *suck, smack, salty.* She screamed louder. Eventually, Rafe grabbed her by the arm and tried to pull her up, but Iridian was dead weight, a shrieking heap. Rafe was dragging her across the carpet. Her shoulder twisted, threatening to wrench out of joint, but Iridian kept screaming. She vaguely heard Rosa telling Rafe to let go, but Rafe wasn't listening. He bent over Iridian and told her—*shouted*—into her ear, "If only your mother—God rest her precious soul—could see this."

"*Stop!*" Rosa yelled.

Iridian was able to turn her head and see that her sister had pulled a nearby lamp from its electrical socket. She held that lamp in both her hands, wielding it like a baseball bat. Its cord dangled to the ground.

Outside, someone honked the horn of their car.

Then, Iridian felt something unmistakable: wind.

It was warm, and it was so strong that it blew back the loose strands of her hair. Iridian had to tilt her face away to protect it from the grit she felt flying into her eyes, but there was nothing she could do to avoid the smell of oranges that the wind carried with it.

In the next instant, the television blinked off. A high, whining sound came from its screen, and Iridian watched as the glass shattered on its own, radiant, as if a fist had been slammed in the center of it.

"Leave, Iridian," Rosa commanded, tightening her grip on the lamp. She was focused on Rafe. "Go outside. I'll take care of this."

Once outside, Iridian heard Jessica shrieking from her car. Through the open passenger-side window, she saw her sister thrashing against her seat, and John was trying to keep her pinned down. A different kind of wind blew through—rain was coming—but a piece of Iridian's hair got stuck in her mouth, and she could taste the dry dust. She thought of Rosa, always swooping in to save her, as she'd just done seconds ago with Rafe. She could still hear the both of them, behind her, yelling at each other in the house. Rafe was yelling, "This is my house!" but Iridian knew that wasn't true anymore. Her father had no control over what was happening in those walls.

Iridian ran toward Jessica's car—toward Jessica's shrieking. She was determined to be the hero for once. She was fed up with men trying to leave their bruises all over her and her sisters.

Jessica

(early Monday, June 17th)

THE PASSENGER DOOR opened, and John was being yanked from the car. Jessica could see Iridian behind him, her arms around him, tugging him backward. John quickly found his feet, however, then spun around and backhanded Iridian across the face. She fell hard against the side of the car, her head whacking the metal frame, and then crumpled to the curb.

All the air left Jessica's body. She couldn't have possibly seen what she'd seen. She blinked, and there was Iridian, on the ground, grimacing, her hand coming up to press against her temple and her thigh scraped from where she'd skidded against the concrete.

Jessica was out of the car, stalking John around the

front end. There was a sound in her head, like a pulse, like a *whomp, whomp, whomp.* Pressure was building behind her ears, in the palms of her hands. She was about to explode.

"I will fucking kill you," she said to John, her voice hoarse. "You hit my sister, and I will *fucking* kill you."

Jessica shoved John in the chest with both hands, but all he did was stumble, laugh, then spit on the street. Too fast, John reached out and grabbed a chunk of Jessica's hair, right at the root. She yelped as he gripped her hair tighter and attempted to push her back into her car.

Jessica's eyes watered from the sudden burst of pain, but she could still recognize the blur of red fabric that had suddenly appeared in her vision. Rosa was there, swinging some kind of weapon at him. After the sickening thud of metal on meat, there was a noise, a grunt. John fell away, yanking out strands of Jessica's hair. Again, Rosa brought her weapon up over her head and swung it at the soft part of John's side, right under his ribs. This time, John bellowed, gripped his torso, and landed hard on one knee.

Jessica heard the bang of a storm door, then another. She looked around and saw her wish from before had come true. Her neighbors were out of their houses. Mrs. Moreno from next door was on her front porch in her bathrobe, yelling into her cell phone and gesturing wildly with her free hand. Teddy Arenas was out in the driveway, cradling his little dog. Mrs. Bolander was at the front edge of her yard in a matching pajama set—pink with watermelons.

Hector and his friends were there. They were out of breath, like they'd just sprinted down the stairs. Peter wasn't with them. He must've been at the pharmacy.

At last, Jessica turned to her own house and saw her father, standing in the open doorway clutching paper in his hand. He hadn't come out to help—he never, ever helped them.

Rosa was still gripping her weapon—a lamp without its shade, Jessica now realized. Its cord dragged across the patchy grass. Rafe slumped against the doorframe, placing his hand over his heart, and that's when Jessica noticed he was wearing one of Ana's old bracelets on his wrist. It was made out of yellow string and a couple of beads. Where on earth had he found that?

It had just been a little over a week ago that Rafe had been in the middle of the street, bruised and crying out, needing help. Jessica had rushed to his side. She'd stopped her car in the middle of the road and had thrown herself at her father. And this is what she got in return, when she was the one who needed help—nothing.

Jessica could see, at the edge of her vision, her neighbors taking slow steps closer to her house, to her yard, to her and her sisters. She remembered, half-remembered, the night that Ana died. It was sticky out—just like now. Rafe was slumped in the doorway—just like now. Jessica and her sisters had needed help, and the neighbors had come rushing from their houses. She remembered screaming against a woman's body. She still didn't know whose. She just remembered the woman's shirt smelled a little bit sour-sweet, like red wine.

"We're leaving," Rosa said to her sisters, dropping the lamp in the grass. She bent to pick up Jessica's phone and keys from where John had pitched them in the yard, and climbed into the passenger seat. "Iridian, are you all right?"

"I'm fine," Iridian muttered. She hauled herself to standing.

"In the car, then," Rosa commanded. "Now."

Iridian did as she was told. Jessica started the engine, and Rosa leaned out the passenger window.

"John, hey," she called out.

John scowled up at Rosa. It was the scowl of a wounded animal. He had his hand pressed against his side. Jessica knew there would be a bruise there. She wanted his whole body covered in bruises.

"You broke my ribs, you little bitch!" John spit out.

"Good," Rosa said. "And if I ever see you on this street again, I will break your spine."

Iridian
(early Monday, June 17th)

WHEN IRIDIAN'S HEAD had hit the side of her sister's car, she'd accidentally bitten down on her tongue. There'd been a gush of hot blood, so sudden Iridian had nearly choked. She'd turned her ringing head and spit bloody gobs onto the curb. Now, as she sat in the back seat of Jessica's car, her tongue was swollen and tender, still bleeding. She had nowhere to spit, so every so often, she was forced to swallow a mouthful of blood. Somehow those mouthfuls of blood went down easier than when her dad had called her a "nothing person."

Of all the insults Iridian had hurled at herself in her bathroom mirror, she'd never thought of calling herself "nothing." It was the worst insult of all—worse than being called ugly or miserable or bird-thin or stupid. It was as if Rafe had taken a hot metal spoon and cleanly scooped out her insides. She'd been left feeling hollow and hungry.

Then, when the TV screen had shattered and Rosa had come to her rescue, Iridian hadn't felt relief. Or fear. She had cried out in desperation and grabbed for paper as if paper could save her life. Rosa had told her to leave and go outside, and Iridian had the time for one last attempt. Rafe had been disoriented, and Iridian had leapt forward. Her fingers had closed around a page from her notebook. There'd been ripping—holes being torn from the metal spiral. She'd been left with a shred, less than half a page. She'd held on to that shred as she'd bolted outside. She'd still held on to that scrap of paper as John's knuckles had crashed into her cheekbone and her head had chimed with the impact.

That scrap of paper was still wadded up in Iridian's sweaty fist, where it was safe, and where no one else could reach it.

Jessica's phone rattled gently in the cup holder in the center console. It had been doing that off and on since they'd left the house.

"You should have left it in the yard," Jessica told Rosa.

Iridian clenched her fist tighter and looked out to the flashing night sky. Cool winds buffeted the car. Jessica's windows were rolled down like they always were, and little leaves were blowing into the cabin. They would come in one window, spin in a tiny roller-coaster loop-de-loop, and then go out the opposite window. Jessica's car had always been as much of a mess as her room, so bits of trash—plastic straw wrappers and old receipts—were flying around in loops as well. Outside there was a storm coming, and inside it was a mini-cyclone. It had rained so much over the course of the last week, Iridian half hoped that by the time she and her sisters returned to their house, there would be no house, or that maybe just the peaks of the roof would be visible. She imagined the soft, rain-soaked ground swallowing the wood and the bricks, sucking it all down with a burp.

"I'm not sorry." Rosa turned toward Jessica and tried with little success to tuck the long strands of her hair behind her ears.

"I know," Jessica replied. "I just wish I were the one who had done it. Everyone's been fighting my battles lately." She paused and looked to Iridian in the rearview mirror. "What happened at the house?"

"He found my stories," Iridian said. "He read them. He wouldn't give them back."

"Then Ana got mad," Rosa said, smirking. "She broke the TV."

"Did you know about John?" Iridian blurted. She met her sister's sharp glance in the rearview mirror.

"Did I know *what* about John?" Jessica asked.

"How he drove off." Iridian paused to nibble on the inside of her lip, where the skin had split and blood was still trickling out. "After seeing Ana slip, he left her there in the yard."

Jessica's eyes slid back down to the road. "Who told you that?"

"Peter," Iridian replied. "He said he and his friends had watched it all from the window."

"That's not what he told me," Jessica said. "He said they didn't see the car. And when were you talking to Peter Rojas?"

"I was at Hector's," Iridian replied.

She then told her sister about what had happened with her notebooks, the smell of oranges, and the hyena.

Fat drops started to fall on the windshield, and Jessica turned on the wipers. Several seconds passed, and the only sound was the *click-swish* of the blades skimming across the glass.

"What else did *Peter* say?" she urged.

Rosa shifted in the passenger seat.

"He said he and his friends saw Ana's ghost," Iridian replied. "Last summer. She was outside, tapping on Dad's window. Rosa knows."

"They left me a note," Rosa said.

Jessica's expression was unreadable, which meant she was furious—because maybe she'd learned the truth about John and Ana, but also because the boys had seen the ghost and had thought to tell Rosa and not her. Jessica had always believed that Ana belonged to her and only her. There'd been the insistence on moving into her room and smoking her cigarettes, but Iridian knew Jessica had also spent the weeks immediately following Ana's death building shrines. She refused to throw anything of Ana's away, and would pile up used mascara tubes and hair ties and half-eaten boxes of SweeTarts all over the floor. They were tiny ofrendas, built there as if to welcome Ana back, as if she'd just momentarily lost her way out the window that night. So, no. Jessica wouldn't have liked hearing that Ana had appeared to the boys across the street—and not her—an entire year ago.

"Where are we going?" Rosa asked.

Good question. Iridian had been so stunned by everything that had just happened, she'd failed to realize they were driving farther and farther away from her house, her street, her neighborhood. She started to panic a little. She didn't know how far the chain on her anchor would stretch before it snapped.

"To the pharmacy," Jessica said. "Iridian's bleeding. She needs stuff."

Again, Iridian tongued the wound in her mouth. Then she tapped her fingertips up her thigh. The skin there was pricked and torn. It burned when she touched it, so yes, she guessed she needed *stuff.*

"You two can just wait in the car if you want," Jessica said. "Let me know if you can think of anything you need—anything for the house."

"I need a new notebook," Iridian said. "And another pen."

Jessica
(early Monday, June 17th)

FOR THE LAST year, Jessica had heard all kinds of things because most people didn't have the decency to wait until she was out of earshot before they ran their mouths. They'd accused Jessica of being desperate. They'd wondered what she could have possibly been thinking. Of course, she'd known John and Ana had been seeing each other for months up until the time Ana died. That was the reason she'd pursued John in the first place. Jessica coped with her sister's death by *becoming* her sister. She'd wanted Ana's room, her clothes, her makeup, her boyfriend. Looking back, that all seemed so stupid. Maybe not stupid. Maybe more like grief-sick. Now all this time had passed, and Jessica was still stuck hard in the role as Ana-Not-Ana-Not-Jessica.

And then there was Peter. *Fucking* Peter. Peter got everything, and Jessica got nothing. Peter got to see Ana knocking on a window at night. All Jessica got was a shadowed hand and wicked laugh. Peter got the glory of fighting John and winning. Peter got to take a quick trip to Mexico and then wash his hands of Southtown.

As she pulled her car into the parking lot of the pharmacy, Jessica itched at her scalp, then between each of her fingers. She wished she could scratch off all of her skin and start over.

With her sisters waiting in the car, Jessica stalked across the parking lot. Before she'd even made it through the pharmacy's doors, her phone chimed once, then again. She tugged it out of her pocket and chucked it into a trash can.

Cotton squares, hydrogen peroxide, a tube of Neosporin. She'd just bought these things for John, and here she was, buying them again for Iridian, who had gone outside twice in two days and had been damaged each time because of it.

When Jessica turned into the school supply aisle to grab a pen and another notebook, there was Peter, just a few feet away, bent over and hacking at a taped-up box with a cutter. She knew that blade. The handle was cracked and held together with bright blue duct tape.

"I used that box cutter on Evalin Uvalde's tires," Jessica said.

"Everyone knew it was you," Peter replied, with a glance over his shoulder. He said it like it was no big revelation, like it was no surprise Jessica was a petty vandal. "No one could prove it, though."

"I should've slashed your tires, too," Jessica added.

Peter's blade stilled. He sat back on his heels.

"Are you fighting with me again?" He looked to the basket in Jessica's hand and rose to his feet. "What happened?"

Jessica still itched like she wanted to peel off her skin, and now the spot on her head where John had grabbed her hair started to throb. She was so tired of boys pulling on her, attempting to invade the life she'd tried so hard to keep protected.

Again, Peter eyed the contents of Jessica's basket and then did a quick scan of her body: her bare legs, her wrists, her throat, her face. As he breathed out, his lips separated slightly. He was concerned. Jessica didn't want him to look at her like that. She wanted him to look at her like that. *She* wanted to look at *him* like that. She had no idea.

Jessica needed a foothold. She needed to feel strong again, and the only way she knew how to do that was to make someone else feel weak.

"Did you know?" Jessica began. "Did you know that a couple of months ago, I actually managed to get Iridian out of the house? We went to the mall. For a while, it went okay. We walked around, went into a couple stores. But when we stopped at the food court for sodas, Iridian froze. She thought she'd seen someone from school. It turned out it wasn't who she thought it was, but still. She refused to move. She just sat there. At one of the tables, for hours. *Hours.*"

"What happened?" Peter repeated. "Jessica, what's going on?"

"I sat there with her," Jessica continued, "until the mall was closing and all the people were leaving, and I was finally able to convince her to walk with me to the car. That is the kind of sister I have." She paused. "*You* did that to her."

Peter held Jessica's gaze. "You're right. I didn't say anything. I could've helped her, but I laughed like an idiot. I'm sorry."

"Have you told *her* you're sorry?" Jessica urged. "The other day, maybe? When she was over at Hector's house?"

Jessica was so, so angry. It wasn't just about John and the pain he'd left behind. She was angry that the ghost of her older sister was playing tricks on her and her sisters and that Iridian had been quasi-hunted in their front yard by a zoo animal gone feral, but she was also angry—more than she could ever describe—that Iridian had gone across the street and sought help from the boys who'd proven over and over again they were no help at all—that they were, instead, meddling little shit cowards.

"No," Peter replied. "I did not."

"Of course you didn't," Jessica scoffed. "But I bet you asked what you could do to help. Since you're so fucking helpful."

Peter tried to say something, but Jessica cut him off.

"What happened in the lunchroom wouldn't have ever happened if you and your friends hadn't decided to *help* us last summer." Her voice was rising. "Iridian doesn't need your *help*. *I* don't need your help. We'll never need your fucking help, Peter. It is *not* your business what happens in *my* house, to *my* family."

"Okay," Peter insisted. He paused. "Jessica, what is this about? Are you okay?"

Jessica cackled, full-throated. "You can't have her! Ana's *my* sister. You can't have her!"

"I-I . . ." Peter stammered. "Jessica. It's not . . ."

"She's *my* sister!" Jessica slapped a hand to her chest. "And *you* saw her! You saw her, right? Her whole body, from head to toe, out in front of the window?"

Peter nodded.

"I've seen her *hand*," Jessica said. "And I've heard her laugh. Just once. That's it. Why is that? Why would she come to you and not to me? How is that fair? How is that fucking fair, huh?"

The movement was slight, but Peter's gaze caught on something over Jessica's shoulder. Jessica turned and saw Mathilda standing in the aisle, looking alarmed.

"Everything okay here?" Mathilda asked.

"Fine," Peter replied.

"I heard about what happened to your sister." Mathilda gave Jessica a sympathetic smile. "It was this time last year, wasn't it?"

Jessica bit the inside of her cheek to keep from screaming. Everyone, *everyone* knew everything. Everyone had pieces of Ana, and no one deserved them.

Jessica felt Peter's arms around her—not around her like to bring her into an embrace, but to steer her away from Mathilda and through the back door into the stockroom. Jessica wanted an embrace, though. She wanted one so badly. She swiveled toward Peter, colliding with him. She pressed her forehead into his shirt and sobbed. Then she pressed her lips against his shirt. She felt his heartbeat, beneath the fabric, beneath his skin. Peter didn't belong to her, Jessica knew, but in that moment, she was claiming him. She had never done anything so wonderful as kiss Peter's shirt. She pushed and pushed against him, but he didn't waver.

Even as she pushed against him, she was saying, "Please, just leave me alone."

Peter didn't let her go, though, and she didn't let him go, either.

Iridian
(early Monday, June 17th)

"WHAT ARE YOU holding?" Rosa had shifted in her seat and was looking at the wisp of paper edging out from Iridian's fist. There was static in the pre-storm air, causing the strands of Rosa's hair to lift and stick to the headrest.

"Is it from your notebook? Were you able to save something?"

Yes. It *did* feel like Iridian had saved something. It felt like she was keeping something alive and warm, egglike, in the palm of her hand.

"Read it," Rosa said. "I'd like to hear it."

Iridian said nothing. Outside, a bright ragged line cut across the sky, and the corresponding boom of thunder made Iridian's head throb.

"Please," Rosa urged.

Iridian looked to her sister, her kind sister, who was waiting patiently—as if Rosa would wait any other way. Her static-puffed hair was a brown halo. Rosa had captured the energy of the oncoming storm, sucked it inside her, and made it beautiful. Just minutes ago, Rosa had attacked John, and possibly Rafe before that. That had also been beautiful.

When Iridian glanced down at her fist, she again saw the long, angry scrapes on her leg, extending from her knee up to the middle of her thigh. The blood was dry, but the scrapes still stung. The hurt was deeper than it looked. She'd been struck by a boy, and she'd never forget it. Her stomach hurt. Her head hurt. It beat like a heavy heart. Her tongue hurt. It was swollen and, if she read out loud what was on the paper, her words would maybe sound funny.

"I was jealous," Rosa said.

Iridian looked to her sister, confused.

"When you told me about the hyena," Rosa clarified. "I was upset that you saw it and I didn't. I didn't know what I was feeling because I don't think I've ever felt it before. I was mad at you and wanted to pull your hair. I'm sorry. I don't feel that way anymore, by the way."

"Oh," Iridian said. "Okay."

"Will you please now read what you have?"

Iridian loosened her fist a fraction, then all the way.

The paper was wadded and damp from her sweat, but in the glow given off by the lights in the parking lot, she could still make out her handwriting—chicken scratches, an ugly mash-up of print and cursive she'd attempted to make beautiful with bright blue ink. She hadn't even looked at what was on the paper until now. She could've torn anything from her father's grasp. It could've been a long description of how a tongue feels against another tongue or a series of incomplete sentences. It could've been blank.

It wasn't blank. Or about tongues.

On one side there was a cut-off sentence that started with *I want*, but then after that, *I'm sorry I'm sorry I'm sorry* was written at least ten times.

Iridian passed the paper up to Rosa and then told her the story—about finding the pregnancy test, about turning Ana's crisis into *her* crisis, about calling her favorite sister a dumb whore. She could barely get those last words out. She hadn't said them for a year, since saying them to Ana.

"I tried to tell her I was sorry, like right then," Iridian said, "but she wouldn't accept it. She told me I'd fucked up. Sometimes it's all I can think about."

Rosa put a cool hand on Iridian's knee and was about to say something when Jessica opened the car door and tossed a plastic bag into the back seat. Iridian folded the scrap of paper and smashed it back into her fist, and with her free hand searched through the bag. She found cotton squares and hydrogen peroxide and Band-Aids that were too small for her cuts. There was no pen—no notebook, either.

She was going to tell Jessica to go back, but then she saw the pink tracks of tears that streaked down her sister's cheek, and the way she was white-knuckling the steering wheel.

"What happened?" Rosa asked.

"Nothing," Jessica replied.

As Jessica pulled out of the parking lot, tiny raindrops started to fall, but neither Jessica nor Rosa rolled their windows up. Iridian quietly tended to her wounds in the back seat, while Rosa extended her arm out the window to wiggle her fingers in the rain.

Even though her leg stung when the hydrogen peroxide hit the scrapes, it was a pain she could manage.

"Iridian," Rosa called back. "Have you ever touched someone's hand? Like, really studied it?"

Iridian had written so many descriptions: what it was like when a hand brushed against another hand, or stroked hair, or pinched tender skin. She'd had lines and lines, pages and pages. And now she could describe what it was like to care for broken skin—the soft pressure; the cool, gentle burn of the peroxide; the feeling of being very close but not all the way close.

But, no. She'd never touched someone's hand, not the way that Rosa meant, anyway.

"I hope you get the chance sometime," Rosa replied, watching raindrops bounce off her fingernails. "It's wonderful."

"Uh-huh," Iridian replied. It was all she could say. Maybe that was true—she was sure that hands could do wonderful things, but all Iridian could think about at the moment was hands doing destructive things: smashing against cheekbones, pulling hair, tearing book pages.

Iridian kept applying the peroxide until there was no more burn and her wounds stopped fizzing. Jessica kept driving, directionless, in circles it seemed. The winds were picking up. The receipt from the pharmacy flew from the back seat and out the window before Iridian could catch it.

"Where are we going?" Rosa eventually asked.

"Nowhere," Jessica replied. "Just around. Peter said he'd come by the house after his shift was over, and until then I'm just killing time." She paused. "He said he thinks Ana is trying to get us out of the house. That's why she's scaring us, ripping up Iridian's things, sending Rosa to search for the hyena."

"Leave the house and go where?" Rosa asked. "Where does Ana expect us to go?"

"Anywhere." Jessica let out a dry little laugh. "Or maybe she's lonely. Maybe she wants some company."

That wasn't funny. Iridian immediately thought of *The Witching Hour*, which doesn't have a happy ending. Whenever Iridian got close to the last few chapters, she always hoped that things would turn out differently. She didn't understand how a story could bring two characters together only to pull them so hopelessly apart. Why create something great only to destroy it? Even though the ending broke Iridian's heart every time, she never skipped it. She felt like the story was punishing her, but that it was a punishment well earned.

At the end of *The Witching Hour*, the ghost wins.

Jessica

HERE'S A SECRET: Something interesting happened four days after Ana died. Jessica was taking a shower. Just after turning on the water, she crouched down and peered into the drain. As the hot, hot water rolled down her back, Jessica pulled a clump of her older sister's hair from the trap. She knew it was Ana's because it was longer than hers was, and because a few of the strands were gray at the root. Jessica held the wet strands between her fingers for a few moments before putting the hair in her mouth and swallowing it.

Jessica
(early Monday, June 17th)

PETER SMELLED LIKE lemons, fake lemons like laundry detergent. Jessica could still smell it, even in her moldy old car, even over the dirt-smell of the rain. The lemon scent had been sucked up in her nostrils as she'd gasped and snorted against Peter's work shirt. She imagined it mixing with her cells and entering her bloodstream. She imagined it scraping against the walls of her organs and changing them, the way acid eats away at rock.

When Jessica had clung to Peter, she'd dug her nails into his lemon-scented shirt—*through* his lemon-scented shirt—and into his flesh. She'd created little hooks to hold him in place. She wondered if he still felt the impression of those hooks and if the small crescents made by her nails were still there in his skin. She wondered what she smelled like—she hoped it wasn't moldy like her car—and if her smell still hung in Peter's nose.

After almost an hour of doing loops through the neighborhood and the rain-soaked, near-empty streets of downtown San Antonio, Jessica stopped for gas at a corner store. She stood with her hand on the pump, leaning her hip against the back end of her car. There was an overhang that was supposed to protect her from the rain, but the spray was still hitting her sideways. The wind gusted and sent the raindrops swirling. Jessica was standing in a puddle. A wrapper from a red Starburst floated by her left shoe.

Rosa ran up, splashing across the parking lot. She'd gone into the store to get herself a bottle of water. She handed Iridian a small carton of chocolate milk through the window.

"Either save it for later or drink it all right now," Jessica told Iridian.

"What?"

"Save it, or drink it all right now and throw the carton away. I don't want you spilling and getting that smell in my car."

What she meant was that she didn't want the smell of milk to mix with or overpower the smell of lemons.

"What smell?" Iridian shot back. "I'm not a child. I know how to drink milk without spilling it."

Jessica waited as Iridian opened the carton and drank the milk all at once, in three large chugs. Then Iridian climbed out of the back seat to shove the empty carton into the overflowing garbage can between the pumps.

"There you go, princess," Iridian said, getting back into the car.

Jessica also got in, turned the ignition, and checked the time. Peter's shift ended at 6 a.m., in a little over thirty minutes. Peter hadn't told her what they would do once he got to her house. Maybe they would just sit on the floor and wait for Ana to tap on the window again. Or break something. Honestly, she'd settle for either. Or anything, really.

"We should go home now," Jessica said.

She expected at least one of her sisters to protest, but neither did.

Jessica pulled into the driveway, into the empty space where her dad usually parked his truck.

"Where do you think he went?" Iridian asked.

Jessica didn't answer. She realized she didn't really care anymore.

The sisters bolted out of the car and hustled through the rain to the door. Iridian was running so fast, she slid through the wet grass and lost her footing. Jessica and Rosa both reached out to catch her before she fell.

"Jess!"

Jessica spun around to see a rain-soaked John jogging up the sidewalk. Had he been lurking around this whole time?

"It's okay," Rosa whispered. "I can take care of it."

"I don't need you to take care of it," Jessica replied.

"I've been calling, sending messages," John said, crossing the yard. "Why haven't you answered?"

Jessica balked. John hadn't even acknowledged her sisters: one who he'd struck and the other who'd struck him. Instead, he was reducing everything that had happened that night to a little quarrel about Jessica not answering her fucking phone.

She thought back to the night she'd first kissed him, in front of everyone, in Evalin Uvalde's entryway. She'd wanted John to taste magical, cool like sweet tea, but he hadn't. She'd wanted him to tell her that she smelled like Ana—she'd doused herself in what was left of Ana's cotton-scented perfume before she'd left that night, screwing off the cap and slapping the liquid directly on her belly. She'd wanted John to tell her that she felt like Ana, that their skin was the same temperature or that they made the same sounds when naked.

He'd never said that. He'd also never told her what *she*, Jessica the individual, tasted like, felt like, sounded like. Instead, he always wanted to know, *When are you coming over?* and *Why aren't you answering your phone?*

Jessica wanted John to answer one question, and then she wanted nothing to do with him ever again.

"Did you see my sister die?" she asked.

John narrowed his gaze, pretending to be confused. Oh, she knew that look. It was one of Rafe's go-to expressions.

"Jessica," John said, "can we go inside, please?"

"Did you see her?" Jessica urged. "Did you *hear* her? She shouted. We heard her cry out."

John spread his arms wide, in a way that also reminded Jessica of her father. It was this big lost-for-words T-shape. It meant, *What do you want me to say?*

Jessica handed Rosa her keys. "Can you two wait in the car?"

"In the *car?*" Iridian balked.

"I'm going to take John inside to dry off," Jessica said. "I'll just be a minute. I promise."

Rosa's eyebrow hiked up.

"Bathroom's off the kitchen," Jessica said as she opened the door for John. "To the right. There are towels there."

John trudged through the dark house, and Jessica was left alone. The living room was a disaster. Pages from the notebook she'd given Iridian were strewn about, on the carpet and on the couch. The television screen was smashed to crystals, as if someone had pitched a bowling ball into the center of it.

"You're mad," Jessica whispered. "I get it."

She took a step forward, and paper crunched lightly under her foot.

"But I don't think you're mad at us."

Jessica waited for a sign that she'd been heard. Iridian had mentioned smelling oranges, but all Jessica could smell was the dust and mildew that always clung to the walls and old carpet.

"I brought someone for you," Jessica said, just as John came out of the back bathroom, rubbing his head with a towel.

Jessica made sure she was between John and the front door. From where she was standing, she could see through the living room and back into the kitchen. She could hear the fridge buzzing, and an ice cube drop from the door to the floor.

"I know you saw her," Jessica said. "You had to have. You watched Ana die, and then you drove away."

There was a shadow—a blur—that appeared at the right edge of the door to the kitchen. It was a figure, a dark, girl-shaped figure in a dark doorway, about Jessica's height.

Jessica had to force her eyes back to John, had to force her feet to stay rooted and her hands from flying up to her racing heart.

"I was scared," John said. He hung his head and shook it. "I didn't know what to do."

The figure behind John glided fully into the doorway

and stopped. It wasn't as clear as a person, but it was more than a hand on a curtain.

"You were scared?" Jessica asked. She started to tremble as laughter built up inside her.

Peter had told her she needed to fight for herself. She didn't need to do that, though, because she had her sisters.

"I don't want to lose you." John reached for Jessica's hand.

She let him take it, but only for a moment. "It's not that you don't want to lose *me*," she said, pulling away and stepping back. "It's that you're scared of being alone. Wait here," she added. "I just need to get something out of my car."

As Jessica turned to the door, John, for the first time, looked around and took in the destruction around him— the paper and broken glass. He started to say something, but by then Jessica was already outside, pulling the door closed. She had her key out, ready to thrust and twist into the lock. She was ready to seal John into the house. It was a terrible thing to do—lock a person in with a ghost—but Jessica was a terrible person.

But then the bolt clicked on its own. Jessica knew she'd always remember that smooth sound: the heavy thunk, heavy like a long, satisfying exhale.

John hit the door and called out, but Jessica backed away from the house, taking ankle-deep steps into the mucky yard. The storm was now in full force. Rain struck her from every direction, and the sky was booming, lit up gray and bright white by the lightning. She heard Rosa and Iridian running toward her from the car.

"She was there," Jessica gasped. "I saw her."

John called out again. The pitch of his voice was higher now. It was like when she was hiding in the church, and he was growing frantic when he couldn't find her. She'd done nothing then, and she'd do nothing now. Jessica closed her eyes and tipped her face up to the rain.

Rosa came up to her side and linked their arms together. "You did the right thing," she said.

John pounded on the door again, over and over. Suddenly, he stopped. Then the screaming started. Only someone standing close to the house could hear it, though. The roar of the storm was so loud.

Iridian

(early Monday, June 17th)

JESSICA'S EYES WERE closed. She looked peaceful, like she was listening to music, like the storm was her favorite song.

Linked together with Jessica, Rosa's eyes were closed, too. Their lids were sealed tight. Rosa dropped her sister's keys into the grass. Jessica might have been soaking in the sound of John's fear, but Rosa was fine-tuned to something else farther away.

Finally, Rosa exhaled, long and slow, like she was deflating. Then her eyes popped open.

"I'm sorry," she said. "I have to go."

Rosa unlaced herself from her sister and took off across the yard. Within moments, she'd vanished between two houses. Without Rosa, Jessica seemed to sway, like she'd lost her anchor. She stared at the front door, then in the direction in which Rosa had run, then back to the door.

"We should find her." Iridian picked up Jessica's keys from where Rosa had dropped them. "Jess!"

Iridian yanked her sister's wrist, but Jessica jerked away, causing Iridian to tip back. She tried to dig her heels into the ground but slipped and fell palms-first into the mud.

"What's your problem?" Iridian barked, wiping the splatter from her eyes.

"She'll be fine!" Jessica replied. "She goes out by herself all the time."

"Not during a *thunderstorm*!"

Lightning silently split the sky, and for a moment longer, Jessica stood facing the house. John's screams had died out, and Iridian imagined him, curled up in a ball just inside the front door, with his head in his hands, weeping. When she had a pen and paper again, she'd fill up line after line describing him there—his body position cramped, his breathless paralysis caused by fear.

"You're right," Jessica said. "Let's go."

Jessica took her keys and then grabbed Iridian by the waist and hoisted her up to standing. Together, they marched to Jessica's car, but at a clap of thunder so close and loud, Iridian startled and again lost her footing. She threw her hand out to check her balance and realized it was empty. The piece from her notebook—the one that she'd been holding in her fist—was gone. Frantic, she fell to her knees and started to claw at the wet grass.

Jessica tried again to pull her up. "Are we going or not?"

"Stop!" Iridian yelled. "Just give me a second."

Iridian's limbs were slick with rain and mud, but still Jessica managed to wrestle her up off the ground and drag her the few feet to her car.

"Wait!" Iridian cried out.

Thrust into the back seat, and without her scrap of paper, Iridian folded forward in half and covered her head with her hands.

Iridian had no heart for John. She didn't care about the low moans and high whines she heard before Jessica closed the door to the house, sounds that mimicked the wind. She cared about that paper more than she cared about almost anything. In that moment, she cared about that paper more than she cared about her sisters, including Ana. As they drove through the neighborhood, Iridian half-heartedly looked for Rosa while mourning the loss of her piece of paper. Occasionally, Jessica would call back to her and ask if she could see anything, and Iridian would just shake her head and mumble.

Eventually, Iridian peeked at her empty hand and saw blotches of blue ink. *I'm sorry* had transferred to her skin. The words were blurry and backward, but they were there.

"Jess. My paper."

"I'm not going to—"

"Please just turn around," Iridian croaked. "My paper. I dropped it. We can find it, and then we'll find Rosa."

"Iridian!" Jessica shouted. "Shut up! This was your idea. This isn't about your fucking piece of paper right now."

Iridian bolted upright and reached forward across the console to grab the steering wheel. She pulled it clockwise, in the direction of the curb, but instead of stopping, the car went into a skid. Jessica shoved Iridian away and was able to pump the brakes and prevent the car from going into a spin. They were stopped, at a diagonal, in the middle of an empty intersection. Iridian was wheezing and could feel the hard thuds of her heart.

"*What the fuck?*" Jessica shouted. "Don't fucking do that again!"

"I'm sorry," Iridian said. "I'm sorry. I wasn't thinking."

Iridian wanted to fold back into herself, crawl into the fabric of the seat. She met Jessica's eyes in the rearview mirror.

"It's okay," Jessica said, easing the car through the intersection. "Just . . . I'll get you another notebook. Let's find Rosa first, alright?"

Rosa

AT THE HEART level, all animals are different. Birds have small hearts that beat very fast. Once, at a petting zoo, Rosa held a chick up to her ear, and the sound it made wasn't like a *thump, thump, thump* but more like a *whoosh, whoosh, whoosh*, like water tumbling around and around in the washing machine. The birds that flew around Southtown during the summer had hearts like tiny engines. They were always moving. They propelled themselves from tree branch to tree branch and telephone line to telephone line. Rosa imagined their heartbeats were so fast that, if she could hear them, they would sound like drumrolls. If their hearts beat that fast, then maybe, sometimes, they conked out mid-flight, and then dropped straight to the ground.

Squirrels also have small hearts that beat fast, though obviously not as fast as birds'. Rosa had never held a squirrel up to her ear, but she'd watched them. Like birds, they propel themselves off tree branches and telephone lines. Sometimes they freeze mid-step because they hear something in the distance or notice something out of the corner of their eye. Their arms and legs and head stay motionless, but their hearts still pound against their ribs. Also, their tails never stop swishing. It's like they can't help it.

Fireflies have tiny hearts that create electricity. Crickets have tiny hearts that fuel tiny legs that scrape together to create a song that will bring them a mate.

The crickets at night are not just chirping, and the birds in the morning are not just chattering. The sounds they make come from their hearts.

When Rosa first started sitting in the backyard on Sunday mornings and her sisters asked what she was doing, she told them she was trying to talk to the animals. She wished she hadn't ever said that. It sounded kind of ridiculous. She didn't want to *talk* to the animals. That was impossible. It also made no sense. Maybe *communicate* was a better word? She just wanted to be able to hear things, and she wanted the creatures of this world to know they were being heard. That's all. When a squirrel sat up on the telephone wires, flicking its tail, Rosa didn't know what it was thinking, and she didn't need to know what it was thinking. If anything, she wanted him—the squirrel—to know that *she* was thinking of *him*.

The Torres family had never had a dog, and, until Rafe hit that one a week ago, Rosa had never been able to lay her head against a dog's silky fur and listen to its heartbeat. At first that dog's heart was beating fast, but then it started to rumble. Then it lurched and twisted. The dog was bleeding pretty bad, and whining softly, and if Rosa could've done something to make it hurt less in its final moments she would have. Finally, its heart beat once more—*hard*—and shuddered. The dog exhaled and then was silent. Rosa counted out a full fifteen seconds, and the dog didn't move. That's when she knew it was dead. She wished she'd done the same thing with Ana, a year ago in the front yard, but she'd been too scared. Before the ambulance came, she should've put her ear to Ana's back, up between her shoulder blades, and counted to fifteen. She should've listened to her heart and said *please*, as if a heart could hear her request. But she didn't.

People were animals, too, and when they got sick or scared, their hearts gave out.

Rosa

(early Monday, June 17th)

THERE WAS NO doubt the hyena was close—in the neighborhood somewhere, maybe in one of the alleys. Rosa had heard it laughing. When she was standing in her yard with her sisters and all the lights in the house had gone out, she'd heard the animal's wild laugh, clear as day.

So Rosa ran into the dim space between two houses. She stopped in a patch of waterlogged grass. Thunder cracked. The sky flashed bright white, and then the sound rose up again, like a bobbing chuckle.

With the humidity in the air, Rosa felt like she weighed an extra twenty pounds. The heavy, electric air tugged at the tiny hairs on her arms.

Storms, she knew, brought out certain instincts in animals. The birds, normally quiet at this time of night, were getting nervous. They squawked and flew around in crazy loops. They heard thunder, and they saw those flashes of lightning, and they got scared. They wanted shelter in a warm and comfortable place.

Jessica used to do the same thing. If a thunderstorm broke out in the middle of the night, she'd run down to Ana's room to seek shelter. Jessica thought no one else in the family knew about that, but of course Rosa did.

The dogs were barking so loud and from so many different places. They were driven mad by the thunder. Rosa could still hear the hyena and its laugh, but she couldn't tell where it was coming from. She'd turn down an alley, thinking she was on the right track, and then the sound would come from right behind her. She'd spin around, and the laugh would suddenly seem far away. Rosa cried out in frustration. There was another clap of thunder, and after that, Rosa thought she heard another laugh, but not the hyena's laugh. It was, undeniably, Ana's laugh.

It was different from the high, cruel laugh she and her sisters had heard back at the house on the day of the block party. That one was meant to frighten, Rosa thought, but this one was genuine and joyful. Ana would laugh like this when the four of them were little and would be playing in the yard together in the summer, barefoot in the grass, racing one another from the edge of the back porch to the fence, chasing one another with the hose or having cartwheel contests.

Rosa heard Ana's laugh again, coming from the street. She swerved and ran back toward it. She could help. She *would* help. It's what she was made to do.

Human hearts are very complicated. They can pull a person this way, then that. They can convince someone easy things are hard, or cloudy things are clear.

Jessica
(early Monday, June 17th)

JESSICA'S WIPER BLADE flicked across her windshield. Nothing was there. The blade flicked again across her windshield, and there the animal was, standing perfectly still in the road. A gray hyena against a gray sky and gray street. Her headlights caught the reflection of two eyes. They weren't startled or scared, but intense, as if they were urging her onward. It was only when Iridian gripped the seat in front of her and shouted that Jessica braked hard and braced for the impact. The sound of the animal colliding with the car was quieter than Jessica would've expected, and it came in two parts. First, there was a wet thud against the front bumper, and then another, more violent thud as the meat of the body was pulled under the tires.

The car went on a few more feet before skidding to a stop. Jessica bucked forward in her seat and clung to the steering wheel for balance. Squinting through the windshield, she saw the wipers still swishing, uselessly tossing sheets of rainwater side to side. Her headlights were feebly illuminating the empty street.

"Shit," Jessica breathed. She looked into the rearview mirror and saw the hyena's dark, unmoving form. "What the fuck just happened?"

"It was a dog, I think," Iridian said.

A howl, animal-like but not quite, cut through the night and rose over the thumps of rain. Initially, Jessica thought the piercing sound came from the hyena, and she half expected to see it rise, all herky-jerky, and stumble out of the road. But when the howl rose up again, louder and more mournful, Jessica realized the sound came from a person, a girl, her sister. In the rearview mirror, Jessica watched Rosa run out from between a couple of houses and into the middle of the street. She was lit up an oozy blood red by the taillights and the rain, and then dropped to her knees in front of the hyena. She swept the long rope of her hair over one ear and leaned down over the animal.

In the back seat, Iridian sucked in a hard breath. She

was staring in horror through the rain-streaked windshield at the murky yellow headlights of an advancing pickup truck. That truck was headed straight toward Rosa and the hyena, both of which had merged into one dark mass on a dark road.

"No!" Jessica frantically slammed down on her horn, but the truck didn't halt and Rosa didn't leave her animal. "No, no, *no!*"

Jessica threw open her door and ran out into the road. She heard Iridian shout something, a warning maybe, but she didn't look back. Jessica knew, just as every other person in Southtown knew, that Rosa was the good sister, the one worth saving. Jessica was the expendable sister, the one with the heart too hot, the one who locked boys into houses with ghosts, the one with nothing to give but anger.

She could feel that hot heart, burning rather than beating, as she plowed through the warm rain toward her little sister.

"Rosa! *Rosa!*"

Jessica lost traction. As she fell, her palm slammed into the gritty asphalt, but she managed to push herself up and plow forward. She shouted her sister's name again, and finally Rosa looked up, startled, as Jessica hauled her off the ground and flung her toward the curb. Jessica slipped again—this time falling hard onto both her hands and knees. She heard, too close, the squeal of tires against a wet road. She felt heat, like the hottest wind, push against her and pin her down.

The impact was quieter than she would've expected. There was a dull thud as the front end of the truck collided with her ribs, and then another as she was pulled under one of the tires. It hurt, but she'd felt worse.

Jessica could breathe, but she couldn't swallow. She knew she was on the ground, facedown, and that her head was turned to the side because pebbles from the road were smashed against her cheek and chin, and rainwater trickled into her open mouth. She may have been trying to talk—saying what, she didn't know. There was something wrong with her ears. She couldn't hear the rain or the car anymore, but she could hear what was going on *inside* her body. Her lungs were gurgling. There were lots of little pops. Her blood, its swishing, was so loud, making such a racket. She heard someone's voice. It took a second, but she realized that voice belonged to Peter. The sound of Peter's voice—even though he seemed so panicked about something—didn't make her angry. She saw his shoes, the off-white sneakers he always wore to work, and she tried to move her mouth, puckering her lips like she was trying to give those shoes a kiss. The air smelled sort of like oranges. She saw the muddy toes of rubber boots and a flash of red fabric. It was Rosa. Jessica's whole spine shivered. Rosa was safe. Her sister had been saved. Jessica tried to cry out with happiness and relief, but she couldn't get the sound to rise from her throat. Rosa knelt down in front of Jessica and then leaned forward. The rainwater continued to trickle into Jessica's mouth. Her lungs kept popping. She heard Rosa breathing, and she felt the lightest pressure, at the center of her chest, right there above her heart.

Iridian
(Sunday, July 7th)

IT WAS SUNDAY, so Iridian slept in, then went downstairs to the kitchen to sit on the counter, eat chocolate puffs, and watch Rosa in the backyard. She was still up on the counter when a car blared its horn out front.

"Rosa!" Jessica yelled from the couch in the living room, where she was watching cartoons on a new television. "The Matas are here!"

Outside, Rosa bolted from her chair. She ran into and through the house, calling out her goodbyes.

After finishing her cereal, Iridian went upstairs to her room and started reading *The Witching Hour*. In her days since the accident, Rosa had helped her sister sort through all the pages and put the book back together—mostly back together. Some pages were still missing, as was the back cover, but it was good enough. Iridian read for a couple of hours, and then she started writing. There might be a time when she would write in her notebooks again, but for now, she wrote on the walls. She started with her old stories. She was surprised by how much she remembered. Things were still in pieces—paragraphs were unfinished; sentences were unfinished—but things had always been in pieces when it came to her stories. That was fine. At least words were being put down. She could see them, and, if they wanted, her sisters could see them, too.

At first, Iridian wrote standing, at eye level, in as straight a line as she could for as long as she could. Eventually, she would come up against an obstacle— a piece of furniture or a window—and she would write around it. After a while, she was forced to sit and write on baseboards and on the molding that went around the doors. She wrote on the back wall of her closet and on the inside of her bathroom cabinet doors. At a certain point, her stories leaked out into the hallway, toward Jessica's room, then on the staircase railing, and on the stairs themselves. There was peacock blue everywhere.

It would take some time, but eventually there wouldn't be a surface without words on it. That was the goal. She knew in time the ink would fade, and in even more time, the walls of the house would split and crumble, but as she scrawled down her scraps of stories, her descriptions of hair and voices and the smells of skin, her growing list of possible character names, she felt like she was constructing a monument, something that would be there forever. Iridian didn't know if she was happy, but at least she felt like she was doing something significant. Doing something significant made her feel significant.

Iridian had been sitting in the hall upstairs, writing on the bathroom door, when she heard Peter let himself in. There were no rules about boys in the house anymore because there was no Rafe anymore. After Ana had smashed the television, Rafe had fled to Norma's, spent the night, and then, before sunrise, made off with a shoebox containing four thousand dollars. Jessica had maybe seen him late one night when she was in the hospital, recovering from a punctured lung and broken femur. She thought he'd been standing by her bedside, weeping loudly into his hands, but that could've been a drug-hazed delusion. Regardless, the girls hadn't seen their father in three weeks, but a few days ago a brand-new television had been delivered to the house, so they knew their father was out there somewhere, feeling guilty and spending Norma Galván's money.

Peter had canceled his trip to Mexico. He and Jessica were trying to whisper to each other, but Iridian could still hear what they were saying. She wrote as fast as she could, trying to copy their conversation word for word.

"You're late," Jessica said.

"Traffic was bad," Peter replied. "I didn't know what kind you wanted, so I got you chocolate."

Jessica slurped a straw and then said, "Vanilla next time."

"Wow," Peter said. "Ungrateful."

"I know. I suck. Someone should run me over with his truck."

Jessica laughed at herself, then immediately winced from the strain.

Iridian kept writing, but she could see, out of the corner of her eye, light starting to flicker from the lamp in her bedroom. The light was from the same lamp Rosa had ripped from the wall downstairs and swung at the men who hurt Iridian and her sisters. They'd brought it up to their room. It was theirs now. The light blinked out, then came back on. It did that sometimes.

Rosa
(Sunday, July 7th)

ROSA WAS IN church, and her attention had started to falter. Father Mendoza tended to repeat certain things in sermons and drive home the same points over and over. They were good points—about the virtues of being humble and forgiving—but still.

Rosa was thinking about how, on the way to church, the Matas' car had passed Peter Rojas's truck. He was coming to check in on Jessica again, which was nice. Peter was nice, but he hadn't been right about Ana. Rosa had never believed Ana's purpose in coming back was to get her and her sisters out of their house. That would've meant they would've had to split up, or split up even more than they already had in the year since Ana died. Rosa knew that Ana had come back to convince her and her sisters to stay together. They needed one another. Rosa knew this for a *fact*, and she'd known it since she'd placed her ear against her sister's chest and heard her heart stop beating. Jessica had shuddered. Several seconds had passed. Rosa had whispered *please*, and Jessica's heart had started to beat again. Rosa had made a heart beat. Before that, she'd only made a heart stop.

There was movement on the pew. Walter was there, next to her. His hand was spread out, palm-down on the wood. Rosa's hand was also there, also spread out. Walter's pinkie finger wiggled a little, then shifted toward hers until it brushed up against the side of Rosa's hand. Rosa didn't smile, but her whole body felt warmer. There was so much magic in small things.

After church, when Walter's mom had dropped her off back at her house, Rosa nearly stepped on a piece of paper in the front yard, wedged between two blades of grass. The paper was lined, but the lines were pale, bleached from the sun and rain. Most of the blue ink was completely faded. As she crouched down to pick it up, she saw that there were only two legible words: *I want*

It could've meant anything.

Acknowledgments

Thanks to my teachers, my students, my colleagues, my family (Guy!), and my friends. This novel was a tricky one, loosely bound for a long time by the idea of combining three sisters, the confining setting of their house/neighborhood, and a ghost. A huge amount of thanks goes to my agent, Claire Anderson-Wheeler at Regal Hoffmann, for seeing a story worth pursuing and being patient with me as I figured it all out. Of course, thanks to Krestyna Lypen and Elise Howard at Algonquin Young Readers (and everyone at AYR), for *also* seeing a story worth pursuing, and for their wisdom and enthusiasm. Courtney Summers and Stephanie Kuehn read early versions of this novel and offered kind words, and for that, I am grateful. A major source of inspiration for this story was *How the García Girls Lost Their Accents* by Julia Alvarez, and, as such, I am stunned and honored to have her give praise to my Torres sisters.

Other sources of inspiration: The chorus of the boys across the street at Hector's house is a nod to *The Virgin Suicides* by Jeffrey Eugenides. Iridian's favorite book, *The Witching Hour* by Anne Rice, is a book I wish I'd written and have read over and over again. The ultimate source of inspiration for this novel, though that may not seem so obvious now, is Shakespeare's *King Lear*. In the play, the phrase "tigers, not daughters" is hurled out as a harsh insult against Regan and Goneril, but I've always loved this line, and wanted to write a story about daughters and their father in which those words perhaps meant something completely different, and weren't an insult at all.

Lastly, thanks to all who have read or boosted my stories. I appreciate you more than you'll ever know.